City of Darkness, City of Light

Émigré Filmmakers in Paris 1929-1939

Alastair Phillips

Amsterdam University Press

For my mother and father, and in memory of my auntie and uncle

Cover design: Kok Korpershoek, Amsterdam
Lay-out: JAPES, Amsterdam

ISBN 90 5356 633 3 (hardback)
ISBN 90 5356 634 1 (paperback)
NUR 674

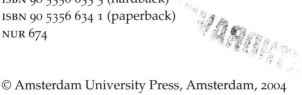

© Amsterdam University Press, Amsterdam, 2004

Contents

Acknowledgements

The research for this book was supported principally by the British Academy but also by the Humanities Research Centre at the University of Warwick and the Research Endowment Trust Fund at the University of Reading.

I would like to express my continuing deep gratitude to my former PhD supervisor, Professor Ginette Vincendeau, for her exemplary support, encouragement and sensitive guidance. Her enthusiasm and sense of engaged pleasure has been constant throughout the long gestation of this project and I am delighted to acknowledge her critical engagement and professional and personal friendship.

Many people have assisted me over the years in various capacities. Among them are: Dudley Andrew; V.F. Perkins; Richard Dyer; Charlotte Brunsdon; Ed Gallafent; José Arroyo; Doug Pye; Jim Hillier; Alison Butler; Mike Stevenson; Lib Taylor; Susan Hayward; Adrian Rifkin; Richard Kilborn; Valerie Orpen; Rachel Moseley; Julianne Pidduck; Andrew Higson; Erica Carter; Michel Marie; Wolfgang Jacobson; Steven Ungar; Michael Temple; Mike Witt; Geneviève Sellier; Janet Bergstrom; Iris Luppa; Sheila Whitaker and Peter Owen; Clive Snowden; Robert Muir and family; Jacques and Janine Volkmann; Gro Ween; Lisa Meekason; Noa and Dror Wahrman; Michael and Colette Casey; Richard and Karen Phillips; Pat and Alex Kurzemnieks and all the respondents to my presentations at seminars and conferences at the Universities of Exeter; Birmingham; Reading; Glasgow and London. Special thanks to all those involved in the Picturing Paris conference which I organised at the University of Warwick in 1998.

I am especially grateful for the kindness and hospitality of Peter Graham without whom I might never have made many of the discoveries mentioned in this book.

My thanks too to the library staff at the University of Warwick; the British Film Institute; the Bodleian Library, Oxford; the BIFI library and the Bibliothèque Nationale in Paris including the Bibliothèque de l'Arsenal.

Earlier drafts of some material contained in this book have appeared, or will appear, in the following publications and I am grateful to their respective editors and publishers for their kind permission to include this work: *Screen* vol. 40 no. 3 (Autumn 1999); *Modern and Contemporary France* vol. 8 no. 2 (August 2000); Michael Temple and Mike Witt (eds.) *The French Cinema Book*, London: British Film Institute (2004) and Douglas Pye (ed.) *Fritz Lang*, Moffat: Cameron Books (2004).

I am also delighted to be able to acknowledge the support given by Professor Thomas Elsaesser to this book. Thank you to the all the staff at Amsterdam University Press including Jaap Wagenaar and Magdalena Hernas.

Last but by no means least, I must mention my partner and own émigré filmmaker, Mark Kurzemnieks, who has accompanied me on this and so many other journeys these last years. Thank you for everything.

Oxford, Autumn 2003

I Introduction

> "With cities, it is as with dreams: everything imaginable can be dreamed, but even the most unexpected dream is a rebus that conceals a desire or, its reverse, a fear".
>
> (Italo Calvino 1974, 44)

Diversity and Exchange – Rethinking the National in European Cinema

In 1931, the French painter Maurice Vlaminck wrote that he now tended to "avoid going to Paris. It has become for me like a train station, a kind of Western Constantinople, a junction [and] a bazaar" (in Golan 1995, 88). Vlaminck's acerbic description of the bustling and cosmopolitan nature of Parisian life points to the fact that the French capital did indeed become a terminus or junction for various groups of émigrés in the 1930s. Among the people drawn to the possibilities of the City of Light were a succession of European filmmakers who arrived in Paris from the internationally successful studios of Berlin. Some like Fritz Lang and Billy Wilder stayed only a brief time. The director Robert Siodmak, on the other hand, ended up working in France for a number of years. This book looks at the significance of this moment in film history through a detailed analysis of the émigrés' various on- and off-screen relationships with their adopted home.

"Home" is not the correct word. The truth is that many of these émigrés were displaced figures on a journey that remained, as it must always be for the exile, both "composite and evolutionary" (Naficy 2001, 222). The time that filmmakers such as Wilder, Lang and Siodmak spent in Paris, in what fellow émigré Siegfried Kracauer has termed "the near vacuum of extraterritoriality" (in Koch 1991,105), was, for many, but one episode of a larger trajectory. To extend the railway analogy, Paris was a "waiting room" (Elsaesser 1984, 278): a place of temporary refuge before their journey onwards to the more rewarding terrain of Hollywood. Because of the glamour of this final destination, and despite the fact that the émigré filmmakers clearly made a significant contribution to French cinema, there is still little written in English about this unique and fascinating phenomenon. My book seeks to redress this imbalance.

To examine the cinematic representation of Paris by émigré filmmakers in the French cinema of the 1930s means to engage with the ways in which European national cinemas are currently being reconceptualized as discrete discursive and economic phenomena. As Tim Bergfelder has rightly stated, the history of these cinemas should necessarily be "characterized by two simultaneous yet diverging processes, namely the film industries' economic imperative of international expansion, competition and co-operation (often accompanied by a migration of labour), and the ideological project of re-centering the definition of national cinemas through critical discourses and national film policy" (in Higson and Maltby 1999, 139). My book explores the ramifications of this phenomenon when the two processes described by Bergfelder are especially accented by political and economic upheaval.

Any sense of a national cinema which seems fixed, fully fledged and dependent on static territorial boundary definitions clearly obscures what Andrew Higson has called "the degree of cultural diversity, exchange, and interpenetration that marks so much cinematic activity (in Hjort and Mackenzie 2000, 64). As this book will demonstrate, these notions of "diversity, exchange and interpenetration" become crucial in an exploration of that privileged site of spatial representation in 1930s' French cinema: the French capital. Definitions of place, belonging, and adaptation – vital, of course, to any exilic experience – have also been fundamental to the ways in which French cinema has located its indigenous traditions. An exemplary way of documenting the émigrés' various encounters with the French film industry is thus to examine how their films made and set in Paris actually represented the city. How, for example, did they engage with pre-existing modes of Parisian representation, both on film and in other media such as photography, song, literature and the performing arts? To what extent did they then refract these modes to produce a distinctive contribution to the picturing of the city? What was at stake politically in this cultural activity, and thus, how were these films received? By referring to Paris in this way – as both a site of social activity *and* a sphere of cultural representation – a more nuanced understanding will emerge of French national cinema during this turbulent period of European film history.

Cinema and the City

Previous critical work on the culture of urban space has argued that the general relationship between the cinema and the city is a complex one. In a tradition going back to the early nineteenth century, cities like Paris have been perceived as texts to be explored or deciphered in their own right. In Ludwig Börne's *Schilerungen aus Paris* (*Depictions From Paris*) (1822-4), for instance, he described the French capital as "an unfolded book … [so that] wandering through it streets means *reading*" (in Gleber 1999, 66). James Donald more recently, has argued that "the city (…) is above all a representation (…) an imag-

ned environment" (1992, 422), whereas Raymond Williams has even suggested, more broadly, that the "fictional method is the experience of the city"
in Caws 1991, 1). Coupled with these claims has come the suggestion that as
an imagined environment," the city is "shaped by the interaction of practices,
vents and relations so complex that they cannot easily be visualized" (Don-
ld, 457). As a result, a preponderance of metaphors exists to describe the vari-
us facets of urban experience. As both Italo Calvino's quotation and the title
f my book suggest, these metaphors may be both positive *and* negative. The
ity, for instance, has been seen as a theatrical stage – a place of transformation
nd possibility – but it has also been seen as a corrupt and corrupting machine
t odds with the rural certainties of the past.

If the city is a metaphorical text, it is unsurprising that much of the critical
liscussion about urban culture and its meanings has centred around the fields
f perception and subjectivity. As Michel de Certeau notes, one single person
an never grasp the full measure of the concept of a city. When we walk the
ity, "we adapt it to our own creative purposes; (...) such negotiations produce
different space (...) it is not a representation of space but a representational
pace" (in Donald, 436). Instead of describing and analyzing the complex "in-
eraction of practices, events and relations" that make up the city as a tentative
vhole, what results is an interpretative practice which privileges the individ-
al's perceptual encounter with the urban. The cinema, as the pre-eminent ur-
an based visual medium of mass communication, clearly fits in with this in-
erest in sight and the city. There is surely an analogy between one's viewing of
he textual spaces of the cinematic narrative, and the walker's encounter with
he created spaces of the built city environment. Writing in the 1920s, for in-
tance, Carlo Mierendorff observed that the "flash-like and disjointed succes-
ion of movement characteristic of early silent cinema seemed to correspond to
he receptive disposition of the city dweller" (in Gleber, 1999, 141). Both ele-
nents clearly concern a broken and fragmented mode of vision which disrupts
n apparent pre-modern sense of the unity of space and time. In the case of the
ity walker, this way of seeing is achieved by the relationship of the moving
ody to the street and its attractions. With the cinematic spectator, it is
chieved by means of the mobility of the camera and the fragmentation of
pace and time through editing.[1]

A problem with this line of enquiry, fascinating though it is, is that by con-
inuing to pursue chains of metaphorical association, one ends up potentially
egating the possibilities open within a more specifically grounded historical
erspective. Fundamental to this perspective are the ways in which particular
ocial, economic, political, and cultural factors force one to consider not just
ow the city was seen, but by whom and when. This book will therefore move
eyond the generalities of much that has been written on the cinematic city

and rewrite an undervalued aspect of film history in a hitherto unexplored fashion. If one accepts that the city as a social space might be multi-layered and open to contradiction or disjuncture, then so too might the ways in which it has been represented on the screen. By making the deliberate shift from the city as text to the cinematic city as text, I will still embrace the productive possibility of a set of tensions. The most significant of these will be concerned with the central question of what happened to the representation of one city – Paris – when filmmakers from another major urban film capital arrived and began to take part in that city's own film industry.

Paris and the 1930s

Paris in the 1930s was in many ways a divided city. As Marc Augé (1996) has demonstrated with evocative precision in his discussion of an anthology of Parisian photographs of the era, the city was marked strongly by currents of continuity and change. Now, with the hindsight of an historical perspective which can view the war about to happen, as well as the one that had just ended, the city appears as a site of various temporalities. Behind the aesthetic facade of the two international Parisian exhibitions of the decade – the Exposition Coloniale of 1931 and the Exposition Internationale des Arts et Techniques of 1937 – lay a society uncertain of itself; a society that kept one eye on the traumas of the First World War, and one eye on the gathering political problems in the rest of Europe. Marred by a succession of short-lived governments, the French capital was riven by political tensions which brought citizens onto the streets in riots, strikes, and demonstrations throughout the decade. One indication of this insecurity was the way in which the vocal supporters of the French right laid claim to individual national pride whilst at the same time genuflecting to an imported ideology from a former military enemy. Another was the way in which the French capital handled the progression of modernization in terms of its built environment. Despite the growth of the greater Parisian region in the 1920s and early 1930s, with its expansion in housing, factories, and railways, the city was still a place which took pride in traditional social mores. If Norma Evenson (1979, 255) is right in suggesting that Paris lies at the crossroads in Europe between a Mediterranean and a Northern lifestyle, it appears that in this decade, at least within the cultural discourse, the more Southern model of the Parisian *quartier* as family community was still dominant. This tradition was carried over into the spheres of popular entertainment; especially within the cinematic representation of urban life.

These observations therefore suggest a broader means of understanding the title of this book. By referring to Paris in terms of darkness and light, I am doing more than acknowledging the prevailing terms by which the French capital has conventionally been discussed. Paris became both the City of Light and the City of Darkness in the nineteenth century as rapid urbanisation and radical restructuring of the built environment produced new ways of viewing and new ways of understanding the city's social structure. This legacy was carried over into the twentieth century in various forms of cultural expression including, of course, the nation's cinematic output. But the example of the arrival of the German émigrés within the French film industry of the 1930s provides a new means of understanding this established dichotomy. Paris was also the city of darkness and light for political reasons. Many of the émigrés were fleeing the darkness of a right-wing political regime in Berlin for the refuge of a European capital which had been seen, since the French Revolution, as a beacon of light for the continent's dispossessed. For various economic and ideological reasons, their reception was not unanimously favourable: it had a dark side embodied by the rising tide of French nationalism. As Thomas Elsaesser has argued (2000, 405), the filmmakers were thus caught up in a "threefold insecurity [since] they were enemy aliens, administrative embarrassments and refugees persecuted for their race or convictions." To add to this, seeing Paris in terms of lightness and dark also involves various interchanges between historical and contemporary interpretations of urban life. In this instance, the French city films of the German émigrés may suggest more than just a meeting point between Berlin and Paris. They also present a new way of understanding the important wider interaction between the past and the present in Parisian culture of the period.

Paris and French Cinema of the 1930s

By the 1930s, with the population of the intramural city stabilised at around the three million mark, and the subsequent rapid growth in the rim of suburban development encouraged by the development of tramlines and rail networks, Parisians were beginning to make use of the advent of paid holidays to view non-urban France. The fact remains though that representations of the city remained enormously popular for the French film-going public. It is still surprising, despite the centrality of the French capital in terms of cinematic production, exhibition, and representation, that there is so little sustained analytical writing about film and Paris. Art history has long privileged Paris as a site of meaning – especially in the case of French nineteenth century painting –

but film studies has yet to fully engage with the city. The French cinema of the 1930s abounds with titles suggesting an affinity with the French capital. Many of these are now forgotten, but they suggest a range of locations and genres. They include: AUX PORTES DE PARIS (Barrois, 1935), AVENTURES DE PARIS (Allégret, 1936), CENDRILLON DE PARIS (Hémard, 1930), ENFANTS DE PARIS (Roudès, 1936), JEUNES FILLES DE PARIS (Vermorel, 1936), MÉNILMONTANT (Guissart, 1936), MINUIT PLACE PIGALLE (Richebé, 1934), MOULIN ROUGE (Hugon, 1939), PARIS MES AMOURS (Blondeau, 1936), QUARTIER LATIN (Colombier, 1939), RENDEZVOUS CHAMPS-ÉLYSÉES (Houssin, 1937), RIVE-GAUCHE (Korda, 1931), LE ROI DES CHAMPS-ÉLYSÉES (Nosseck, 1933), TOURBILLON DE PARIS (Diamant-Berger, 1938), TROIS ARGENTINS À MONTMARTRE (Hugon, 1939), TROIS ARTILLEURS À L'OPÉRA (Chotin, 1938) and LA VIE PARISIENNE (Siodmak, 1936). Various anthologies have featured short written pieces on Paris and the cinema, and writers like Adrian Rifkin (1995) have introduced film in their discursive analysis of Parisian entertainment culture.[2] The two books which specifically deal with the topic, Charles Ford and René Jeanne's *Paris vu par le cinéma* (1969) and Jean Douchet and Gilles Nadeau's *Paris-une ville vue par le cinéma, de 1895 à nos jours* (1987), still remain inadequate. The former pursues the question of film adaptations from well-known Parisian literary texts and provides scant textual or historical detail. The latter is more comprehensive, but it is primarily concerned with being a pictorial illustrated survey of what is still a field largely dominated by the canonical texts of poetic realism and the *Nouvelle Vague*. This book will provide the first sustained discussion of a number of popular cinematic interpretations of the French capital.

Thanks to the work of a number of scholars, we now *do* have a detailed understanding of various facets of the French cinema of the 1930s. Survey texts such as Pierre Billard's *L'Age classique du cinéma français. Du cinéma parlant à la Nouvelle Vague* (1995), Raymond Chirat's *Le cinéma français des années trentes* (1983) and *Atmosphères: sourires, soupirs et délires du cinéma Français des années 30* (1987) and Jean Pierre Jeancolas's *15 ans d'années trente: le cinéma des français* (1983) have documented key moments in the era's history by providing a descriptive analysis of indicative texts and individuals. Writers such as Frances Courtade (1978), Colin Crisp (1993) and Paul Léglise (1970) have sought to examine the logistical economic, political, and technological determinants of the cinema as an industrial practice. Michèle Lagny, Marie-Claire Ropars and Pierre Sorlin (1986) have investigated the character roles and narrative structures which dominated the decade's film output. For the purposes of my exploration of the cultural representation of Paris and the significance of the German émigrés, I have particularly drawn upon the recent work of Richard Abel (1993), Dudley Andrew (1995) and Ginette Vincendeau (1985 et al). The former has provided a useful introduction to the many written debates circulating at the time about the nature of the French film industry and its place within the overall culture of the time. Andrew's rigorous and sustained analysis of one key facet of 1930s French cinema – poetic realism – has provided a serious example of how to write film history on the basis of what he terms "concrete cultural manifestations" (1995, xi). Andrew has sought to locate a historiography somewhere between the poles of the formation of an auteurist canon and a model of social analysis predicated on a mode of reductive social determinism. Borrowing from Roland Barthes' term of *écriture*, he has suggested the analytical model of an *optique* which helps "make concrete the mysterious operations of the auteur (who chooses a particular aesthetic option before contributing personal style), while at the same time [specifying] the aesthetic and cultural fields within which artworks make their mark" (19). According to Andrew this always suggests "a limited set of possibilities alive at a given moment in a specific cinematic situation" (19). Whilst finding myself in broad agreement with many of his conclusions, it will become evident that I have also shifted the terrain of analysis. Several of the films that I discuss were projects many of the filmmakers concerned were probably reluctant to make. Their outsider status dictated choices motivated by important economic, as well as aesthetic, factors. Despite the fact that the émigrés clearly "opened up stylistic options that would be crucial for poetic realism" (Andrew, 176), they also made city-based musicals, operettas, caper movies and melodramas.[3] These films should not be seen as less interesting because of this. Rather, as well as being suggestive evidence of the heterogeneity of popular French film culture of the time, they also provide valuable new perspectives on the depiction of the French capital. Finally, Vincendeau reminds one of the dangers of "going back to a history of how French society of the 1930s [was] reflected in its films" (1985, 11). Her ongoing project of uncovering the inter-textual nature of 1930s French film practice has allowed one, instead, to see how the category of the "socio-historical" was actually "inscribed within filmic texts" themselves (11). I have largely followed the example of her model in this book and will also show that any history of the cinema of the period is, at least in part, also a history of that epoch's popular entertainment culture.

France and the Émigrés

The early years of the 1930s were marked by the transition from silent to sound film production. As many have pointed out, the "introduction of speech, dialogue, and an actor's verbal performance reframed the question of how the French cinema could differ from and challenge of the American cinema" (Abel

1993, 9). This notion of what a nationally specific French sound cinema meant is an ongoing reference point in my discussion of the émigrés. As I have already mentioned, Paris was more than the émigrés' temporary home. It was also the symbol of the French nation and, as such, it became one of the key sites where definitions of the era's cinematic production became determined. The arrival of so many filmmakers from another European capital clearly provides a fascinating historical opportunity to contextualise this process. We will see, for example, how apparently stable notions of national identity in relation to the city were troubled or refracted by the arrival of the émigrés. A question still remains over the degree to which the émigrés were either seen negatively because they were not French enough, or were seen positively because as fellow Europeans they could contribute to the ongoing trade battle with the economic hegemony of the United States.

The waves of émigré filmmakers from Berlin in the 1930s must be understood within the overall context of the twentieth century rise in immigration into France. After the first decade of the twentieth century, France was the leading host country in the world for newly arrived migrants. In 1930, exceeding its nearest rival, the United States, France had a foreign-born population of 515 out of every 100, 000 people (Noiriel 1996, 146). This rise had primarily been necessitated by the depletion in the male workforce after the First World War, but it was also linked to the modernisation of the Paris region. In his study of France and its non-indigenous population, Gérard Noiriel (1996, 151) has argued that because of the "myth of origin that was built upon the events of the Revolution (...) French immigration [has] always [been] approached as a question extrinsic to the country's history. It [has been] seen as a fleeting phenomenon, something fleeting and marginal". As I have indicated, this has certainly been the case regarding the ways in which the Parisian work of the German émigrés has been discussed. Conventional film history has tended to bypass the passage of German exiles and émigrés in France in favour of providing an account of their subsequent work in Hollywood.[4] Recent books such as Anthony Heilbut's *Exiled in Paradise* (1997) and Stephanie Barron's *Exiles and Emigrés* (1997), which also look at the broader dimensions of European artists' exile to United States, largely do so from a high cultural perspective. Existing work on the German émigrés in Paris (Gilbert Badia et al. and Jean-Michel Palmier 1988) tends as well to only consider such fields as literature, political philosophy, and journalism. There is still a lack of critical material on the time filmmakers spent in the French capital. Was this, as Elsaesser (1983a, 1) has already suggested, due to "the apparent lack of success" of the films that the émigrés actually made?

Elsaesser has been one of the pioneers in readjusting the focus of study of this neglected aspect of film history. His documentation with Vincendeau

(1983) provided the valuable corrective to the notion that the Berlin émigrés were a uniform grouping. As I shall also demonstrate, it is important to distinguish between the political phase of emigration after the Reichstag fire in 1933, and the previous wave of economically and technically related emigration. Much that has subsequently been written about the émigrés has tended, understandably, to privilege the difference of their work from conventional French film practice (Elsaesser 1984a and various essays in Jacques Aumont and Dominique Païni 1992; Heiner Gassen and Heike Hurst 1991; Sibylle Sturm and Arthur Wohlgemuth 1996). By reiterating this difference and linking it to the émigrés' prior work in Berlin, these accounts still contribute to the problematic assertion that the émigrés failed while in the French capital. The considerable importance of the place of the émigrés in French film culture of the 1930s has yet to be fully documented. While I am not interested in the inadvisable task of measuring the relative greatnesses of the émigré French films, I do, nonetheless, believe that it is essential to also account for how successful the émigrés were in "fitting in". To this extent then, I agree with Noiriel (1996, 169) who argues that if the "collective memory" of immigrant communities can be analysed, it can only be done so according to an ongoing sense of contestation. This would involve what he calls "a never ending struggle between what Émile Durkheim called 'native dispositions,' which impel the individual to turn back to his native traditions; and everyday life in a foreign land, which requires some form of adaptation, that is, a sacrifice of the past for the sake of the present and future".

As Hamid Naficy has recently observed, this sense of contestation is often markedly present in exilic cinema; both in terms of how we conceive of its modes of production and how we perceive its means of visualization. What Naficy calls "accented cinema" (2001, 4) resonates for him because it is "created astride and in the interstices of social formations and cinematic practices" (4). It may work against and within dominant forms of cultural representation to the extent that the exiles's own hybrid sense of cultural and personal identity is also somehow visualised and expressed through a similarly hybrid mode of filmmaking. This sense of hybridity – which Salmon Rushdie, in another context, calls being "at once plural and partial" (in Naficy, 13) – is useful in relation to the history of the émigrés in Paris, especially in a stylistic sense. However, we must also be aware, of course, of the then problematic production context of mainstream French cinema of the 1930s. Questions of adaptation and integration were obviously more significant in this period than in the case of the more contemporary conceptualisation of an independently financed diasporic or exilic mode of filmmaking. Elsaesser's model of a "lateral history of 'interference'" which can replace "a linear history of 'influence'" (2000, 428) is therefore also pertinent to my series of case studies. Rather than necessarily seeing the Berlin émigrés as separate and thus inflected simply with the sense of being influential, shouldn't we also see the potential of a hybrid cinema in terms of what could be termed as a dialectical process of oscillation? That is to say, the history of the German émigrés in Paris was never a uniform phenomenon. Perhaps, instead, it fluctuated between "creative mismatches and miscognition on the one hand (with many a comedy of error and some lost illusions), and over-adaptation, assimilation and over-identification (this too, often with a grain of comic or tragic irony)" (431).

City of Darkness, City of Light

I have divided the book into six chapters. The following chapter, "The City in Context," examines the social, political, economic, and cultural backgrounds which inform my subsequent analysis of a number of the Paris films made by the émigrés. It proposes a complex and mutually informing set of contexts which, taken as a whole, present a fruitful way of situating the cinematic relationship between France and Germany over the period in question. The nature of my analysis, the result of synthesizing existing research with new readings of primary source material, varies according to the questions I ask. At times, I provide a wide-ranging and chronological perspective; elsewhere I have found it useful to home in on a particular moment or individual in order to illustrate some of the broader themes under discussion.

I begin by going back to the nineteenth century to situate a general discussion of the shifting permutations of Franco-German relations. I then move to the specific question of the different ways in which France and Germany made sense of the crucial inter-relationship between the city and modernity. If one of the key features of modern urban experience was a disruptive perceptual encounter with the new, an understanding of the specific intertwining of place and memory in the capitals of Berlin and Paris may result in new ways of understanding the discussion and representation of urban life within the cities' respective film cultures. How, in particular, did the defining moment of the First World War affect these matters? The war also left a significant material legacy in terms of the future directions of the European film industry. I therefore go on to uncover how links and rivalries between the Franco-German film industries over this period helped to pave the way for the subsequent patterns of emigration from Berlin to Paris in the late 1920s and the early to mid-1930s. As well as fully drawing upon relevant trade sources and personal memoirs to provide the general picture, I also present a number of more biographically detailed and discursive case studies. These serve a secondary purpose in that they introduce specific aesthetic and political themes which I develop later in the course of my film analyses. The chapter ends with a discussion of the matter of the émigrés' arrival and reception in France. Here, I consider the émigrés' place within 1930s French film culture in the light of their ethnicity and cultural identity in order to examine how these apparent outsiders related to the symbolically important site of the national capital. A complex picture emerges regarding the notion of a homogenous national film culture at a time when, in many quarters, that very notion had such political and economic significance.

In Chapter Three, "City of Light", I begin my discussion of the French films made by the German émigrés by examining three hitherto neglected examples of émigré film making in detail: LA CRISE EST FINIE (Robert Siodmak, 1934) (See Appendix Eight); LA VIE PARISIENNE (Robert Siodmak, 1935) (See Appendix Nine) and MAUVAISE GRAINE (Billy Wilder, 1933) (See Appendix Ten). I contextualise this work by privileging the way that the films intersect with many of the cultural conventions by which "light Paris" has historically been understood. How, for example, did the émigrés negotiate the entertainment milieu of "light Paris" and its sense of spectacular pleasure? Did the émigrés conform to a way of viewing the capital which was in itself spectacular? How did the émigrés foreground existing city mythologies in their use of Parisian stardom and performance? I draw upon a wide range of written source material to understand not just the textual processes of the films, but the subsequent ways in which the films were then discussed.

Chapter Four, "City of Darkness," deals with three other case studies of émigré city films which concern themselves with prevalent mythologies of the French capital: COEUR DE LILAS (Anatole Litvak, 1931) (See Appendix Eleven); DANS LES RUES (Victor Trivas, 1933) (See Appendix Twelve) and CARREFOUR (Kurt Bernhardt, 1938) (See Appendix Thirteen). Here, I consider the obverse of the notion that the city was the centre of spectacular pleasure by engaging three methods to perhaps better understand Paris as a place associated with the dark. Firstly, I look at the Parisian street as a site of literal, metaphorical, and moral darkness to discuss how we may understand nationally specific concerns about both French sound cinema and the wider progress of urban modernity. By placing the work of the émigrés at the heart of these debates, we are able to see more clearly why their representation of Paris mattered, and how it related to a broader inter-textual history. This history is crucial to my related discussion of the ways in which a number of the émigrés contributed to the picturing of Paris as the geographical heart of poetic realism. Secondly, I examine the significance of the Parisian night, especially in terms of its associations with urban entertainment and crime, and consider how the émigrés mediated various representational tropes relating to the spaces of the city where crime and pleasure occurred – notably the Parisian *café*, the *bal musette* and the nightclub. Finally, I return to some of the concerns introduced in Chapter Two by re-examining the inter-relationship between place and memory in the context of the past itself as dark. Here, I assess how the arrival of the émigrés mattered to the ways French cinema of the 1930s remembered Paris, and how this related to broader questions facing French society of the time.

My penultimate chapter, "Divided City," consolidates the previous chapters' discussion of the representation of Paris by means of a detailed case study of the ways in which two specific émigré films – PIÈGES (Robert Siodmak, 1939) (See Appendix Fourteen) and LILIOM (Fritz Lang, 1934) (See Appendix Fifteen) – pictured the city in terms of both light and darkness. I begin with an extensive production and reception history of the features which examines how they were split, like so much émigré work, between seeing Paris as the centre of a domestic film production system and Paris as a place of temporary exile. I then go on to examine how this sense of division is consolidated by the way the films employed, and then played with, two conventional male Parisian star personas in the sense that an instability in male identity actually foregrounds the overall representational instability inherent in the films' narratives. Finally, I conclude this section by turning to the way in which the theme of mobility in émigré city narratives is reconfigured in both texts to shed new light on Parisian representational myths of gender and place.

Mobility is a dominant motif in this book. In his study of ethnographic discourse, James Clifford (1992) noted how many of the French Surrealists spent their time in hotels or hotel-like accommodations. He extended this observation to suggest that, in many ways, the cultural history of Paris in the early twentieth century can be written in terms of seeing the city as "a place of departures, arrivals and transits" (104). To some degree, of course, all cities, at all times, have been "sites of dwelling and travel" (105), but I also believe that the question of journeying has particular significance for my discussion of the representation of the French capital by the waves of German émigré filmmakers in the 1930s. The idea of the journey can be uncovered in many of the actual narratives of the films I look at, but what also strikes me as particularly resonant is the way in which the émigrés' own journeys as filmmakers then became inscribed in various extra-textual legal, economic, and critical discourses of the period. Beyond the notion of what was undoubtedly, in many ways, an alien production and reception environment, lies the pressing issue of identity and the revealing journey of cultural transformation. For the émigrés, as we shall now see, the crucial issue remained the crucial distinction between cultural difference and cultural assimilation; in other words, what Albert Dreyfus, writing in 1930s' Paris, simply termed "the ability to adjust" (in Golan 1995, 141).

2 The City in Context

An Historical Ambivalence

In his evocative and modestly tempered account of the complex nature of the relationships formed between Parisians and their German occupiers during the Second World War, Richard Cobb rightly seeks to demonstrate the range of feelings available within the framework of this situation. Instead of painting a picture which conveys an unambiguous clash between the values of lightness and dark; he argues that, certainly at the metropolitan level, "relations between *occupants* and *occupés* were obscured, twisted and complicated by all sorts of nuances of personal relations, ranging from mutual trust to a jarring acrimony" (1983, 60). This question of cultural ambivalence frames the history of the encounters between the two countries. If one goes back to the beginning of the nineteenth century, for example, Napoleon formally banned Madame de Staël's enthusiastic collected writings on the literary and philosophical culture of the German states entitled *De l'Allemagne* (1810). An interest in German intellectual life persisted, however, with the founding of the *Nouvelle Revue Germanique* in 1829 by Marquis Edouard de Lagrange. Meanwhile, for many German cultural figures such as Ludwig Börne, and Heinrich Heine who first moved to the city in 1831, Paris represented a beacon of free intellectual and literary expression. In Heine's writings, he referred to its "gracious and civilised air" (in Kruse and Werner 1981, 97). Like many others, he saw the city as more than just the capital of one nation. For him, Paris, then the largest city in Europe, also stood as the capital of the enlightened values of the European world. A sequence of travel books and memoirs followed from German writers based temporarily in Paris (Gleber 1999, 6-12). Throughout the nineteenth century, admiration within the Parisian intelligentsia for the liberating currents of German idealist philosophy was consistently tempered by a sense of trepidation regarding the military strengths of their near neighbour. Michelet wrote of "my Germany, the scientific power that alone has made me study questions deeply, and given Kant, Beethoven, and me a new faith" (in Zeldin 1993, 116); yet it was this same national culture that fought with such vigour and animosity during the campaign of the 1870 war to annex Alsace-Lorraine. France's divided perception of the German nation became, by the end of the nineteenth century, split in two once more. This time it was along the lines of political allegiance. As Zeldin has argued, while "the left admired liberal, intellectual, anticlerical Germany, and regretted only that this was unfortunately balanced by the Hohenzollern, despotic Germany; [t]he right admired its monarchist power, and regretted that it was materialist and Protestant" (121).

Despite these guarded feelings and geo-political resentments, relations in the spheres of culture, finance, and commerce continued to prosper well into the twentieth century. The 1900 Paris Universal Exhibition was attended by more German citizens than the total of all other foreigners put together and Paris was an obligatory destination for any poet or painter wishing to cultivate themselves. In Berlin, those working in visual culture were keen to keep abreast of developments in the French capital. In 1911, for example, Kandinsky invited Robert Delaunay to exhibit at the first Blaue Reiter exhibition. Afterwards, the German painter commented on what he saw as a clear difference between the two artists. Kandinsky interestingly points to an abiding set of criteria recognizable, to some extent, in the later perception of differences between German and French cinematic depictions of the city. While Delaunay was interested in the multifaceted play of light on surface conceptions of the texture of modern, everyday urban life, Kandinsky saw himself drawn inwards to the complexities of picturing the life of the mind. In the field of literature, the success of Romain Rolland's lengthy saga of German-French relations, *Jean Christophe* (1904-12), helped to underscore the material nature of contact between the two nations. In the period leading up to the First World War, for instance, Germany was France's main supplier of coke whilst at the same time it provided a significant export market for France's own raw materials and agricultural produce. Even during the onset of war, elements of Germanophilia were still apparent amongst sections of France's aristocracy. Gilberte, for example, in Proust's *Le Temps retrouvé*, praises the "perfect breeding of the staff officers" (Proust, 1981 edition, 774) and approving mentions are made by several characters in the novel of the work of Wagner and Nietzsche.

The bitter legacy of the German occupation of the northern swathes of France and the years of traumatic struggle during the First World War colours the affective history of the period. One only has to consider the brute statistics of the conflict fought on French soil to recall the lasting impact it must have had on the nation. 1.4 million French soldiers were killed amounting to over ten per cent of the active male population. Three million others were wounded with a third of these suffering from permanent disablement (Zeldin 1993, 1084). The additional loss of the lives of all those who were then never born remains incalculable. In the post First World War period, few ordinary Germans and French met each other. Exchanges were limited to the spheres of culture and commerce. Business relations continued to be clouded by the issue of war reparations which failed to heal despite the United States instigation of the Dawes Plan of 1924 to invigorate the German economy and thus allow it to pay its dues along the terms of the May 1919 Treaty of Versailles. In the worlds of literature and the visual arts things were different. Franz Hessel, who was to later work on a translation of Proust with his friend Walter Benjamin, published a nostalgic account of pre-war life in Paris entitled *Pariser Romanze* (1920). In it he evoked what was for him "true old Paris ..not that of the famous sights, but the secret one we discover in passing old corners" (in Gleber, 1999, 95). There were also stimulating exchanges between the Surrealists. The catalogue to Paul Klee's first exhibition in Paris, for example, had a forward by the French surrealist writer Louis Aragon. Many French intellectuals also took a keen interest in the satirical, urban caricatural work of the Berliner, Georg Grosz.

For the French writer Pierre Mac Orlan, who wrote a preface to the Parisian Grosz exhibition of 1924, Grosz's work spoke of the common situation that the city dwellers of France and Germany now found themselves in. "The social classes who ten years ago possessed respective traditions, which differentiated them from each other, are now merging in new combinations under the lights of the street", he wrote. "If people since the war can be distinguished from those that preceded them, it is by their passive obedience to the laws of speed. (...) The whole of the street and its intermediaries are animated in the magical, dirty and brutal frenzy of everyday life" (in Metken, 1992, 47).[1] Along with the architectural and design links between Le Corbusier and Mallet-Stevens and their German counterparts, there was a gradual renewal of interest in German literature with the founding of *La Revue d'Allemagne* in 1927. Erich Maria Remarque's *All Quiet on the Western Front* was a phenomenal bestseller. It had sold nearly half a million copies within six months of publication in 1929 (Weber 1995, 18). Among popular film audiences, the emotional reckoning of VERDUN, VISION D'HISTOIRE (Léon Poirier, 1928) enjoyed enormous success. The following quotation from the French film trade press of the time gives, however, a flavour of the still simmering antagonisms. The journalist has noted how Poirier's film was generally praised in Germany but no mention was made of national culpability. In fact, a Frankfurt newspaper has even gone so far as to criticise the French attitude towards the war. It is quoted as saying "If there were no French politicians and no French newspapers the Frenchman would be the most honest man in the world". "Well!" sniffs the French journalist, "if there hadn't been the 'Deutschland über alles' mentality, perhaps the same could be said of a German!"[2]

In many of the films of the 1930s such as Raymond Bernard's LES CROIX DE BOIS (1931), mention of the war surfaces directly and indirectly.[3] Among the films I will discuss in detail, it actually forms the core narrative impulse of CARREFOUR since the central character is an amnesiac war veteran. War widows feature in the same film and also in DANS LES RUES, which signals the fact that by the middle of the decade, women in the age group between twenty and forty years old outnumbered their male counterparts by more than one million (Weber 1995, 14). In his account of the French nation in the 1930s, Eugen Weber even argues that the decade began in August 1914 with the time frame in question simply being divided between mainly a sense of *"après guerre"* and *"avant guerre"*. Although this formulation might be seen as overtly determinist and certainly benefitting from the privilege of hindsight, it remains true to say that the effect of war – whether it be remembered or anticipated – significantly affected the dealings of the French with the Germans over this period. It altered the ways the French saw themselves in relation to Germany, and the ways the French then represented themselves to each other through the medium of cinema.

Modernity and the City

The period leading up to the various departures of the émigrés from the German film industry to Paris saw the continued rapid expansion of the two national capitals. The post First World War era in France was when the nation went from being a predominantly agrarian society to one in which the majority of its members could count themselves as urban based. By 1930, 66 per cent of the population lived in towns (Weber 1995, 37). Similarly, the population of Berlin went from 2 million residents to almost 4 million between 1910 and 1925 (Kaes 1998, 184). In both cases, the cities' populations swelled through migration from the rural provinces and beyond the borders of the state from the Jewish communities of central Europe who were then escaping violent waves of persecution. Many of the most important filmmakers of Weimar Germany actually came to Berlin from elsewhere: Fritz Lang from Vienna, F.W. Murnau from the Ruhr District and G. W. Pabst from Bohemia.

The crucial difference between the two places was the relationship between an overall history of the city and the timing of this expansion. In the case of the French capital, modernity already had a set of nineteenth century connotations going back to the official expansion of the city boundaries during the Second Empire and the work of Haussmann in redesigning the appearance of the city's built environment. As the capital of the French nation and the City of the Revolution, Paris already possessed a vital political, cultural, and architectural history. Berlin, on the other hand, only became the metropolitan center of Germany in 1871 and thus Germany's particular "turn to the city" was seen as representing something else. Whereas Paris had expanded in a piecemeal fashion, or had even literally uncoiled, if one looks at the metaphoric possibilities suggested by the circular pattern of the *arrondisements* on the map, Berlin's growth was more linear, seamless, and rapid. Its very reason for being was to suggest the possibilities of the industrial age. "Berlin has not grown; rather it has undergone a transformation. Chicago on the Spree is emerging", wrote Walter Rathenan in 1899 (in Müller, 1990, 40). As Anton Kaes has suggested, the consequence of this relatively sudden development was that by the mid- to late-1920s, Berlin "was considered the paragon of modern living – both intriguing and terrifying in its tempo, diversity and moral laxity" (1998, 186).[4] For many cultural observers, including Siegfried Kracauer, there was an inherent correlation between the characteristics of the modern city and the features of its most contemporary form of entertainment: the cinema. Both represented a sense of "continuous mobility, rootlessness, nervousness, loss of concentration, and the resulting relativity and meaningless of traditional values" (Kaes, 186).[5] For the Berliner Tristan Tzara, the city was even becoming like "a serial film. (...) Events are unravelling so rapidly that I have the impression that the whole of Germany is acting in front of an enormous lens", he wrote (in Metken 1992, 29). In his review of a key Berlin *Straßenfilm* of the 1920s, DIE STRASSE (Karl Grüne, 1923), Kracauer specifically noted how it conveyed a "wordless and soulless coexistence of directed automobiles and undirected desires" (in Kaes, 187).[6]

An important distinction between German and French film culture of the period is thus signified in debates about the nature of the cinematic representation of social life where the city becomes largely viewed in negative or positive terms as the locus for a set of questions about work, leisure, gender and modernity. In his discussion of the internationally successful urban German cinema of the 1920s and early 1930s, Jonathan Munby has argued Robert Siodmak's appropriation of the *Kammerspielfilm* in a film like STÜRME DER LEIDENSCHAFT/TUMULTES (1931) was the direct result of a search for "an aesthetic appropriate to the intimate and interior crises brought on by modern urban life" (1996, 78).[7] In a variant on the ways in which Expressionist filmmaking externalized the disturbances of the inner psyche through heightened set design and lighting set-ups, the overtly subjective mobility of the camera in the *Kammerspielfilm* "projected the intimate psychology of individuals onto a world of external objects" (79). Settings were more naturalistic, less abstract than the Expressionist model, but "in the context of Weimar Berlin, this externalised subconscious was hemmed in by the milieu of run-down apartments, producing a characteristically pessimistic, sparse, dark, and claustrophobic effect" (79). The result, from Munby's perspective is a filmmaking practice which sees the city not as a neutral site of social documentation, but as an oppressive state of mind. The physical "body" of the city actually becomes one with the protagonist's imagined relationship to it.

This idea of a highly subjectivised reading of the experience of urban life is also present in earlier films. Janice Morgan (1996), unlike Kracauer, actually sees the city in the *Straßenfilm* in a less pessimistic fashion. She suggests that in this instance the street was posited as "a liberating 'other' place, the scene of random encounters, excitement, spontaneity". The "deep shadows, rushing traffic, circulating bodies, and flashing lights" of the city at night were contrasted negatively with "[t]he claustrophobia of the bourgeois household" (33). This might be so, but by picturing the city after dark as a libidinous and unsettling environment, the city's identity as object of desire is only read as an expression of the extremities of a subjective male consciousness. In any case, the city may become the site of transposition for all the protagonist wants to succumb to, but he does eventually renounce this option. Whether one views the street as imprisoning or liberating, the gender of the implied urban subject is still being universalised as male. As Patrice Petro (1989) rightly cautions, simply reading urban cinematic space as a male domain is absenting one half of the equation. By assuming "the narrative clash of bourgeois and criminal elements [is] an allegory for [Weimar male] subjectivity" (xxi), one is forgetting the place of women in both the urban melodramatic narratives and, in turn, the contemporary audience. In DIRNENTRAGÖDIE (Bruno Rahn, 1927), just to give one telling example of another key city film, the street might also be read as a new site for women, albeit one which is an expression of "the precariousness of Weimar's much vaunted economic and sexual liberation" (164).[8]

A fruitful way of refining an exploration of the relations and differences between Berlin and Paris leading up to the 1930s, lies in focusing on the matter of the crucial inter-relationship between place and memory. Berlin – at home and abroad – was clearly perceived as the European city on the edge of contemporary urban development. Its architecture, wholesale residential redevelopment and concentration of industrial and commercial innovation led many observers to bemoan the way its relationship with the past was changing. For Kracauer, Berlin was the place "where one quickly forgets". "Indeed", he wrote, "it appears as if this city has a magical means of wiping out all memories. It is the present and puts its ambition into being absolutely present (...) Elsewhere, too, the appearance of squares, company names, and store names change; but only in Berlin do these transformations tear the past so radically from memory" (in Hansen 1995, 385). Commenting on the pace and momentum of this change in Berlin, Kracauer called Paris "Europe's oasis" (in Hansen, 386). This emphasis on an equation between the materiality of the moment and the loss of a spiritually informed sense of landscape fuelled the critique made by German anti-modernists. Their thinking had its origins in the almost metaphysical associations between the rural landscape, individual subjectivity and national identity found in the tradition of German Romanticism. The term "asphalt culture" was coined to describe the ill-effects of urban life and the forgetting of the past that the modern city meant. According to the sociologist and economist Werner Stombart, "asphalt culture" extended everywhere, forming "a species of human being that leads its life with no genuine affinity with living nature .. A species with pocket watches, umbrellas, rubber shoes and electric light" (in Frisby, 2001, 246). Wilhelm Stapel, editor of *Deutsches Volkstum*, argued that "Today's battle cry must be 'The resistance of the landscape against Berlin'"(in Natter 1994, 215). Nowhere was this disapproving emphasis on the moment more true than in the field of Berlin cabaret entertainment where songs and performances made witty reference to the multitudinous phenomena of modernity such as the city's transport system, cinemas and open-air amusement parks. Its "secret" was summed up by DER BLAUE ENGEL's composer, Friedrich Hollaender. The pithy and topical skepticism of the Berlin cabaret meant, for him, a "two-minute song of our times, the sweetness of love, the heartbeat of unemployment, the bewilderment of politics [and] the standard-issue uniform of cheap amusement" (in Dimendberg, Jay and Kaes 1994, 566). Erich Kästner, the author of EMIL UND DIE DETEKTIVE (1927), meanwhile, complained that it was natural that the cabaret made Berlin its home. In an astonishingly negative rebuke of its pleasures, he commented that "[t]he metropolis in its natural form is an inhumane place to be and inhumane means are required for it to be endured. (...) Such dreams purify people for their doings by the light of day" (in Dimendberg, Jay and Kaes, 562-3).[9]

Looking at Paris, on the other hand, means taking on board an already complex and very different representational history. Because of the lack of the intense emotions of "blood and soil" Romanticism in French culture, the idea of the city is also less partisan than in the German example. In relation to the metaphorical and literal darkness of the backward provinces, Paris has historically stood for the pleasures of display, sophistication and progressive social change (Corbin 1996). The French capital from Balzac to Flaubert has always meant an escape from the stifling boredom of provincial life. There was a thread of misgiving about the ill-effects of urban life – in a number of French nineteenth century literary accounts of the city and industrial change, for example – but Paris, unlike Berlin, had by then a stable tradition of being seen as an approved symbol for the nation. The 1789 revolution was central in consecrating the French capital as the unified centre of liberty and progressive social and political values. The centuries of commerce, learning, and infrastructure, not to mention the heterogeneous influx of residents from different regions, had all produced a sense of a map which through its distinctive areas could also serve as a metonymic map for the country as a whole. Modern Germany and American companies may have been literally harnessing the power of light to dominate the electrification market and its ancillary industries (including the potential of sound cinema), but Paris continued to stand for the intellectual and political connotations of light in the metaphorical sense of enlighten – ment.

In 1930, we therefore find the French writer Louis Reynaud conducting an enquiry entitled *L'Âme allemande* into the character differences between France and Germany. His speculations concluded that if the German temperament re- lied on a knack for combining instinct and organisation, the French could, on the other hand, be justly celebrated for their elevated sense of taste and reason. His findings match the racially motivated distinction Norbert Elias was later to make in *Über den Prozess der Zivilisation* (1936) between Parisian "civilisa- tion" (meaning intellect and artistry) and Berliner *Kultur* (meaning modern- day socially minded politics). These thoughts find their echoes in the writings of the likes of Walter Benjamin and Kracauer, as well as the French surrealists. They all noted an enthusiasm for the modulated temporal layerings of Pari- sian existence, and marked this with an acute awareness of the processes of change.[10] This fascination with the passing of time and the fleeting nature of the modern urban moment goes back of course to Baudelaire's seminal thoughts on the "ephemeral, the fugitive [and] the contingent" quality of Pari- sian modernity in *The Painter of Modern Life* (1995 edition, 12). It also fuels Louis Aragon's and André Breton's detailed interlinking of subjective mem- ory and urban space in their surrealist novels *Paysan de Paris* (1926) and *Nadja* (1926). In his fascinating essay, "Analysis of a City Map", also dated 1926, Kracauer evocatively described the accumulated sense of social inheritance found in the archetypal Parisian *faubourg*: "Some of the Parisian faubourgs are giant shelters for all sorts of ordinary people", he wrote. " ... The way in which they have cohabited over the centuries is expressed in the form of these shel- ters, which is certainly not bourgeois but is not proletarian either, to the extent that the latter term evokes smokestacks, tenements and highways. It is impov- erished and humane at the same time" (1995, 41). Kracauer could as well be writing of films such as DANS LES RUES and COEUR DE LILAS.

These comparisons have fascinating repercussions. This different cultural inheritance of the town and country dichotomy meant that the ambivalent im- age of the city, apparent in so many German films, did not translate well in the French cinema of the 1930s. There was simply not the same intrinsic disap- pointment regarding a sense of the loss of national purity. Instead, the rural re- gions appeared to sit, at least to some extent, with the metropolitan. Indeed, for Paul Morand who returned from the United States in 1930, horrified by the impersonal, mechanised and streamlined character of American city life, the talent of the French was to combine the two. "In the past, I wished Paris looked like New York", he wrote. "This is no longer true. (...) While I wrote a few years ago: 'France has no choice but to become either American or Bolshevik', I now believe that we must avoid with all our strength these two precipices. (...) The genius of Paris is precisely that of the meticulous peasant" (in Golan, 1995, 81).[11] That is not to say that there wasn't a perceived set of differences between the city and the country in French cultural discourse over the period in question. Romy Golan notes a complex vein of tradition and regionalism running in tandem with more progressive tendencies in the fields of public architecture, design and visual representation. Her argument hinges on the results of the war between France and Germany. "Whilst the Germans", she suggests, "had no choice but to confront the consequences of war, victory gave France the luxury of a *rappel à l'ordre* whose political and cultural agenda was largely aimed at repressing the trauma of war. (...) [There was] a collective ethos driven toward the restoration of what had been before: a world stilled and a vision infused by nostalgia and memory" (ix). Golan notes a turn to depictions of rural life in the painting of the period which was mirrored in the regionalism of writers such as Maurice Barrès and François Mauriac and the influential appointment of the architectural historian Paul Léon as Chef des Services d'Architecture au Ministère de l'instruction Publique et des Beaux Arts who disliked modern German design because it was too "internationalist" (in Golan, 27). There is even a preponderance of painterly depictions of the French capital – by Maurice Utrillo, for example – which instead of viewing Paris in terms of danger and instability (à la Berlin) portrayed the city in terms of a communal village much in the manner of René Clair in Sous les toits de Paris (1930) and Georges Lacombe in Jeunesse (1934). Indeed, the French early sound cinema may be seen as a crucial site for the visualisation of a certain set of depictions of the capital which relied on past notions of Paris. In this sense, instead of being a place of confrontation with the shock and disturbances of modernity as in Berlin, the French cinema auditorium instead became an important site of remembering. The French cinema, crucially, had no real need for the "blood and soil" mannerisms of the likes of the German "mountain film" genre to act in sharp contrast to the depiction of modern life. Paris always meant a different sort of home.

National Boundaries and Early European Sound Cinema

One of the critical ways in which French and German interests met and intersected with the industrial model of the United States was over the issue of the conversion to sound. Indeed, this triangular cultural and economic relationship continued to haunt the paths of the émigrés throughout the decade. As Icart (1974), Andrew (1983, 1995) and Crisp (1993) have all noted, linguistic frontiers which were formerly of small difference during the silent era suddenly became significant stumbling blocks to industrial expansion in the late 1920s. These blocks, in turn, "radically modified the power relations of the national production systems" (Crisp, 10). The power relations in question became codified along the lines of a battle campaign with the respective sides, the Americans and the Germans, using the terrain of France as a key staging post in the struggle for control of the lucrative market of Europe and its ancillary territories. The reasons the French film industry found itself in a position of subordination are complex. In part, it was a matter of simple economics. Most of the major French studios had only just recently depleted their reserves of financial capital because of the electrification of their infrastructure. Then there was the simple issue that none of the major French companies had any formal links to any of the sound patent holders which were principally Western Electric and R.C.A. for the Americans and the newly merged Tobis Klangfilm conglomerate for the Germans.[12] P.A. Harlé wrote in the *Cinématographie Française* that the French found themselves "at ground zero" regarding "creation and distribution of sound equipment".[13] In the words of Andrew (1983, 57), "France was there for the taking".

Another factor that must also be taken into account here is the one which would colour the nature of the French film industry's subsequent relationship with the German émigrés. A key component of the debate over the control of the production, distribution and exhibition of sound feature films was also to be the issue of cultural identity – the matter of what version of modern life, what kind of nationally specific popular pleasures were to be represented on the screens for audiences enthralled by this new form of entertainment. There were some anxious voices. The critic Georges Altman, for example, noted bitterly that "the films coming out of this new technology and which represent 'landmarks' are coming, for the moment, from America and Germany". He even went so far as suggesting that "*the Latin genius* [might] *be badly suited to the screen*" (in Abel 1988, 82). Altman's pessimism was of course misfounded, but a question remained, for many, over what the characteristics of Paris-based sound cinema were to be.

The history of the inter-relationship between technology, economics and the formation of a specifically European film-related cultural identity goes back to the silent period. During the 1920s, several initiatives were formed between Germany and France in an effort to counteract the hegemony of the Hollywood system. In 1925, the alliance of Westi, Ciné-France and Pathé-Consortium (along with Films Abel Gance) produced the monumental and avowedly European minded NAPOLÉON (Abel Gance, 1927) whilst, in the summer of the previous year, Louis Aubert had entered into an alliance with the German film giant U.F.A. (Universum Film Aktiengesellschaft). These measures followed the League of Nations trade conference of 1924 which had stressed the need for European film co-operation as one of the means to heal the remaining bitterness following the First World War. In 1926, the League of Nations actually sponsored the first of the Franco-German led International Film Congresses in Paris.[14] These congresses were an important part of the so-called "Film Europe" strategy of creating a pan-European film industrial structure to counteract the perceived hegemony of the American organisations. More meetings followed in Geneva (1927), Berlin (1928), Paris (1929) and Brussels (1930). At the 1929 gathering, Charles Dulac, vice-president of the Film Board of Trade of France, summed up the prevailing view. In his mind, there were "but two possibilities for Europe – either we must form a European bloc working jointly among ourselves or we will gradually but surely be colonised by America" (in Gomery and Staiger 1979, 40). As Andrew Higson and Richard Maltby note, the history of "Film Europe" was "simultaneously one of economic strategy and cultural practice. On the one hand, there was the very pragmatic form of trade collaboration ... developed in recognition of the need to compete with the American film industry from the strength of a comparable home market. On the other hand, Film Europe was a cultural project which engaged with the prevailing ideas of internationalism. At times, the two ideas intertwined, at times they were clearly in opposition" (1999, 17). Clearly, networks between producers, directors, tech- nicians and performers were established over this period which continued to influence the nature of Franco-German film relations throughout the 1930s. Jacques Feyder, for example, had a contract with DEFU – Deutsche First National to direct a French and German cast in a Berlin studio production of THÉRÈSE RAQUIN (1928), whilst Ciné-Romans financed LA DUCHESSE DES FOLIES-BERGÈRE (1927) directed by Robert Wiene and shot in Berlin, Vienna and Paris.[15] Extremely influential in fostering cross-border relationships was the Alliance Cinématographique Européenne (A.C.E.), the overseas arm of U.F.A. Established in the Spring of 1926, and based in Paris, it served as more than the main conduit for German export features in the French language markets. Under the leadership of Raoul Ploquin, it was also to be part of the German-financed French-language film production phenomenon of the 1930s.

Despite these efforts to produce a pan-European (or more specifically Franco-German) counterbalast to Hollywood, the fact remains that many of the previously mentioned collaborations were short-lived. This was due to the precarious financial position of many French film companies and the use of American capital to bolster German film interests at the short-term expense of the French following the terms of the Dawes Plan. One only has to look at the following sets of production statistics to see the picture of the relative strengths and weaknesses of the two industries at the end of the 1920s.

Film Production

France	Germany
1926 – 84 films	1926 – 202 films
1927 – 88 films	1927 – 241 films
1928 – 94 films	1928 – 221 films
1929 – 52 films	1929 – 185 films

Film Exports[16]

France to Germany	Germany to France
1926 – 23 films	1926 – 33 films
1927 – 28 films	1927 – 91 films
1928 – 23 films	1928 – 122 films
1929 – 15 films	1929 – 130 films

The Paris studios, somewhat symbolically, were themselves divided between looking to America and looking to Germany in terms of the slow transfer to sound technology. A company such as Natan epitomises this split with its Epinay studios being equipped by Tobis and its rue Francoeur studio in Montmartre being equipped by R.C.A.[17] On the other hand, despite these problems and despite the material legacy of French pre-eminence in European film production before the First World War, the relative economic weaknesses of the French domestic infrastructure may have indeed actually helped to facilitate specific patterns of creative-inter-relationships between Berlin and Paris. These modes of exchange then served as a crucial formative context for the subsequent ways in which the French capital was soon to be pictured by foreign as well as French artistic talents. The centrality of Paris here also points to the far-reaching way in which the inter-relationship between European and Hollywood film production and distribution would inform the arrival and departure of the many filmmakers who made the city their temporary home throughout the course of the 1930s. In his early article on the German émigrés in Paris, Elsaesser points out correctly that the passage of the filmmakers to the French capital must be viewed, at least partly, in terms of a trade war "in which Germany reacted to Hollywood's attempted colonisation of European markets by pursuing similar tactics towards its European neighbours, notably France" (1984, 281). Andrew (1995, 172) also notes that *Variety* was "full of notices from 1928 to 1931 accusing the French of making exchange deals with Berlin that violated the quotas they had set up to protect their industry against

Hollywood". Certainly, the Germans were prepared to counteract the aspirations of the Americans which were embodied in the likes of the following article published in *Film Mercury* in March 1930. "We will arrive at our goal no matter what the cost", it says. "[T]he foreign market is from now on just as important as our internal market. It will bring in receipts doubled compared to those at home, and it is for this reason that day and night our businessmen work with tenacity to get the reins of control in hand everywhere" (in Andrew 1995, 94). At the 1930 U.F.A. convention, Ludwig Klitzsch, the Director General, noted the advantages of geographical and cultural proximity in combatting the aims of Hollywood. "Since the coming of sound, the American film industry has almost entirely lost its non-English speaking territories", he remarked. "... On the other hand, U.F.A. finds itself in an excellent situation (...) thanks to the central geographical situation which Germany occupies in Europe which allows it to work in common with those countries who are in need of sound films in their own country but don't possess the means to create and maintain a national film industry" (in Icart, 48). In terms of forging links central to the subsequent phenomenon of the migration of personnel, the most significant feature of this trade war was the development of the multi-language version (MLV) film phenomenon.

Paris as Staging Ground for the Early Sound Wars

In 1929, the German company Tobis established an outlet in Paris as a subsidiary to its central operations in Berlin (See Appendix 1). It had three main components: the production company "Société des films sonores Tobis" which specialised ostensibly in French language film production, the distribution agency "Filmsonor" and the former Menchen studios at Epinay which were subsequently equipped with Klangfilm sound recording facilities. In an interview with the French trade press early that year Docteur Henkel, the director of Tobis's German division, went to great pains to stress the co-operative nature of the project and the degree to which it would benefit France's incipient sound film industry. "It is not at all a question (...) of an intrusion into France by our Berlin company", he said, before going to detail how a group of French, Dutch, Swiss and German financiers had purchased the Tobis patents and were planning to lease them to an independent French company which was in the course of being constituted.[18] Henkel also explained that the studios would be equipped by machinery made in France. Tobis's plans chimed with the words of German producer Erich Pommer who around the same time reminded the French film industry that the way to compete with America in Europe was not to take the path of the "false international film".[19] "A director shouldn't imitate the things which are better done by the directors of other countries", he claimed. "Each country must preserve its national character with elements which represent the best it has to offer. (...) A director should never forget his nationality". This was also the point of view of the second Congress of the International Federation of Cinema Directors (3-7 June 1929) which at the same time stressed the need for co-operative foundations for the battle to resist the onslaught of American-led competition.[20] So it was that in the absence of significant domestically financed sound conversion and production, Tobis in Paris was seen as French film culture's best hope in stabilising a sense of nationally specific norms of sound film representation. The influential trade voice of P.A. Harlé called Tobis in Epinay "our European champion". "Let's hope", he said, "that this brilliant outsider will be ready quickly enough to lock horns with the efforts of the Americans and allow us (my emphasis) to produce (...) the first fine French language films".[21] This must have been the thinking behind the recruitment of René Clair who started work for Tobis on September 15th having failed to complete the early MLV PRIX DE BEAUTÉ.[22] Clair developed prestige level productions such as the hugely successful and influential SOUS LES TOITS DE PARIS which is itself an interesting instance of the complexity of Franco-German film relations in the early sound period. Despite the fact that SOUS LES TOITS DE PARIS was evidently a top-level project, with superbly designed sets of the city by the Russian set designer Lazare Meerson to showcase the world of the ordinary citizens of Paris, it originally failed at the box office in its country of production. It was, ironically, only after a gala presentation in Berlin and positive critical reception from the Germans that it then re-opened in Paris to subsequent success.[23] What is also fascinating, reading the contemporary reports of this phenomenon, is the way that the success of the film was perceived to be due to a combination of factors. It was not just the design and character of the reconstruction of Paris that apparently mattered. What was equally significant was the way that this then showcased the perceived splendours and "gentle sweetness"[24] of the French language itself.

Tobis was not the only foreign company to recognise the financial potential of the chance for audiences of hearing the cadences of their native tongue matched to the moving image. Between 1929 and 1930, Paramount spent $10 million equipping the Joinville complex in Paris that had been owned by Ciné-Romans with six sound studios ready for the production of MLV sound versions. The company Production started in April 1930 under the supervision of Robert T. Kane. As Vincendeau (1988) and Courtade (1991) have argued, MLVs were a significant, early but briefly lived method of overcoming the cultural and economic barriers presented by the arrival of sound in the global film marketplace. Usually shot simultaneously in different languages, like those at Paramount, MLVs also consisted of projects which were "made from the same source material, but with a short time gap" (Vincendeau, 26) or even "polyglot" films such as Julien Duvivier's Berlin based Tobis production, Allô Berlin! Ici Paris (1931) and Pabst's Kameradschaft (1931), in which each speaking actor conversed in his or her native tongue.[25] To some extent, Paramount was well aware of national sensitivities in setting up MLV production in the French capital. It set up a French language committee which included Sacha Guitry, Paul Morand, and Edouard Bourdet. At its 9th International Conference, it reminded French trade concerns that its "sound films made for France, even made for Paris, would mean that French theatrical and filmmaking genius could now be employed on its home turf without the sterilising effect of transplantation".[26] The fact remains, however, that as Courtade (1978) has argued, '[t]he Paramount Studios at Joinville represented the most significant effort at colonisation ever attempted in the field of filmmaking. It wasn't only a question of conquering the French market; through multiple versions the entire European market was involved" (63).

Although short films were also produced at Joinville, at the beginning of 1930, Paramount announced a production slate of 51 feature productions. These included a series based on Poulbot's sentimental illustrations of Parisian street urchins. Only two films were made, Les Rois mages (1931) and Sur le tas de sable (1931), but these indicate a keen interest in fitting in with an established, popular iconography of a timeless version of the French capital. Unlike Tobis at Epinay which specialised in prestige ventures, Paramount signed up all manner of entertainment properties which included, in the words of its 1930 press release, "dramas and comedies, operettas and police plays, [as well as] epics of the Far West".[27] Films were shot in as many as eight principal languages: French, German, Spanish, Italian, Hungarian, Swedish, Polish, Czech and Rumanian. In her memoirs, the script-girl Jeanne Witta-Montrobert paints an evocative picture of the phenomenal, international bustle and exchange of life on set at Joinville in the early 1930s. "[O]peretta matelots and fishwives rubbed shoulders with elegant couples in smoking jackets and silk dresses", she wrote; "each person waiting for the time to rejoin their team. As for those who organised these people – the scriptwriters, directors and assistants coming from all corners of the world – they formed a veritable Tower of Babel which had to be united by someone like me who was in charge of scripts" (Witta-Montrobert, 1980, 35). The same biblical phrase was used in Roger Régent's press report in Pour Vous on "Joinville, Babel Moderne".[28]

One of the important and unexpected consequences of Paramount's project was a certain consolidation in relations between French film professionals and their German counterparts. This was a phase in the Franco-German film relationship which prefigured the later wave of previously Berlin based filmmakers who came to work in Paris after 1933. As well as the expected numbers of German sound technicians who were coming to work in many French studios at the time, Joinville also meant a good deal of on the ground co-operation between other sorts of film professionals. A report from the Berlin based Paramount conference of 1931, confirms that only 60 per cent of personnel working on German language productions were German.[29] It follows that there must have been significant contact between French and German practitioners. Witta-Montrobert notes how the Germans, in particular "were preoccupied with matters of technique" (36). This supports Andrew's argument that "the chief long-term effect of [Tobis and Paramount] (...) was the opportunity and training they provided for hundreds of French artisans to learn a craft that they could carry with them to the numerous feeble but native production companies that inevitably sprouted on the newly bulldozed terrain [of the French film industry]" (1995, 99). In any case, however, the experiment was, in fact, short-lived. Tobis almost ceased production after 1933 and Paramount wound down operations the same year due to the Wall Street Crash of 1929 and the rising popularity of dubbing.

Berlin as Prestige Model and Place of Work for French Film Industry Professionals

In 1929, *Le Courrier cinématographique* commented that "all films that are produced in Paris bear the hallmark of that indefinable thing that none can imitate – 'The City of Light', capital of the world!"[30] Yet, at the same time in Berlin, both the U.F.A. studios and Tobis were already starting out to make French sound fictional features as part of the MLV phenomenon, many of which were also, ostensibly, set in Paris. In 1934, A.C.E. even decided, under the auspices of Raoul Ploquin, to establish a department at the Berlin Neubabelsburg studios specialising in films made by an all-French crew.[31] At first, these were to be MLVs but from 1936 they included exclusively French only single-language productions such as GUEULE D'AMOUR (Jean Grémillon, 1937) and L'ENTRAÎNEUSE (Albert Valentin, 1938). The speed with which the U.F.A. Neubabelsburg studios converted to multi-language sound film production had impressed French film professionals. Gregor Rabinowitsch who had come to Paris in 1923 as "the disciple of Franco-German collaboration", and was co-director of Ciné-Alliance with Noë Bloch, noted how directors in Berlin now "had at their disposition an instrument of great beauty – the studios of U.F.A. (...) which in just six months have been completely transformed and equipped for the talking picture. (...) To write off the costs of a full-length sound film it will be necessary to shoot the same version in 3 or 4 different languages. And for that, it will be necessary to hire foreign personnel".[32] A steady flow of French speaking personnel, such as Albert Préjean and Annabella, thus arrived on short contracts in the Berlin studios to produce French language versions of German productions or German versions of French scripts. Throughout this period, the *Cinématographie Française* had a regular section noting the new arrivals to Berlin from Paris. On 19 September 1931, for example, the trade weekly noted that Yves Mirande and Charles Boyer were staying in the Hôtel Eden, Henri Chomette was staying at the Hôtel Alhambra and Florelle was in the Pension Impériale. The French film press of the early sound period widely acknowledged that the German cinema industry remained worthy of the same critical respect and admiration won through the impact of prestige U.F.A. projects such as METROPOLIS (Fritz Lang, 1927) and DIE BÜCHSE DER PANDORA (G.W. Pabst, 1929). In a production report from Berlin on the set of the French MLV COUP DE FEU À L'AUBE (1932), Antonin Artaud was typical in praising the systematic facility with which the U.F.A. production system could engage in producing high quality popular cinematic entertainment. "The Germans make commercial films in the best sense of the word", he commented. "Their films are of a high technical and artistic quality and being also very human they naturally sell very easily".[33] This account is substantiated by André Beucler's impression that "the Berlin workshops do things well: the photography is clever and precise, the sound excellent, the editing sophisticated (...) In all technical matters, our neighbours make no compromises; near enough is not good enough" (in Crisp, 179). The music hall star Florelle, whose first films were shot in the German capital, also commented that the reason working in the Berlin studios was so agreeable was "because everything is organised there in such a precise fashion". She refused, however, to go further and claim, like many did, that actual German technical prowess outshone the work of their French counterparts. "I can't really say, in my opinion, that German directors or camera operators are superior to ours", she suggested. "The superiority of certain German films lies principally with German organisation which knows how to make the best of the same means that we, in fact, possess ourselves".[34] For the novelist and screenwriter Joseph Kessel, a frequent commentator on Berlin affairs in the French press, German organisation even spread to the representation of the social order. In his review of Siodmak's TUMULTES, he claimed that "what gives the underworld [in the film] a unique and obsessive character is the cohesion with which its members are placed in a network (...) [there is] a total discipline which creates a unit of all these ex-convicts and strong-heads".[35]

Whilst this discipline was discussed in largely admiring terms, it was none-theless also the source of a certain amount of tension during production. Cultural differences were reported over meal times. As Alexandre Arnoux pointed out in a report from Neubabelsburg, the Germans considered eating as a subsidiary activity to the practicalities of solving a particular task. The French, on the other hand, saw lunch as an important opportunity to share and discuss ideas over the communality of food preparation and consumption.[36] There was also the matter of different modes of performance. In an interesting commentary on the distinctiveness of both German and French acting styles, a critic from the Berlin-based *Der Kinematograph*, noticed how French acting talents in the German capital tended to perform in a "more theatrical and complicated manner" than their German counterparts. Their style was "less naturalistic".[37] His comments point to the obvious differences in professional back- grounds. Many of the French stars working in Germany were also engaged in the transition from the music-hall to the cinema. But these remarks also suggest a certain difference in the conception of the representation of everyday life. "We should take into account the differences in the delivery of words, in the expression of a gesture", the article continued. "Romance actors sometimes tend to pathos where we tend to a form of sober objectivity".[38]

Importantly, these differences extended to the problems regarding the representation of the city. The journalist and cartoonist Pol Rab, in a report on the French MLV MON CŒUR INCOGNITO (Mandref Nos and André-Paul Antoine, 1930), couldn't help describing Berlin as a "grey and provincial town" which despite the best intentions was unable to conceive cinematically the character and elusive atmosphere of Paris on screen. "A Parisian interior just isn't a Berlin interior", he declared. "The experienced set designer would notice a thousand differences between the two of them".[39] Whilst it is true that this kind of tension seemed to focus on certain issues of national pride, the key point remains that the governing discourse regarding German cinema was the acuity with which German cinema professionals – be they actors or camera operators – could render a psychological intensity to the depiction of the ordinary realities of city life. If one returns to Artaud's comments on COUP DE FEU À L'AUBE, which as the name suggests was a police thriller, the actor's most significant observation was the existence of a group of camera operators who were "without equal" in their talents. "They research the logical effects of light", he noticed. "They try to create a kind of luminous psychological ambiance which matches the state of mind of the scene. (...) You wouldn't be able to imagine the extent of the care they take to achieve picturesque detail and revealing psychology". For some, this rendering of light was ill-suited to the modes of performance. Florelle commented that she would have preferred her work on

Pabst's L'OPÉRA DE QUAT'SOUS (1931) to be lit by a French cameraman. "Certain passages of the film, I find, are not really to my taste", she noted.[40]

Patterns of Exile and Emigration in the Pre-Nazi Era: The Russians and their Relationships to Paris and Berlin

Paris was a site of exile for many of the dispossessed of Europe even before the tenets of the French Revolution enshrined the notion of France as the country of human liberties. As Schor (1989) has suggested, this search for liberty involved many variations of the word ranging from the material to the moral; from the intellectual and artistic to the political. As far as the French film industry was concerned, the wave of emigration from the U.S.S.R. encompassed all of these definitions. In discussing the importance of pre-1933 emigrations to Paris, it is important to recognise the contribution of the Russians. The trajectories of these émigré filmmakers may have preceded the different journeys from Berlin that took place in the early 1930s, but the two passages can not be seen in isolation. Each grouping developed networks which inform the overall tangled processes of émigré film production during the late silent and early sound period. Victor Trivas, for example, who ended up directing the early Poetic Realist melodrama DANS LES RUES, was one of the original White Russian émigrés in the 1920s and came back to Paris via Germany in 1933. The Russian producer Michael Safra, after working in Berlin, also emerged in Paris to produce features for Berlin émigré Robert Siodmak; and Gregor Rabinovitch, another key Russian producer, went to Germany but returned to France in 1933 and, amongst other films, oversaw QUAI DES BRUMES (Marcel Carné, 1938) with émigré Eugen Schüfftan as cinematographer.

The Russian immigrants of the 1920s were fleeing the Russian Revolution. In this sense, their arrival in the French capital was fuelled by a different set of political priorities than those filmmakers who left Germany after the rise of Hitler in 1933. Just as the waves of emigration from Berlin were enabled by various pre-existing structures of exchange and co-operation between France and Germany, so the Russians were assisted by the fact that the French film industry had long-standing links with that part of the world. Gaumont was well established in Russia before the beginning of the First World War, and Joseph Ermoliev (later Ermolieff) had begun work as a technical assistant at Pathé's Moscow branch. The departure of Ermoliev and fellow filmmakers such as Alexandre Volkoff, Ivan Mosjoukine, Nicolas Toporkoff, Alexandre Lochakoff and Nathalie Lissenko was not sudden. Many had worked in Yalta in the Crimea between 1918-1919 after leaving Moscow, and although they fled Odessa

when the city was captured by the Bolsheviks early in 1920, they knew, thanks
to Ermoliev's preparatory visits to the French capital, that opportunities
awaited them on arrival in Paris. Ermoliev set up La Société Ermolieff-Cinéma,
based in the former Pathé studios at Montreuil, with partners Alexandre
Kamenka and Noë Bloch, but in 1922, he moved to Berlin leaving Kamenka
and Bloch to establish Les Films Albatros. What followed is an indication of
the close proximity between the French and German film industries in this period of intense competition with the increasingly hegemonic model of the
United States. Two years later, Vladimir Wengeroff, from the German-based
film consortium Westi, lured Bloch and many of his personnel to set up a subsidiary of Westi to be based in Paris called Ciné-France-Film. Westi, however,
faced financial collapse in the late summer of 1925. Bloch, therefore, moved to
set up an internationally minded Franco-German production outlet, Ciné-
Alliance, with his former colleague Gregor Rabinovitch, now in Berlin, and the
French production company Société des Cinéromans. Kamenka's Les Films
Albatros continued to make features through to the 1930s. Many of these films
were by prominent directors of the period and include such titles as UN CHA-
PEAU DE PAILLE D'ITALIE (René Clair, 1927) and LES BAS-FONDS (Jean Renoir,
1936).[41] In much the same manner as the succeeding émigrés from Germany,
the Russians actually concentrated on making "French" films despite continued nods to their national heritage. As Albera notes, "[t]he general attitude of
the Russians concerned both the desire to integrate themselves, to be the guar-
antee of modernity, and the wish to meet the wishes of the society that welcomed them. In other words, to legitimate the stereotypical folkloric and exotic
image that France had of Russia" (1995, 80). Although one can observe traces
of the Russian traditional cultural heritage in the continuing vogue for Slavic
melodramas of the 1930s, the Russian émigrés should also be remembered for
their ability to adapt to contemporaneous norms of French cultural representation. Russian set and costume designers, such as Lazarre Meerson and Boris
Bilinsky, worked with the likes of Marcel L'Herbier and Jacques Feyder on
French-based productions, which then went on to be well received on the export market as models of French excellence. The German trade weekly
Lichtbildbühne's Paris corespondent believed, for example, that Albatros's FEU
MATHIAS PASCAL (Marcel L'Herbier, 1925)] "definitely belong[ed] among the
few films of French origin which deserve to be placed in the same class with
the best American and German productions"(in Thompson 1989, 55). For
many, the work of Lazarre Meerson, in particular, was a central influence on
the mode of 1930s' French urban representation which saw Paris as an intimate
village. Andrew (1995) claims that Meerson, particularly in Tobis's SOUS LES
TOITS DE PARIS, "downsized the picturesque vistas of the city of light by con-
structing its more picturesque back alleys" (179). A production report, from

the set of the film, comments on the same thing. "Special facilities have been installed to allow René Clair to both take up the panoramic view and comb each of the houses to study more closely the lives of their inhabitants".[42] This sense of scale concurs with the previously noted French aversion to the dominant Weimar German model of urban representation which saw the city as "everyone's nightmare" (Andrew, 180).

Trade and Economic Emigration from Berlin to Paris before 1933

In a chauvinistic article published in the German film periodical *Kinematograph* towards the end of 1931, it was noted that "the German cinema incontestably dominates Europe. (...) The French film industry owes 80 percent of its success to German efforts".[43] The journalist went on to complain that whilst the French "certainly possess remarkable resources from the point of view of actors and directors, they lack one principal thing: precise organisation or what we call in Germany 'business sense'. (...) It is disarming to hear a French director of production, charged with directing a German language film version, shout to the German actor 'It's impossible to faire solche petites ici'". This intemperate tone, which also neatly captures the linguistic and cultural ferment of MLV production at the time, must be seen in the context of the increasingly political, problematic trade relationship between the two countries. Editorials in the French press of the time were constantly lambasting the German film industry for its perceived inequalities regarding the granting of import licenses and other matters of financial co-operation. France, again, saw itself as the losing partner in the triangular competitive relationship between itself, Germany, and the United States. To some, it was apparent that the Germans seemed to be keen on substituting the word "European" for "German" only when it suited them. Colin Reval noted, for example, that French directors were not allowed to bring French technicians to Berlin to make French MLVs, but the French openly accepted the use of German crews in Paris to make equivalent German MLVs.[44] (It should be said though that this was because French directors in Germany worked for the major studios, whilst the Germans working in Paris tended to be employed by much smaller individual production companies).

The German position was informed by more than a need to make off-hand cultural comparisons. The Berlin film industry was facing real economic pressures of its own. Firstly, there was the increasingly predatory nature of the Hollywood studios who were opening outlets in many of the European capitals. As Vincendeau (1988, 30) notes, "[b]y September 1931, all major US studios had established a presence (in terms of production, that is, since most of them were already present as distributors) in Europe: Warner Brothers, Universal, RKO, Paramount, United Artists and MGM in London; Paramount, United Artists and Fox in Paris; Fox and United Artists in Berlin". Then, secondly, the effects of the Great Depression were still being felt with a noticeable downturn in receipts leading to the closure of a number of cinemas. It was no wonder then that a number of important German-based filmmakers decided to take the opportunity to move and work with their non-"business sense" minded French contemporaries in Paris.

Many of those who made the journey to the French capital took advantage of the pre-existing network of links between the two countries. One of the key staging posts, apart from Paramount and Tobis, was the newly established production company owned by Adolphe Osso called Société des Films Osso (See Appendix Two). Osso had resigned from his influential position as Chief Administrator of Paramount Pictures in the United States at the beginning of the decade and returned to France where for a few years his company sustained an ambitious programme of sound features, many of which were developed by émigré personnel. In May 1931, Noë Bloch was named Director of Production and his links with the German film industry, via his previous partnership with Gregor Rabinovitch, must surely have been useful in the recruitment of such names as Carl Lamac, Heinz Hilpert and Max Neufeld. Bloch was also able to make use of family connections and, the same year, put his nephew, Anatol (later Anatole) Litvak, under contract. Looking at the Osso filmography, one also notes the names of other key Russians such as Victor Tourjansky. By the end of 1931, the *Cinématographie française* was able to note a significant number of foreign filmmakers who were now operative in France. As well as the German names already mentioned, these included the Italians Carmine Gallone, the Swiss Robert Wyler, the Czech Karel Anton and the Hungarians Alexander Korda and Paul Féjos.[45] The number of overseas personnel working on French language film production in France was viewed with consternation in some quarters. A shrill editorial in the *Cinématographie française* entitled "No More Foreigners in Our Country!" argued the case that although foreign filmmakers were providing an "indispensable" service, there must be stricter regulation of the number of native French personnel working on any one production.[46] For others, it was a case of the preservation of the right of French filmmakers to make films based on cultural properties of French origin. In his memoirs, Marcel L'Herbier recalls his indignation that "French literature should exercise so powerful an attraction on foreign directors that a Tourjansky should direct *L'Aiglon*, Korda *Marius*, Litvak *Coeur de lilas* [and] Fejos *Fantomas*" (in Crisp, 178). Yet the service that many of these filmmakers provided was indeed "indispensable" precisely because as foreigners they could enhance rather than subvert the needs of the French industry at a crucial period of transition. The interaction of industrial and national-based factors in this wave of pre-1933 emigration can be examined more closely by turning to two individual studies – Anatole Litvak and Kurt Courant.

Case Study One: Anatole Litvak

Anatole Litvak (See Appendix Three) stands as an under-explored but none-theless exemplary example of the wave of émigré filmmakers who arrived in Paris in the early 1930s prior to 1933. His particular importance rests in the way that, despite his evident outsider status, he was able to participate in con-temporary debates over the direction a specifically French sound cinema should take. It was probably market logic that dictated Litvak's decision to come and work in the French capital. He already knew the city, having briefly worked there after deciding to leave the U.S.S.R. in the mid 1920s. Litvak had been an assistant, albeit in a minor role, on Gance's NAPOLÉON, for example. Although on contract to Société des films Osso, he was lent, in the first in-stance, to Fifra – a production company owned by Dorothy Farnum and Maurice Barber which had recently purchased the rights to the 1920s stage play COEUR DE LILAS. Originally Maurice de Canonge was going to direct the film version, but Litvak's success with CALAIS-DOUVRES/NIE WIEDER LIEBE (1931) had persuaded the French that he was a marketable asset. Litvak was something of a cultural chameleon. Indeed, he has actually been described as "the most Parisian of foreign directors" for the number of his features that he set in Paris.[47] In an interview accompanying his subsequent French feature CETTE VIEILLE CANAILLE (1933), based on the play by Fernand Nozière, he claimed that Paris was the place where he worked the best. "Perhaps there is something in the air, in the way that the spontaneous spirit of all the collabora-tors suits my temperament", he said. "The French do the work in an instant that the English, who are nonetheless charming, take two hours to do with sol-emn slowness; or the Germans can only carry out with the most precise orders. The French may grumble but they do it so well!"[48]

Litvak was born and educated in Russia. After a doctorate in philosophy and involvement in the theatre and cinema in St Petersburg, he came to Paris in the mid-1920s to work with Ciné Alliance and Albatros Films. He continued to pursue his connections with the pool of Russian émigré filmmakers and moved to Berlin where he was involved with Alexander Volkoff on features such as CASANOVA (1927). He worked with his uncle, Noë Bloch, and with Gregor Rabinowitch on the U.F.A. funded SHEHEREZADE and THE WHITE

DEVIL (1930) which necessitated journeying to the Victorine Studios in Nice. He became an editor on Pabst's DIE FREUDLOSE GASSE (1925) in Berlin where he also directed his first feature DOLLY MACHT KARRIERE (1930). After COEUR DE LILAS, he worked in Vienna briefly to shoot DAS LIED EINER NACHT/CHANSON D'UNE NUIT (1932) before returning to Paris. His remaining French films after CETTE VIEILLE CANAILLE were L'ÉQUIPAGE (1935) and the hugely successful MAYERLING (1936). The latter film was his passport to Hollywood and there, later, he directed the remake of the seminal French Poetic Realist drama, LE JOUR SE LÈVE (Marcel Carné, 1939) entitled THE LONG NIGHT (1947).[49]

In interviews, contemporary critical references and memoirs, the recurring feature of Litvak's contribution to the French cinema of the early 1930s, was the extreme diligence and ambition he displayed in his aim to make what he called "real cinema". This term "real cinema" may be said to have three main components all of which intersect with prevalent issues facing French cinema of the period. The first of these elements is the question of the direction that the new recorded medium of sound cinema should take in relation to theatrically based entertainment. Talking about COEUR DE LILAS at the time of the film's release, Litvak argued that "real cinema" should circumvent the pull of "filmed theatre" through its attention to "light, rhythm and images". "In COEUR DE LILAS, my cast only speak when the situation demands", he commented. "I simply want to make cinema; nothing more, nothing less".[50] These remarks echo those of Litvak's former émigré colleague Rabinowitch who two years earlier had said, in his capacity as "the disciple of Franco-German collaboration", that the talking film must not become the "theatrical" film, the cinema must stay as cinema; it must be, above all, a visual medium".[51] They also, of course, echo debates about the nature of sound cinema in the French film press of the time; in particular the now famous distinctions drawn between René Clair and Marcel Pagnol. In juxtaposing the novelty of theatrically based scenarios and dialogue with the former glory of silent film production, Clair believed that "[t]he cinema must remain visual at all costs" (in Abel, 1988, 39). Marcel Pagnol, on the other hand – in his article "Cinématurgie de Paris", for example – saw the potential of the new sound medium to make use of theatrical drama to the extent that "the talking film [should be seen as] the art of recording, fixing, and diffusing theatre" (in Abel, 135).[52] Reviews of Litvak's early Parisian work constantly praise the level of technical prowess and the director's facility to let the co-ordination of images speak at the expense of over-laboured dialogue. His use of extensive traveling shots and rythmic editing are frequently singled out. *Cinématographie Française* noted that in CETTE VIEILLE CANAILLE, for example, Litvak had only kept the elements from the stage version that could be rendered cinematic. "The result is that we have a well edited film that is interesting to follow where the images are important in themselves – it is a film which co-

1. Anatole Litvak shooting COEUR DE LILAS on the streets of Paris (BIFI)

mes from the cinema", it declared.[53] This is true, especially in the many formally
inventive links between the various scenes. The virtuoso crane shot which introduces the world of the street in COEUR DE LILAS, and which I discuss later, is
another indication of Litvak's method.

The second aspect of this notion of "real cinema" concerns the specific facility of film, as a popular entertainment, to draw upon the "authentic" immediacies of the social world for its dramatic narratives. Like a number of émigrés,
Litvak was particularly interested in the urban milieux of his adopted environment. In this sense his concerns matched with uncanny precision those outlined in an important article written by Francis Carco in 1930.[54] Following the
success of his screenplay for PARIS LA NUIT (Henri Diamont-Berger, 1930),
Carco made a call for French cinema to make "films of atmosphere" which
made use of cinema's ability to register, in the minutest detail, aspects of the
urban everyday.[55] Exactly one year later, Litvak himself authored a piece entitled "The Film of Atmosphere must replace the 100 per cent talking feature".[56]
Central to Carco and Litvak's concerns was the sense that the visual inspection
of the camera created a spectatorial relationship which differed from that of
the connection between a live theatrical audience and a stage play. Carco sug-

gested that the cinema was "less collective and more direct", meaning that the partnership between the viewer and the screen was as immediate and intense as the intimate bond created between the mind of a novelist and his or her reader. Consequently, what mattered for both figures was the evocation of so-cial atmosphere and detail over the display and artifice of spectacle and per-formance. Carco, for example, wrote in his article about a subsequent film pro-ject which would draw upon his personal knowledge of the men and women of "certain obscure corners" of Paris whilst Litvak, according to the memoirs of the assistant producer on COEUR DE LILAS, René Lucot (1984), made exten-sive searches for authentic Parisian locations prior to shooting the film. Even in the scenes which were shot in the studio, Litvak uses numerous apparently non-professional faces to provide background flavour to the narrative.

The third sense in which the question of Litvak's "real cinema" related to the concerns of the day is an extension of the points made so far. Litvak matters as an important case study of one of the early 1930s film émigrés because of the level of visual sophistication and training that he was able to bring to a natio-nal cinema searching for a way of competing with the models of Berlin and Hollywood film production. Litvak, simply, was able to bring the proficiency of his German training to the Parisian film studio. Lucot, for example, recalls Litvak's extensive preparations for the previously mentioned key traveling crane shot in COEUR DE LILAS which introduces the atmospheric milieu of the *quartier* for the first time. In her memoirs, Witta-Montobert (1980, 56) also makes the point that Litvak "dressed himself with great consideration". "This finesse was found again in the way that he very rarely mishandled performers and technicians", she observed. "He presented a familiar, solid impression whilst on set but this did not prevent him from being demanding. All his films were meticulously prepared. Most of the scriptwriters he worked with had been formed in the German school – they worked with extraordinary care, leaving nothing to chance, checking the script for the smallest detail. (...) Litvak made his plans in collaboration, then he let his co-workers edit the dia-logue. (...) Once the script was done, he checked it and modified it depending on the kinds of lens he wished to use". All of this points also to close levels of collaboration which can be examined by turning to Litvak's key émigré co-worker, the cinematographer Kurt Courant.

Case Study Two: Kurt Courant

As in the case of Anatole Litvak, there has been very little written on Kurt (later Curt or Curtis) Courant despite his important contribution to the French cinema of the 1930s. His first full-length film made in France was also Coeur de Lilas although he had made French language MLVs in Berlin after the coming of sound (See Appendix Four). Unlike Litvak, he was a native German. He had started making films in 1917 – he co-directed Hilde Warren und der Tod (1917) with Joe May – and in Germany worked with a number of names such as Fritz Lang and Hans Steinhoff who were to leave for France later with the rise of Hitler. In a short memoir of his silent period of filmmaking, Courant recalls how he learnt the dramatic and emotional possibilities of the moving picture medium. "I began to look upon photography not as the mere recording of a scene but as an integral part of the drama", he wrote. Hamlet (Glade, 1920), in particular made him "aware of the unrecognised possibilities of creative cinematography" (1956, 18). Courant also had Italian connections. He worked with an Italian director, Palermi, in Germany, and after Coeur de lilas, he was the cinematographer on Carmine Gallone's Un Fils d'Amérique (1932) shot in Paris.

Courant went back to Berlin in 1932 although, by the end of the year, he had returned to the French capital to set up temporary residence at the Hôtel Napoléon. He did briefly visit Germany the following year but, as a letter published in *Cinématographie Française* later in 1933 makes clear; by now, he saw Paris as his home. The letter is somewhat curious. It seems at pains to prove that Courant was not exactly part of the growing tide of politically motivated émigrés who were beginning to cause some consternation in the French studios. Yet the truth was that Courant was Jewish and so he actually falls into both camps of émigrés who came to work in Paris – he worked in France at times for both economic and political reasons. "It was not without interest or feeling that I read the article in your latest issue devoted to French and foreign filmmakers", the letter says. "I wish to inform you that I have been resident in France since December 1932 but I was not mentioned in your list of foreign operators who have been resident in France from the 1st of May 1933. I also want to add that I always work with a French First Assistant".[57] By saying this, Courant was alluding to the widespread fear that talented and well-esteemed newcomers from the Berlin studios, once installed in Paris, would pose a threat to French job prospects. There was, certainly, a broadly held view that German cinematographers such as himself and compatriot Eugen Schüfftan, were responsible for a perceived German "look". In 1931, for example, a review of Courant's L'Homme qui assassina (Kurt Bernhardt, 1931) had found that if the film had a fault, it was because "the atmosphere is too German. (...) the photography has conceived both the interiors and the full daylight exteriors in *clair-obscur* ".[58] Again and again on his arrival in France, Courant's attention to the singular effects of lighting techniques was signalled by commentators. In Cette vieille canaille there is indeed evidence of a deliberate exploration of the way different lighting sources may be exploited for dramatic purpose. In LE JOUR SE LÈVE (Marcel Carné, 1939) the steam from passing trains is specifically lit for its atmospheric potential. Yet this "German" visual style was to be one of the greatest contributions that the émigrés actually made to 1930s French cinema, in general, and the representation of Paris, in particular. In this sense, Courant was right to stress his affiliations with French filmmaking interests. He is a fascinating example of the way in which many of the émigrés worked in Paris by fitting in and enhancing the development of "native" production by at the same time being "different".

Courant, like his other German compatriots, was "different" because of his technically astute understanding of the narrative possibilities of relating character, space and decor within the frame through the control and direction of lighting. As Philippe Roger (1991, 117) has suggested in his general discussion of the German camera operators in France in the 1930s, the key to this was the simultaneous concentration and dispersal of light within the shot. On the one hand, light was directed so that blacks and whites were reinforced at the expense of neutral and even lighting arrangements. Strong light sources meant a kind of sculpting effect within the space of the image. This often produced harsh contrasts between illumination and ink-black darkness so that the contours and outlines of facial features or items of the decor were dramatically defined. On the other hand, light was also actually carefully dispersed so that the direction of a particular light source was obscured in favour of a more diffuse and suggestive use of shadow. This offered multiple possibilities regarding the creation of space and depth in the image and the situating of the actor in relation to the design of the set in the studio. Courant himself was particularly known for the way he worked to soften the texture of this ambient light through the use of fine silk fabric which was attached to the numerous small projectors he used.

Courant is especially interesting as a case-study because of the important role he played in the future direction of French film output. In particular, he was, as he has already suggested himself, adept at playing a teacherly role to native cinematographers. The benefit of being considered "German" was also that he could pass on the fruits of his own indigenous training. This is an important point. The relationship, for example, between the creative use of diffuse and pointed light sources was "German" partly only because of the vast financial and material resources of the German studios. A heightened degree of proficiency and expertise with the available technology had been managed due to industrial strength. Lighting technology had developed rapidly in the late silent era and Berlin was able to invest in the skills needed to manipulate the various projectors now available. As well as knowing how to differentiate effectively between the older and stronger arc lighting and the softer potential of recent incandescent lamp sources, German technicians such as Courant were also skilled in the potential of new film stocks. The widespread introduction of panchromatic film from 1927 onwards allowed a far more subtle palette of greys and washes which proved to be of great potential regarding the illumination of the urban milieu. The fame of the German camera operators was such in France that Courant's fellow future émigré Eugen Schüfftan actually advertised the new Eastman Kodak film with G.W. Pabst in the French film press. This meant that when the German lighting émigrés arrived to work in Paris, they were seen as advantageous to the future growth of the indigenous industry.

This necessity of this pedagogical function, as Andrew (1995, 177) has suggested, was symptomatic of the lack of any consistent artisanal studio-based learning along the lines of the model of the American corporations in Hollywood. Younger French cinematographers were obliged to develop their skills through temporary mentoring relationships which varied from one production to the other. Throughout the 1930s, before and after his interludes in England between 1933 and 1936, Courant consistently worked with native assistant camera operators such as Charles Bauer, Jacques Natteau, André Bac and Maurice Pecqueux. This amounted to a form of non-formalised instruction. In his memoirs, the set designer Georges Wakhévitch concurred. "I was lucky enough to know the great Germans, such as Courant and Planner, who formed the whole group of people like Matras, Kelber, etc.", he said. "Our cinematographers were practically all taught by these people. We decorators also had alot to learn. (...) The lighting, the acting, the intelligence behind the scenarios [of the German films of our youth] was devastating. For us, it was a revelation" (in Crisp, 377).

Claude Renoir, for example, was Courant's assistant on Jean Renoir's celebrated adaptation of Zola's LA BÊTE HUMAINE (1938). The deputy might well have been impressed by the virtuoso way in which light is modelled by Courant in the film for dramatic purpose. The cinematography makes full use of the aesthetic potential of reflective surfaces like water, window panes, shiny black fabric and mirror glass. At key moments in the narrative, psychological tensions registering on the faces of its main protagonists are enhanced by expressive abstract patterning. In an important review of the film, Emile Vuillerme returns to the themes introduced by Carco and Litvak earlier. In so doing, he highlights the way that Courant's "Germanic" visual style actually served the purpose of such a prestige, ostensibly "French" production. Vuillerme describes how the cinematography of the film reminds him of the work emanating from the Berlin studios in the late silent period. In his mind, however, this is proper because "the subject of the film is *noir*". Indeed, "*noir* is currently the colour in fashion in our studios".[59] Vuillerme then goes on to make a fascinating comparison between the success of this visual darkness and the novelistic qualities of the author on which the film is based. He suggests that "the art of Zola [itself] is essentially cinematographic. His realism (...) is exactly that of a *cameraman*".[60]

The Rise of the Nazis in Berlin and the Politics of Departure

For the thousands of German-based émigrés who decided to leave the country after the rise of Hitler in 1933, the decision to emigrate "was determined by motives which were at once political, moral, emotional and psychological" (Palmier 1990, 143). The situation for many German directors, actors, technicians and producers had been worsening throughout the early years of the 1930s as the Nazi propaganda machine steadily produced diatribes against the perceived Jewish bias of the German film industry. In one 1932 pamphlet, the National Socialist Party claimed that "Germany's motion picture distribution companies were 81 per cent Jewish run" (in McGilligan 1997, 169). In early 1933, Joseph Goebbels went so far as to call for a boycott of all Jewish businesses. Just over a week after the Nazis seized power in the March 3rd elections, Goebbels set up the Ministerium für Volksaufklärung und Propaganda (National Ministry for Public Enlightenment and Propaganda). At the same time, because of this political tide, film trade relations between France and Germany were also showing signs of obvious strain. German press articles, reported in *Cinématographie Française*, still tried to stress the mutual interests of the German and French film-going publics despite the ongoing difficulties involved in the technicalities of economic co-operation. "The charm of Annabella and Milton's good humour" had been called France's best diplomatic assets by Film Kurier.[61] Yet, in March 1933, Bernard's LES CROIX DE BOIS was suddenly banned from further distribution in German cinemas. A spate of nationalistic "revenge films"[62] such as BLUTENDES DEUTSCHLAND (Carl Froelich, 1933) was noted by the French with great anxiety. Given this background of rising national chauvinism, it was not surprising that the new German government moved swiftly to make an imprint on such a key feature of cultural production as the film industry.

The now infamous gathering of DACHO (the Association of German Film Producers), chaired by Goebbels, took place at the Hotel Kaiserhof on 28 March 1933. According to Michel Gorel, then a reporter in Berlin, Goebbels was dressed in a brown shirt and displayed a pronounced "Napoleonic air". Speaking to a vast assembly of German film employees, he complained bitterly that they were making "licentious films".[63] What he meant was that the national purity of German film culture was being tainted. "You are employing the French and the Jews", he reportedly said, according to Gorel. "You are sabotaging the German renaissance and all the work of the Führer. I've decided to keep a close eye on you and that is why I am grouping all the German film companies into one vast syndicate with myself in charge".[64] Goebbels' aim was to purge the German cinema of all of its undesirable elements. In another report, he was quoted to have said that "the cause of the crisis in film isn't economic, it is moral. The German cinema needs new men, new artists, new forces and new subjects. The cinema must evolve with the times".[65] Consequently, the next day after the meeting, U.F.A. set about firing all its known Jewish employees and a formal boycott of Jewish filmmakers was instituted on April 1st. A week later, in the German *Film-Kurier*, Gorel noted at least 4 new films with marked Hitleresque themes already in development.

Kurt Bernhardt, the film director, was at the Kaiserhof meeting and in his memoirs he remembers the room being filled with Nazi stormtroopers. "I had arrived with my girlfriend Trude von Molo, star of L'HOMME QUI ASSASSINA which I had just finished shooting", he wrote. "She was a very beautiful woman and Goebbels wanted to greet her in person. Whilst he approached us, I asked Trude 'What should we do?' She replied, 'Let's get out'" (in Elsaesser and Vincendeau (eds.) 1983, 12-13). Bernhardt was one of many to take an early train out of the country though he did return briefly, with specific permission, to shoot some of the exterior sequences of LE TUNNEL (1933). The immediate decision to leave has, however, been over glamourised by some. This is true in the notable case of Fritz Lang whose own departure narrative will be recounted in more detail in Chapter Five. From Jan-Christopher Horak's account, it appears that the Nazis were aware that the sudden withdrawal of Jewish money would have a disastrous effect on the German film industry but he is wrong to suggest that "there were no new films produced in the Summer of 1933 involving Jewish filmmakers" (1996, 375). Although many had left Germany, some like Ludwig Berger and Joe May were still working on French language MLVS in Berlin in July before their departure.[66] The idea of hordes of people getting on the first train out, therefore, seems to be an exaggeration. It was not until July 14th that a temporary Reich Film Guild (Filmkammer) was instituted with a permanent model coming into effect as late as November 1st. Horak points out that although Aryan ancestry was obligatory, exceptions were made in the early months of the enterprise. Indeed, as late as July, the German government seemed to be keen to persuade some of those who had temporarily deserted the Reich to return. In a circular publicised in the French film trade press, Goering, the German Minister for the Interior, noted the fact that "numerous German subjects belonging to the film industry have gone to Paris in search of work in the studios there. Most of their names are known and they figure on a blacklist. If they do not reply to the letter of reintegration, that they can obtain from the Ministry of the Interior, they will lose their nationality and their possessions".[67] Leaving, evidently, was not a simple matter. As Palmier (1990, 143) sensitively notes, the decision to emigrate was affected by "very diverse objective factors" which included "the material and intellectual capacity to abandon Germany in an attempt to construct a new existence abroad". Many émigrés even believed that they were going to return soon. Alfred Döblin, the author of *Berlin Alexanderplatz*, for example, thought that Nazism was just a "storm" that would not last (in Palmier, 146). A significant number of immediate *départees* in the early months of 1933 returned to Germany from France once their tourist visas had expired. Lotte Eisner, the prominent film critic, was, however, one of the few who felt differently. In one interview, she movingly recalls having to abandon everything; even all her books. "I knew that I wouldn't be coming back in a hurry", she said. "Lots of intellectuals thought that Nazism would only last a few weeks. From the beginning, I was more realistic" (in Badia (ed.) 1982, 299).

The Place of Jews in Paris

The process of the displacement of Berlin-based filmmakers necessitated by the rise of the Third Reich in Germany, had ramifications beyond the immediacies of national exile. Because the émigrés were often Jewish and because they were mainly German, they also played a part in the way notions of Frenchness were discussed. This is why an account of the émigré representation of France's capital is of such intrinsic significance. It raises issues about assimilation and cultural differences, which were pertinent beyond the confines of the film industry of the time. Before moving on to a discussion of the specific reception of the émigré filmmakers when they arrived in the French capital, we need to contextualise their arrival by looking at the place of the Jew in Paris. By tracing the historical relationship between Jewish immigration to Paris and questions about national identity and the city, it becomes apparent that the 1930s émigrés actually fell into a continuum of thought about the nature of urban life which goes back to the nineteenth century.

Paris in the 1930s was the third largest Jewish community in the world after Warsaw and New York. Between 1918 and 1939, 150,000 Jewish immigrants arrived in the city. By 1939, Jews constituted 7 percent of the metropolitan population (Golan 1995b, 164). The majority of these residents lived in Belleville, the eastern section of Paris which was also the focus, in several kinds of cultural representation, of a certain form of authentic, working-class Frenchness.

French Jewry was emancipated during the French Revolution. During the course of the nineteenth century, at least on a certain level, it had begun to view itself as distinctive but also somewhat assimilated into the structures of everyday French society. New Jewish migrants, however, continued to arrive throughout the century, particularly from Germany. Most noticeable was the flood of exiles mainly from Alsace and Lorraine after the annexation of these provinces by Germany in 1871. These migrants settled in the areas around St. Paul, Bastille, République, as well as Belleville. They were later followed by migrants from Poland, the Ukraine and Lithuania. As Weinburg points out, Jewish society in the 1930s was therefore, in fact, divided between older generations of immigrants who were able to maintain a bourgeois existence through commercial and industrial interests and a secondary tier of former Eastern European, skilled, artisanal workers from the textiles and furniture trades. "Like the varied population it served", he argues, "Jewish organisational life in the 1930s was a patchwork quilt of competing identities and solutions to the 'Jewish question'" (1977, 22).

The central component of this "Jewish question" was thus the degree to which Jews could act and be perceived as "French". This attempt to settle cultural difference and attempt to fit in also lies at the heart of the ways in which the émigré filmmakers of the 1930s operated in relation to the representation of Paris. Even at the time of the Dreyfus affair, there were distinguishable strands of opinion about the place of Jews in national life. For the older generations of Parisian Jews, integration meant that fidelity to French identity could work alongside religious affiliation to the remarkable extent that, in some quarters, anti-Semitism, could actually be seen as a German import. France's established Jewry perceived themselves as different from more recent Jewish arrivals from Alsace and Lorraine, while in right-wing discourse, there was an important conflation of anti-German and anti-Semitic sentiment. An example of this confusion was the writing of the right-wing journalist and commentator Edouard Drumont who "disseminated the image of the Jew as [both]the newcomer to France and the quintessential German" (Hyman 1986, 14). This tendency to exaggerate the differences between old and new – between having roots and being uprooted – was exacerbated during the early years of the twentieth century, particularly with the influx of skilled workers from the Jewish cultures of Eastern Europe. The image persisted, however, of the relationship between Jewishness and being German and this duality undoubtedly fuelled the elements of xenophobia which greeted the likes of Robert Siodmak on their arrival on French soil.

An important subsidiary element to the continuing critical debates about the place of Jews in relation to French culture, and Paris in particular, was the contention that Jews were perceived as "symbols of the city (...) and of industrialisation" (Hyman, 200). There are a number of significant ways in which this touches on issues concerning the émigrés and Paris. Firstly, the fact that French Jewishness remained largely an urban phenomenon meant that the ideological value of the old and untouched rural version of Frenchness embodied by the peasant worker could remain intact. Secondly, as a result, it was mainly the French capital that became the staging ground for debates about the degree to which modern material advancement related to the question of national identity. The manner in which capitalism and industrialisation meant a refashioning of what it meant to be French was, in fact, contradictory. On the one hand, Jewishness, in particular, could present a set of anxieties about the loss of what the nation once had. The destruction of the old simplicities in favour of impersonal mass production could be simply viewed as someone else's fault. Furthermore, the inequities of capitalism could be seen as something intrinsic to the character of Jewishness. This is certainly the point, to some extent, in the value-system that the likes of Paul Morand perpetrated. This anti-Semitic line of rhetoric was easily extended in descriptions of the French film industry's main competitors. American finance was equated with ex-German Jewish control and thus also anti-French tendencies. Louis-Ferdinand Céline, for example, wrote of the perils of "American Judeo-Gangsterism" and *L'Ami du peuple* just before Hitler came to power, warned of the dangers of "Judeo-German-American finance" (in Weber, 102). On the other hand, it was obvious that the nation needed to keep up with its industrial competitors such as the United States, Great Britain and, of course, Germany whose industrial strength France feared for political reasons after the Franco-Prussian war of 1870. The tragedy of the post First World War Jewish migration to France was that it only fulfilled a temporary economic need in building up manpower lost due to the ravages of war. When economic stagnation and depression set in, in the 1930s, Parisian Jews, once again, became the targets of resentment. This contradiction between an acceptance of the input of beneficial skills, and a rejection based on redundancy or the detrimental effect they may have on the indigenous economy, was paralleled in the reception of the émigré filmmakers. Although highly regarded, as mentioned before, they increasingly became the focus of economically and racially motivated resentment.

The fact that the majority of migrants naturally made Paris their home raised another issue seized upon in anti-foreigner discourse in relation to the city. Reservations about the extent of urbanisation had led to a rhetoric, in some quarters, that involved the city and its associations with disease and filth. As a result of the waves of immigration to Paris, the stigma of cosmopolitanism could be added to these sins. As Hyman points out, it was post First World War "urban migrants who remained most resistant to the treasured simple French virtues best incarnated in the peasant" (67). In his extensive analysis of the critical practices of the right-wing film critic Lucien Rebatet, Faulkner demonstrates how this historical conflation between the Jewish migrant and urban cosmopolitanism worked within the specific terrain of film culture of the 1930s.[68] He suggests that "Rebatet's reviews [reveal] that the Jew is the figure of heterogeneity" (1992, 145). The word "Jewish" thus became "an emblematic epithet, an omnibus adjective of opprobrium, that [could] designate a person, place, attitude, condition, idea, situation, politics [or] behaviour" (145). In Rebatet's writing, "the word 'Jew' is not merely a serviceable epithet of scorn or abuse; it is the floating signifier of Otherness which formulates the division between the same and different, inside and outside, French and non-French" (145). What is so fascinating is the fact that right-wing critics such as Rebatet then went on to link the perceived ill-effects of Judeo-Germanism with the filmic depictions of the realities of city life which began to proliferate in the 1930s. These depictions included the work of indigenous filmmakers. Rebatet detested both the emerging hard-boiled realism of Americans like James M. Cain and the home-grown populist Parisian literature of Francis Carco because they appeared to conflict with his political allegiances. Writing in *Les Tribus du cinéma* (1941), he linked the popularity of this literature to key poetic realist films such as Marcel Carné's JENNY (1936), and LE JOUR SE LÈVE (1939). For Rebatet, Carné "was the most accomplished representative of that Marxist aesthetic which (...) springs spontaneously from the political, financial and spiritual rot that always follows the Jewification of a state" (86). "The leprous and misty *faubourgs* which [Carné and his like] used for settings exuded nothing but sordid feeling" (87). Jewishness then becomes linked to the negative associations of the cultural representation of urban darkness. Right-wing film historians Maurice Bardèche and Robert Brasillach's made the same point in their critical history of the cinema when they conflate morbidity with the national character of German cinema. In their view, "The French cinema slowly lost its national character" in the later 1930s. "The most famous works between 1936 and 1940 resorted to a morbid aesthetic analogous to that which held sway in post-war Germany" (in Vincendeau 1983, 6). Even in his memoirs published in the 1960s, Brasillach was to complain about the way that "the émigrés cried and raised their fists saying to France 'pay attention,' whilst collaborating in doing their best to create the terror that they denounced" (1968, 121). Despite this, one of the challenges of the early sound era for French filmmaking was to manage an effective and nationally specific set of representational codes for the depiction of the national capital which could compete with the successes of its main rivals, Germany and the United States. One of the greatest paradoxes of the involvement of émigré personnel in the French industry of the 1930s was that they partly helped to shape a filmic version of Paris which did compete, but they did so not just because they were able to fit in, but also because of the contribution of the significantly different cultural baggage that they brought with them.

Reception: The Émigrés' Arrival in Paris

During the nineteenth-century periods of emigration from Germany, France had not usually been the German country of choice. In 1933, out of a total Parisian population of 1.25 million, the number of people of German origin only amounted to between 50 and 60, 000 (Badia 1979, 13). In the light of this, perhaps it is not altogether surprising then that the total number of Weimar refugees in France did not exceed 30, 000, 90 percent of whom were male and 75 percent between the productive ages 25–40 (Palmier 1990, 143 and 274). Nonetheless, between 20 April and 7 July 1933, the Préfecture de Police de Paris noted the arrival of 7,195 German refugees (Thalmann 1982, 150).[69] The émigrés from Germany can be divided into three major categories: Jews fleeing racial persecution; political opponents of the National Socialist regime; and lastly, literary, artistic, or intellectual figures who were motivated and prosperous enough to refuse the terms of the new dictatorship. They included, apart from the names already mentioned, the following filmmaking talents: the directors Karel Anton, Hans Steinhoff, Adolf Trotz, Joe May, Robert Wiene, E.A. Dupont, Richard Oswald, Ludwig Berger, Berthold Viertel, Fedor Ozep, Wilhelm Thiele, G.W. Pabst, Max Ophüls, Richard Pottier, Hermann Kosterlitz, Leontine Sagan and Alexis Granowsky. There were also the producers Seymour Nebenzahl, Eugen Tuscherer, Joseph Somlo, Joseph Lucacevitch and Hermann Milkowski; the writers Hanns G. Lustig, Ernst Neubach, Friedrich Kohner, Emeric Pressburger, Walter Reisch and Billy Wilder; the composers Franz Waxman, Max Kolpe, Friedrich Hollaender and Oskar Straus; the cinematographers Hans Androschin, Franz Planer, Otto Heller and Georg Krause; the actors Peter Lorre, Felix Bressart and Walter Rillo; the editor Jean Oser; and the set designers Otto Erdmann, Ernö Metzner, Hans Sohnle and Emil Stepanek.[70] Many of these film industry professionals passed through the Hotel Ansonia, 8 rue de Saigon, near the Arc de Triomphe.[71] This trajectory was later written about in Erich Maria Remarque's novel *Arche de triomphe*. A small number of wealthy exiles found rooms at the Majestic Hotel, avenue Kléber, which ironically later became the main headquarters of the German military command during the Occupation.

At first, the émigrés were treated sympathetically by the French government. A circular from the Ministry of the Interior, dated 20 April 1933 (in Palmier, 277), gave instructions that French consulates were to treat German Jewish requests for visas liberally. Even at this stage though, the move was opposed by hostile journalists in right-wing publications such as François Coty's hugely popular, anti-Semitic *L'Ami du peuple* which, as early as 1930, had a circulation of one million copies and claimed a readership of three million (Weber 1995, 88). In June for example, it criticised the "hurried tide of Jewish-socialist-Germans" who had descended upon the French capital (in Badia 1979, 26). Paul Morand (in Badia 1979, 26) writing in *Le Temps*, also noted the "veritable Biblical" nature of the photographs appearing in the newspapers that depicted the scenes at the Gare de l'Est and its environs. At the end of October 1933, the French government took its first steps to rein in this flow of German refugees. The Minister of Foreign Affairs asked the French ambassadors in Berlin and Munich to no longer issue visas to Germans unable to provide all the required documentation. Extra vigilance was advised along all frontiers. A report in the *Pariser Tageblatt* of 20 December claimed that the German consulate was no longer issuing new passports after expiry "due to fresh instructions" (in Aurich et al. 2001, 224). With an increase in xenophobia exacerbated by the Stavisky affair of January 1934, the Ministry of the Interior advised prefectural chiefs in the Autumn to stop granting extensions to foreigners who had obtained only short-term visas from French consuls.[72] On 6 February 1935, the French government formally passed a decree which limited the validity of identity cards for overseas emigrants. At the same time, foreigners were disqualified from taking on salaried work without first obtaining a work contract. This degree of administrative uncertainty is reflected in Siodmak's account of the time that he spent in France. "I didn't have a passport and my wife had only a German one which could have been cancelled at any moment", Siodmak wrote. "Not having a work permit meant that my presence was only barely tolerated. I don't know how many days we spent at the Préfecture. We were part of the hundreds of people from all nationalities sitting on wooden benches. We never knew if our permit to stay would be extended" (in Elsaesser and Vincendeau (eds.), 13).

The émigrés were well received in some quarters of Parisian society. Jewish refugees were subject to welcome committees such as the *Comité national de secours aux réfugiés allemands victimes de l'antisémitisme* organised by the Consistoire israélite de Paris under Robert de Rothschild. In February 1934, the committee decided to organise the *Bibliothèque des livres brûlés*. It opened on 10 May of that year. Entertainment such as the Franco-German cabaret Die Lanterne was established to provide twice-weekly revues of songs, dance and sketches between 1933 and 1939 at various locations around Paris including the Caveau Camille Desmoulin at the Palais Royal. At one time, Joseph Kosma, the film composer, was its music director. Various press organisations such as the daily *Pariser Tageblatt* and the weekly *Les Nouvelles d'Allemagne* kept the newcomers informed and assisted them in the formation of a sense of

place. Artists and intellectuals were also befriended by politically minded
French compatriots. The case of populist novelist Eugène Dabit who was the
intimate of many émigré writers, is particularly interesting. His most famous
novel, HÔTEL DU NORD (1929), was filmed in 1938 by Marcel Carné in a production supervised by the former U.F.A. producer Joseph Lucacevitch.[73]

Lucacevitch was just one of the many Berliners who arrived in Paris to be
praised by sections of the French film industry for their skills and professional-
ism. In a later interview, Louis Daquin recalls Lucacevitch's singular tenacity
in getting each scene just right. "As for the school of French cinematography",
he recalled, "their skills were perfected [by the arrival of] the German camera
operators; all the assistants battled to work with them" (in Vincendeau 1983,
5). Despite these comments, the idea of Paris as the City of Light – a kind of urban lighthouse beacon signalling the values of liberty to those in distress –
needs to be seen in a fuller context. Just as this book explores the culturally
coded notions of darkness as well as light in relation to the filmic representation of the French capital, it is as important to acknowledge the shadows of xenophobia and racism behind the glow of goodwill. According to the German
idiom, the definition for contentment is to be "as happy as God in France". That
certainly was not always the case for those filmmakers who found themselves
exiled in Paris.

Reception: The French Film Industry

From the perspective of the French film industry, the presence of foreign professionals working alongside French workers on French-language productions was consistently viewed with a certain amount of ambiguity. By the early
years of 1933, it was evident that a number of directors who had achieved popular success with the French public with productions based in Berlin, were
viewing Paris as a destination due to increasing political difficulties in Germany. Nino Frank touted this potential in a report which suggested that the
French capital could soon amass a group of talents which "Hollywood would
be able to envy us for".[74] One of the directors mentioned was Victor Trivas.
Trivas's enthusiasm for working in Paris may well have been tempered by the
reports which began to regularly appear in the French film press. A typical editorial in *Pour Vous* deplored the persecution of minorities in Nazi Germany
but, at the same time, it cogently emphasised the growing anxieties of native
French filmmakers. "Several French directors have been coming to see us", it
reported. "The current situation is worrying them. There is so little work in
France but [they say] you can see yourself calmly removed from directing a

production in favour of a stranger, freshly arrived from Germany who is unknown in this country".[75] To this extent, the magazine applauded a decision by the Employment Minister on 7 April 1933 to further regulate the percentage of foreign workers permitted to work on a French film production. This decree followed earlier versions issued on 10 August and 19 October 1932 which specifically addressed the Americans. It stated that no more than 10 percent of the major artistic personnel, and no more than 25 percent of minor staff members on a single film project could be foreigners.

Previous scholarly attention to the phenomenon of German emigration to France has not fully recognised the level of ambivalence in the French reception. Throughout the summer of 1933, the Parisian film press was making ever-sharper distinctions between genuine political refugees and those who were coming to work in France for economic reasons. In an article entitled "The Great Exodus of Cinema Jews", Michel Gorel drew a line between the moneyed "carpetbaggers" (as he saw them) and the "real victims of the Hitlerian terror". "Among these German Jews, I know two or three directors of real talent, a dozen excellent camera operators, several magnificent actors and a number of authors and scriptwriters of real sensibility", he commented. "We have to set them to work – and fast!"[76] Lucie Derain pointed out, however, in an article which bore the headings "The Overseas Invasion" and "French Directors First", that every overseas talent such as Anatole Litvak and Kurt Bernhardt who found employment, there was the risk this would put a French director out on the street.[77] Similar arguments were consistently made for the number of French cinematographers facing unemployment. This point underlines, again, the perceived strengths of the German émigrés. Paradoxically, it appears that little critical attention was paid to the influx of Berlin producers who, as previously mentioned, were in a position to galvanise their contacts and revitalise the French film industry. Derain's article, in particular, specifically bemoans the lack of native French talent in this domain to match the contributions of Germany and the United States. "It is imperative that we rapidly acquire this sense of organisation that is so lacking", she complained. Derain, at this stage, had yet to realise the impact that the likes of Seymour Nebenzahl, producer of several Siodmak features amongst others, would have on French film production.

By 1934, France's economic situation had worsened and the German film émigrés increasingly became the subjects of organised hostility from disenfranchised sections of the French film industry. Most famously, the studios at which Robert Siodmak's prestigious musical LA CRISE EST FINIE was being shot were picketted by protesters bearing placards with the motto "Siodmak Go Home!" In May, the Justice Minister specifically rejected requests that the émigré filmmakers be naturalised whilst the Employment Minister Adrian Marquet announced that no further work permits would be issued to foreign film personnel. Gaston Thiery captured the thinly veiled tone of antagonism in an article published in *Paris-Midi*. In a dig at the enthusiasms of the likes of Victor Trivas, he noted that "We learn that a film with a 'truly French' subject and title is currently being shot in a Parisian studio (...) where the producer of this film is one M. Apfelbaum (or some such name). (...) If we think about this carefully, will this really be a French film? (...) When one notes that half of the French film workers are unemployed, the worry is whether the facilities offered to foreigners aren't perhaps a bit much" (in Jeancolas 1983, 115). This type of criticism was just the polite version of an increasingly harsh line of politically motivated rhetoric which held sway over segments of parliamentary discourse and, more widely, in the proliferating right-wing press. The pejorative term *métèque* began to appear more frequently in articles along with the word "invasion". Jacques Feyder complained that "Jewish invaders had taken over the French cinema" (in Weber 1996, 93).[78]

A key example of this anxiety over national pride in the sphere of cultural activity was the publication of Paul Morand's *France la doulce*, first printed in serial form in 1933 and then published by Gallimard in 1934. The novel satirises the place of the foreigner in France's film industry by telling the story of the manipulation of a Breton aristocrat by a bunch of scheming foreign Jewish financiers who want to set up a film production company. In the publicity attached to the novel, Morand denied any intentions of ill will. "To prevent any misunderstandings", he wrote, "I declare that the rabble who swarm around here bear no relation to the big international names which we have welcomed on their journey. I am only asking for a place for our compatriots; just a small place in our national cinema". Nonetheless, the following description of the supposed current state of French film production speaks volumes. "This was a new dimension, without any depth, where logic, form and normal relations had disappeared in favour of a never-ending Tower of Babel in which words and the simple ideas of ordinary human exchange were emptied of their original sense. Only the word 'money' was capable of stirring this heavy spirited but powerful world" (1934, 122). Morand's theme of the corruption of French cultural production was later reiterated in Marcel Pagnol's self-reflexive cinematic representation of the film industry, LE SCHPOUNTZ (1938). The film featured a Jewish producer and a director, Bogidor Glazounov, who because of his undetermined nationality, Russian name and Italian accent was sarcastically allowed to be defined as a "great French director" (in Billard, 207).

As seen earlier, France's Jewish population became a particular part of the way that definitions of the French nation state were fought over by both sides of the political spectrum in the 1930s. For the Right, the Jewish film émigrés, amongst others, represented an unwarranted threat to a pure and homogenous version of nationhood, whilst for some Leftist elements they could stand as a symbol of organised capitalism. Faulkner (1992) has even gone as far as arguing that the Parti Communiste Français's (PCF) scornful but nationalistically motivated rhetoric of the "two hundred families" during the period of the Popular Front actively contributed to the eventual success of the right-wing argument. The "two hundred families" were the unjustly favoured ruling elite of the nation whose interests were naturally hostile to the programme of Léon Blum's short-lived Popular Front reform government which came to power after the elections of April-May 1936. Faulkner's suggestion is that the PCF "created room for a competing interpretation" by allowing "the Right to supply its own anti-patriotic equivalent of the Left's 'two hundred families' in naming Jews and foreigners as enemies of the nation and the state" (139-140). Be that as it may, it is true that the reprieve offered by the Popular Front regarding anti-foreigner legislation ended with the fall of Blum's government in July 1937. Restrictions on immigrants and quotas on the number of foreigners employed in the film industry were re-enacted. In March 1938, illegal aliens were even formally barred from Paris. They were given the choice of either leaving the country or going to work on a farm in the provinces. In the year that the Second World War broke out, Rebatet's column in *L'Action française* produced a black list of Jews and foreigners who had directed films in France in 1938. Yet in terms of many people mentioned in this book, Rebatet was in a way beating a dead horse. Several of the émigré filmmakers were already on their way to the United States, a place whose film industry, unlike its French counterpart, was from its earliest beginnings made up of migrants.

Case Study Three: Erich Pommer

In many ways, Erich Pommer is an emblematic example of the interrelationship between the French, German and American film industries that characterises the general history of the German film émigrés. Before arriving in Paris in 1933, he had already had extensive experience as a film producer in all three countries. This trajectory provides an insight into the shifting positions of strength and interdependence between the different localities. It also explains two further points: the course Pommer's career took after his arrival on French soil when Hitler came to power, and the extent to which it was actually viewed, in some quarters, as a source of national pride that such an international figure should make Paris his temporary home.

Thanks to the recent research of Ursula Hardt (1996), we now have a clearer and more detailed picture of the course of Pommer's international career. Pommer had started work for the Berlin-branch of Gaumont in the pre-First

World War period at a time when Franco-German film relations were skewed in favour of Paris. The main French companies had important subsidiaries in Berlin and the majority of films exhibited in the German capital then were of French origin.[79] He started to have direct contact with Paris whilst working in Berlin for Eclair, and before war was declared, he was put in charge of an Eclair production unit in Vienna. Marcel Vandal, Pommer's collaborator in the Austrian capital, served as a co-producer with him on Fritz Lang's émigré Paris film LILIOM (1934). During the First World War, France's subsidiaries in Berlin were placed under military supervision, but the Franco-German film relationship survived through the creation of innocuous sounding "front companies" set up in neutral countries. In the immediate years after the First World War, Pommer was at the forefront of the reorganisation of the nation's film production as Germany's film industry faced strengthened economic pressure from Hollywood. Arguing that Germany needed to control capital because of the pressure of war reparations, Pommer advocated the previously mentioned system of import quotas for French film exports. He took on Fritz Lang as a leading directorial talent and after his significant domestic and overseas success with Robert Wiene's DAS KABINETT DES DOCTOR CALIGARI (1920), he became increasingly concerned with overseeing the high-production quality, "artistic" end of German film production. Pommer became famous as the producer of the so-called *Großfilm* such as DIE NIBELUNGEN (Fritz Lang, 1924) – the large-budget, export market driven features which are remembered today at the expense of the vast majority of less-expensive, popular genre films, which mainly targeted the domestic mass audience. By the mid-1920s, he had a powerful holding in the eyes of his European competitors. *Cinématographie Française* called Pommer "the soul of the gigantic [German] cinematographic organisation" (in Hardt, 82).

Following the fallout from the controversial trade agreements between U.F.A. and Paramount and M.G.M. in 1925, Pommer resigned from his position in Germany and went to the United States for two years.[80] It was there that he encountered, first-hand, the material differences and advantages of a modern industrial infrastructure and consumer society that so interested the Berlin intelligentsia of the time. When he came back to Europe, he brought with him an enthusiasm for the possibilities of new production techniques. Pommer had been fascinated with the superiority of American lighting techniques and opened the door for Kodak and Eastman Panchromatic negative film to be made available for German films. The subsequent degree of facility and expertise in the possibilities of managing the exposure of light on negative film was to be a significant contribution of the German émigrés to French film production. As well as introducing the novel concept of a shooting schedule, Pommer also began exhibiting a greater degree of American showmanship which as

Hardt points out, became crucial to the German advantage in the transition to sound. In 1929, Pommer declared that the task of his native film industry "is not so much the cultivation of the absolute artistic film, as it is the raising of the artistic level of the entertainment film" (in Hardt, 113). This comment provides a clear indication of where he also stood in relation to his short-lived output in France between 1933 and 1934.

Two key successes overseen by Erich Pommer in the early sound era reveal the two directions that the export-led component of German cinema took in the years leading up to Pommer's decision to emigrate to Paris in 1933. Firstly, there was the cycle of the light musical *operettenfilm* established by Germany's first sound feature, MELODIE DES HERZENS (Hanns Schwartz, 1929). As Elsaesser points out, "many of the émigré directors obtained their first contracts and assignments in France, Europe and Hollywood" because of their work in this genre (2000, 336). Secondly, there was the phenomenal success of the darker dramatic elements of DER BLAUE ENGEL (Joseph von Sternberg, 1930). As already mentioned, many of these features were MLV productions and Pommer became adept at allaying the costs of some productions by creating short-term partnerships with foreign business partners (See Appendix Five). Given his demonstrable business flair, it is not surprising then, that Pommer had already made provisions for his professional future by the time the U.F.A. board met on 29 March 1933 to decide the fate of its Jewish employees. Unlike the majority of Pommer's fellow Berlin émigrés, the move to Paris was for him, just his continuing of business as usual.

Ludwig Klitzsch had apparently assured Pommer in 1932, that U.F.A. would not discriminate against Jews, but by the beginning of 1933 Pommer had entered into discussions with American Fox Film Corporation's Sidney Kent about setting up a European production subsidiary in Germany or France the following Autumn. Clearly, Pommer was hedging his bets about the outcome of the political developments in his native country. After his dismissal from U.F.A., he remained in Berlin until the third week of April but when his son began to encounter anti-Semitic discrimination at school, Pommer immediately began making plans to take the Berlin-Paris train as far as Hanover. The Pommer family was then driven into France at a more obscure border crossing. Although Pommer rightly feared for his wife and child, there is evidence that he was still cognizant of his status within the now highly politicised world of German film production. He might well have been considering returning briefly, for he left preparatory work on the Fox German outlet with an assistant, Eberhard Klagemann. Certainly, as with certain other prominent German Jewish filmmakers, Nazi authorities were prepared to turn a blind eye to the producer's ethnicity for the time being. During his stay in Paris, probably for propaganda as much as practical reasons, German authorities offered Pommer the chance to become an honourary Aryan. As late as 1935, he was granted a curious renewal of his German passport in New York which did not identify him as Jewish.

Pommer spent his early months in the French capital settling in and expanding his contacts. In August 1935, the formation of Fox Europa Productions was announced in the French trade press. In an indication of how earlier Franco-German collaboration had provided a grounding for the subsequent French output of the German émigrés, Pommer's appointed assistant was André Daven. Daven had been a production supervisor for Paramount at Joinville under Robert Kane and supervisor of French-language versions of U.F.A. films in Berlin. They commenced with two projects: LILIOM, directed by émigré Fritz Lang, and an adventure film starring Henri Garat. This second feature turned out later to be ON A VOLÉ UN HOMME (1934). It was directed by fellow émigré Max Ophüls and was based on a script by René Pujol and Hans Wilhelm.[81] Judging by the admiring comments published in sections of the French film press, the arrival of Erich Pommer on French soil again was perceived as a matter of great potential. Referring to the successes of both "dark" films such as ASPHALT (Joe May, 1929) and TUMULTES (Robert Siodmak, 1931), and "light" films such as LE CHEMIN DU PARADIS/DIE DREI VON DER TANKSTELLE (Wilhelm Thiele, 1930) and LE CONGRÈS S'AMUSE/DER KONGREß TANZT (Erik Charell, 1931), Roger Régent reminded French readers that Pommer's films had "a definite personality, a concern for detail and a degree of technical perfection".[82] Pommer reciprocated. "I want to favour in all possible ways the French industry", he told Régent. "I want to devote my efforts to discovering the young gifted individuals who should tomorrow constitute the real backbone of French cinema". By now, Pommer obviously didn't expect to return to Germany. "I am starting my life again", he said. "Everything is finished [in Germany]".[83]

Pommer and Daven had initial plans for further productions in Paris which included a Jerome Kern and Oscar Hammerstein operetta to starring Garat and Lilian Harvey.[84] In a later interview in *Cinématographie Française*, Pommer detailed his plans to create a "serious Franco-American collaboration" with the idea of pooling technical and artistic resources from both countries in a Paris-based production outlet to rival the German industry.[85] This new and ambitious reformulation of the triangular film relationship between the United States, Germany, and France is a powerful reminder of the changes in European film culture that the Nazis necessitated, but ultimately, Pommer's dream failed. Both LILIOM and ON A VOLÉ UN HOMME failed at the box office and Fox pulled out of Europe, partly because of these failures and partly because of the currency difficulties America experienced after it decided to abandon the gold standard. In any case, France was now experiencing the worst of the Depression and xenophobic sentiments were running high. Pommer's status as a particularly international émigré was beginning to count against him. In relation to Liliom, Lucien Rebatet was to note in a sneering fashion that "by virtue of the 'cleaning' of the German studios, the Jew Erich Pommer has installed himself with us. (...) M. Pommer may wish to make France the new centre of cosmopolitan film production, but he has only brought us a yid film in both technique and spirit".[86] Pommer was also suffering from health problems and decided to take move to the United States. He was to return to Germany only after the war, where he took a job initially turned down by fellow émigré Billy Wilder; that of overseeing the reconstruction of the shattered Berlin film industry during the American Occupation.

Case Study Four: Robert Siodmak

In terms of the scale of his work, Robert Siodmak is probably the most important of the German émigré filmmakers who came to Paris in the 1930s. Apart from the scale of his output whilst in France, Siodmak is also noteworthy because of the number of other émigrés with whom he worked. Like Erich Pommer, he was a well connected and well respected member of the former Berlin filmmaking fraternity. Accounts of his personal history have played up the apparently shifting nature of his identity. Like his compatriot Fritz Lang, Siodmak was not averse to an element of self-mythologising. Contrary to personal legend, the director was actually born in Germany and not the United States to where his father had emigrated at the end of the previous century. Siodmak liked to refer to the accident of his so-called American ancestry especially after emigrating to America himself, but he was of firm European origins as a descendent of a group of Hasidic Jews in Poland. He worked as an actor in the theatre and briefly set up an illustrated revue magazine before moving to Berlin with his brother Curt in the mid-1920s with the aim of getting a foothold in the capital's film industry. Central to Siodmak's place in this book is his association from an early stage with the cinematic representation of the modern city. In 1929, along with fellow café-life associates Billy Wilder, Edgar George Ulmer, Friedrich Zimmerman and Eugen Schüfftan, he was responsible for the influential *plein-air* city documentary Menschen am Sonntag which depicted the activities of the residents of Berlin during the course of their day of rest. All of these filmmakers were to emigrate from Germany in the 1930s with Wilder and Schüfftan both working in Paris. Wilder stayed just long enough to make Mauvaise graine (1934) whilst Schüfftan continued to be part of the French

film industry until the 1960s. He was Siodmak's cinematographer on LA CRISE
EST FINIE (1934).

Following the success of MENSCHEN AM SONNTAG, Siodmak was subsequently taken on by Erich Pommer at U.F.A. where he worked as a director on
a number of high profile, mainly Berlin-based films. In the course of this short
period, he was to become one of Germany's most celebrated directors (See Appendix Six). Siodmak's first sound feature, shot with Schüfftan, was the natu-
ralist urban melodrama ABSCHIED (1930). It was written by Emeric Pressburger who also served as a scriptwriter on LA VIE PARISIENNE. Set in a dingy
Berlin boarding house, the drama apparently exemplified Siodmak's predilection for establishing the precise social context of his narratives through an attentive use of camera movement and decor. Shortly after completing the film,
he wrote a number of articles in German film periodicals extolling the new
dramatic potential for the visual and aural components of film to capture the
realities of the ordinary urban dweller. Like his fellow émigré Litvak, he
wanted to produce a cinema which referred to the complexities of city life as it
was actually led. For Siodmak, the technical and aesthetic potential of "real
cinema" similarly meant a conflation of the medium of sound film with the details of "real life". Arguing for the virtues of actorly and directorial improvisa-
tion only after the benefits of careful rehearsal and planning, he suggested that
dialogue "must be natural, 'popular' in the true sense of the term. No gesticu-
lation, no recitation, no pathos but life itself in all its simplicity" (in Dumont,
1981, 46).

After the satirical black underworld comedy DER MANN DER SEINEN
MÖRDER SUCHT (1931), scripted by Billy Wilder, Siodmak turned to his first
MLV production, the prestigious VORUNTERSUCHUNG/AUTOUR D'UNE EN-
QUÊTE (1931). The French version of the film was shot simultaneously and
starred Pierre Richard-Willm in the part played by Gustav Frölich. It also featured Florelle, Annabella and Gaston Modot. René Clair's brother, Henri
Chomette, was appointed co-director and French dialogue supervisor.
Chomette was nicknamed "Clair-Obscur" in the trade, essentially meaning
"the lesser known Clair" but whilst this may have been true, the term also has
a secondary ironic meaning which points to the significant difference between
the French and German depictions of the city at that time. Unlike the lighter,
more romanticised version of capital city life achieved by the more famous
Clair, VORUNTERSUCHUNG was primarily indebted to the atmospherics of
"clair-obscur" lighting which emphasised the social entrapment of an impoverished world of urban shadow and darkness. The melodramatic crime narrative takes place in a series of poorly lit boarding house rooms, city offices, underground train carriages and dingy streets. Through its investigation of the
inter-relationship between the bourgeois world of a judge's son and the tene-

ment life of a female prostitute it may have born a resemblance to DIRNENTRAGÖDIE. As Dumont suggests, however, Siodmak's film was actually more a forerunner of the spate of realist city films that appeared in Berlin that same year. These included Piel Jutzi's adaptation of Alfred Döblin's BERLIN ALEXANDERPLATZ; Lupu Pick's GASSENHAUER/STREETSWEEPER and Hans Tintner's ZYANKALI/CYANIDE. The following year, Siodmak was to have his greatest German success with the MLV urban underworld drama STÜRME DER LEIDENSCHAFT/TUMULTES, which starred Emil Jannings and Charles Boyer, respectively. The script was actually written in Paris by Siodmak and co-workers, Robert Liebmann and Hans Müller. As Dumont has noted, the film bears some similarities to the German street film as well as to American early sound crime dramas like CITY STREETS (Rouben Mamoulian, 1931) and PUBLIC ENEMY (William Wellman, 1931), but it differs from these prototypes in way it represents public morality. In the case of Siodmak's film, there is no redeeming conclusion in which bourgeois codes supplant those of the urban criminal underclasses. In TUMULTES, we see ample evidence of Siodmak's facility to marry psychological detail with social texture. Through the effective use of lighting and decor in particular, the city emerges, despite the additional use of location footage, as a claustrophobic and heightened environment for the consequent outpouring of criminal and emotional passions. The film was a great success and managed to seal Siodmak's French critical reputation for producing a certain kind of city-based realist cinema. It was still playing in Parisian auditoriums in the Autumn of 1933, months after the director's arrival on French soil.

After a light costume comedy appropriately called QUICK (1932) for U.F.A., Siodmak joined its main competitor, Deutsche Universal-Film AG to shoot an adaptation of Stefan Zweig's BRENNENDES GEHEIMNIS/BURNING SECRET (1933). Deutsche Universal-Film AG, a former branch of Universal Pictures, was becoming an increasingly indispensable place of hospitality for Jewish filmmakers. In 1932, one could count fellow future Parisian-based émigrés such as Franz Waxman, Hermann Kosterlitz and Kurt Bernhardt among its luminaries.[87] The company was also, at the time, responsible for the distribution of the films of Siodmak's cousin, Seymour Nebenzahl's Nero-Film company (See Appendix Seven). An indication of the problems facing Berlin's Jewish filmmaking population is provided by the fact that the premiere of BRENNENDES GEHEIMNIS was delayed several times. It finally took place in Berlin on 20 March 1933, but the film was projected without any production credits as stipulated by Goebbels. Only the cast credits were shown. The following day, the Nazi party paper *Der Angriff* pressed for a formal ban arguing in a typical harsh editorial that Siodmak had produced a film with "a sickly and stifling climate". It went on to claim that "[t]oday we must demand a cin-

ema that is clean and decent so that we may be spared from now on these un-
healthy erotic disturbances" (in Dumont, 85). Not long after Goebbels' Hotel
Kaiserhof speech on 28 March and the formal call for a boycott of all Jewish
businesses on 1 April, Siodmak made the understandable decision to leave for
France with his wife-to-be, Bertha Odenheimer. Perhaps on the basis of his father's American citizenship he managed to enter the country on a simple visa
without any problem, but for the duration of his stay until 1939, he was never
formally granted a residency permit by the French authorities.

Siodmak's two main biographers to date have focussed primarily on the
significance of his American films, especially those which make a contribution
to the post-war noir cycle. Disappointingly, Deborah Lazaroff-Alpi simply
transcribes her predecessor's brief chapter on the director's French career
meaning that a need remains for a more detailed consideration of Siodmak's
Parisian output. Before analysing and contextualising the director's French
films specifically set in the French capital, a broader survey of his place within
French film production of the 1930s is necessary. By May 1933, Siodmak was
being interviewed in the Parisian press about his future projects in the French
film industry. At this stage in his career, it appears that Siodmak truly believed
that his chances of obtaining American residency had expired and so the "famous director of TUMULTES" was described as "for the moment without nationality". "I don't know how long I am going to be here. For a long time I
think", he told Jean Barois in *Paris-Midi*.[88] None of Siodmak's early projects
amounted to anything, but they reveal a previously unrecognised consistency
in that they suggest a sustained desire to fit in with the codes of French culture.
They included screen adaptations of Julien Green's *Leviathan*, Maupassant's
Bel-Ami (with Charles Boyer) and perhaps most interestingly, a version of
Edouard Bourdet's lesbian drama *La Prisonnière*. Siodmak also turned down
the screen adaptation of Flaubert's *Madame Bovary* on the basis that he didn't
"know the French provinces well enough".[89] The project went to Jean Renoir
instead. Finally, in July 1933, Siodmak was offered a contract with Seymour
Nebenzahl's Nero-Film and his first film in France, an adaptation of another
Bourdet play, *Le Sexe faible*, went into production. It starred many of the original stage cast including Pierre Brasseur and Victor Boucher. The script was
written by Yves Mirande, the dialogue supervisor on TUMULTES. Mirande's
work was partly amended by fellow émigré Hermann Kosterlitz.

A highly revealing interview with Lucien Rebatet at the time, provides a
fascinating glimpse into life on the set of an émigré production.[90] It also suggests ample evidence of the simmering xenophobic resentment of the right-
wing press. Siodmak is evidently anxious to demonstrate his credentials as an
unthreatening European – rather than a specifically German – filmmaker. He
doesn't want to appear like some problem-making political figure, but Rebatet

remains unconvinced. As the interview progresses, Siodmak stresses that he was not completely qualified to tackle a popular Parisian stage comedy. "I haven't done any thing without the advice of M. Edouard Bourdet", he reassures his interlocuter. He also praises the French film industry. "It is possible to make excellent films here. You've got everything it takes. It is as good as in Germany and I really like your actors". The only fault that Siodmak discerns is the frequently noted aspect of professional organisation. "You simply lack discipline and method", he comments; before adding approvingly "but we'll bring that to you". This must have been exactly what the likes of Lucie Derain wanted to hear, but Rebatet intervenes and questions Siodmak about his notion that French directors have been very anxious since the arrival of the German émigrés in France. "I know", Siodmak says, "but there is no need for alarm. What am I going to do? Two films a year. In your national output, that doesn't amount to much". At this point, Siodmak apparently searches for a word and calls an interpreter. Rebatet sarcastically notes that there's no shortage of possible translators working on the set. The journalist then moves to provide apparent evidence for the assertion that French film industry professionals have every reason to be worried about the émigré presence. Bourdet's brother reveals that despite being employed as an assistant on the film, there is nothing for him to do on the set. "With the exception of the camera operator", he notes, "all the major figures around Siodmak are German". "They work as a team. Normally there should be only one foreigner per film crew". As if to prove this point, Rebatet then goes on to detail a police raid on the set. One German employee without proper working papers, is questioned but to the journalist's evident disapproval, the matter is seemingly resolved.

The negative feelings engendered by Rebatet's barely concealed hostility in the Autumn of 1933 were exacerbated by the congruence of both political and economic upheaval the following year. Siodmak's subsequent project for Nero-Film, the depression-era musical LA CRISE EST FINIE, was picketted at the Joinville studios in May 1934 by the National Federation of French Cinema. Its representative, Siodmak's former-assistant Henri Chomette, spent several weeks lobbying the French Ministry of Justice for Siodmak to be taken off the project. According to Dumont (99), the matter was settled when the girlfriend of a member of the aforesaid ministry was appointed as an extra. Nonetheless, Seymour Nebenzahl still felt it necessary to advertise the fact that only seven foreign employees essential to the project, had been employed out of a total of 90 production workers.[91] The film was a moderate success and subtitled prints were made for the English-language export market. Despite this, it was not until the Summer of 1935 that Siodmak was to work again on a proper feature-length project – another musical, this time based on the Offenbach operetta LA VIE PARISIENNE. He had to make ends meet by working uncredited on the

Buster Keaton vehicle LE ROI DES CHAMPS-ÉLYSÉES (Max Nosseck, 1935) in the Winter of 1934. LA VIE PARISIENNE (1936) was a lavishly funded production. As an indication of its anticipated box-office returns, dozens of sets were constructed at the Pathé-Nathan studios and there was an expensive publicity campaign. In spite of these efforts, the film was not a commercial success. This might well have been due to Siodmak's attempt to alter the scenario of the original which was set in the heyday of the French Second Empire. The ironic, temporally layered nature of the narrative combined with the relative lack of original music from the stage production may well have led to the French public's disenchantment.

Next Siodmak worked on another music-related project with Métropa-Films entitled LE GRAND REFRAIN (1936). It was written by Yves Mirande and scored by the celebrated German composer Richard Werner Heymann. Since Heymann had written the music for two of the previous models for LA VIE PARISIENNE – the German FLV operettas DER KONGREß TANZT/LE CONGRÈS S'AMUSE (1931) and DIE DREI VON DER TANKSTELLE/LE CHEMIN DU PARADIS (1930) – this could have been an effort to meet audience expectations more directly. Siodmak's subsequent film, MISTER FLOW (1936), was shot in the summer of 1936 in curious circumstances. The project, previously turned down by Pierre Chenal, was based on the crime novel by Gaston Leroux and featured a number of Paris's most prominent stage talents such as Louis Jouvet and Edwige Feuillère. It was written by the prominent screenwriter Henri Jeanson and financed by Nicholas Vondas, an impecunious Greek producer, and so the production was marred by the fact that many of the actors were only paid on a daily basis. Often only one of the major actors was on the set at a time necessitating some awkward camera manoeuvres. Siodmak was obliged to use his own furniture for the decor. Despite these setbacks, the film was a critical and financial success and it appeared, from then on, Siodmak's currency within the French film industry was secure. His next project, the white slave trade drama, LE CHEMIN DE RIO (1937), was also written by Henri Jeanson and starred Jean-Pierre Aumont, Suzy Prim and Jules Berry, but it was his last with Nero-Film. Siodmak's cousin had apparently taken advantage of his precarious position and consistently refused to pay the director properly for his efforts. The two never spoke again.

MOLLENARD (1938) saw Siodmak reunited with Eugen Schüfftan on a prestigious adaptation by Charles Spaak of the Prix de Paris-winning adventure novel. It starred Harry Baur, Albert Préjean, Pierre Renoir and Gina Manès and was made for producer Edouard Corniglion-Molinier. Like LE CHEMIN DE RIO, the film had an ostentatiously international setting for its dramatic narrative. Again, it combined the work of a prominent French script-writer who paid particular attention to atmospheric visual details in both lighting effects and set design. In this case, MOLLENARD boasted the contribution of the Hungarian set designer Alexandre Trauner who, like Schüfftan and Courant, also eventually worked with leading French directors Jean Renoir and Marcel Carné towards the end of the decade.

We can now see what happened to the German émigrés who stayed in France to weather the original storms of racial disdain and economic difficulties during the period of 1933-4. Many were clearly beginning to integrate themselves by becoming major forces in French film production. It is noticeable, for example, how many of the reviews of MOLLENARD refer to its distinctively French character. *Le Petit Parisien* wrote that the film "honours French production" whilst Pierre Gignac claimed that Siodmak's film "marked a red-letter day in the progressive output of the French film industry" (in Dumont, 118).

MOLLENARD was not a box-office success, but perhaps the level of critical acclaim that Siodmak now enjoyed persuaded him to embark on his most directly political French film. In the early Summer of 1938, he was engaged in negotiations with the Austro-Hungarian émigré novelist and playwright Ödön von Horváth to shoot a version of his novel *Jugend ohne Gott* about the conflict between a German school teacher and a class of Hitler Youth. In a truly bizarre turn of fate, the writer was suddenly killed when a tree fell on him in front of the cinema showing SNOW WHITE AND THE SEVEN DWARVES (1937) where he was due to meet Siodmak's wife. After completing the unfinished portions of two features, ULTIMATUM (Robert Wiene, 1938) and LES FRÈRES CORSES (Jean Tarride, 1939), Siodmak turned to his final French film, PIÈGES, made between April and May 1939 against the backdrop of a seemingly inevitable war with Germany. PIÈGES was to be the director's most successful film in France, although it did attract criticism from some quarters keen, once again, on emphasising Siodmak's ethnicity. *L'Action Française* complained about how national treasure, Maurice Chevalier, was used by the director and the co-scriptwriter. "Two foreigners, Messers Siodmak and Companeez, have played this dirty trick on him", it wrote (in Dumont, 123). The film obviously benefitted from the star performance of Maurice Chevalier, but it also saw a return to the conflation of careful social detail, atmospheric visual style, and an interest in the undercurrents of urban criminal psychologies which marked Siodmak's earlier Berlin successes. By now, Siodmak, one of the longest established of Germany's French-based Jewish émigrés, was making plans to leave his country of asylum. Upon discovering that he was in fact still eligible for American citizenship, he organised his departure to the United States, sailing from France on the very day before war broke out. He had an advance for a Dutch-based film to be made the following year in his pocket, but like so many other émigrés from Berlin, he never returned. Instead, the world of the American city now became his subject.

3 City of Light

Paris as Spectacle

"The Avenue de l'Opéra inundated with electric light; rue Quatre Septembre shining with a thousand gas jets (...) a crowd coming and going under a shower of rosy and whitest light diffused from great ground-glass globes (...) that mass of gleaming streets which lead to the Théatre Français, to the Tuileries, to the Concorde and Champs-Elysées, each one of which brings you a voice of the great Paris festival, calling and attracting you on seven sides, like the stately entrances of seven enchanted palaces, kindling in your brain and veins the madness of pleasure"
(E. de Amicis in Clark 1996, 76).

This delirious quotation was, unsurprisingly, *not* authored by one of the émigrés from the German film industry who arrived in "the City of Light" in the early 1930s – it comes from the pen of a male visitor in the 1870s – but the phrasing does suggest a number of issues that concern the relationship between various émigré films set in Paris and the mythical status of Paris. Firstly, it introduces the notion of spectacle which was as appropriate for a visitor as it was for a native resident. According to T. J. Clark (1996, 63), the term "spectacle" pointed "to the way in which the city – and social life in general – was presented as a unity in the later nineteenth century, as a separate something made to be looked at – an image, a pantomime, a panorama". How did the émigrés, as temporary residents of Paris, refer to this "highly coded" (Clark, 63) aspect in their own cinematic representations of the capital? In what ways did this suggestive condensation of looking and performance lead to the related issue of pleasure and entertainment? Despite Robert Siodmak's pronouncement that he hated "operetta and vaudeville because they represent hollowness, flashiness, and artificiality"[1], he directed two musical films during his time in Paris. These two films relied substantially on a fascinating integration of prominent cinematic techniques and popular French theatrical form. What exactly was the relationship of these émigré films to the pre-existing live city entertainment which de Amicis makes such an intense allusion to? The visitor's words suggest an equation between these codes of knowledge regarding "the great Paris festival" and the specific matter of light. How was the "City of Light" represented by the people who came from the very different urban film culture of Berlin? To what extent did the émigrés picture the city in ways which subscribed to the conventions of popular Parisian cinematic practice, and to what extent did they also contravene existing norms?

It is unlikely that many of his fellow émigrés shared Max Ophüls' rhapsodic impressions regarding their place of exile. In a nostalgic account of his film career in the French capital in the 1930s, he reminisced that "Paris which had always amused me on holiday, was too lovely (...) It captured me with its pleasant carefreeness (...) The night porter down in the plush entrance hall [of the hotel] (...) invited me to a *coup de rouge* and prophesied 'it will sort itself out, sir, I am sure of it. Everyone in the world has two fatherlands: his own and Paris'" (in MacDonald 1996, 101).[2] Nonetheless, Robert Siodmak's musical films, LA CRISE EST FINIE and LA VIE PARISIENNE and Billy Wilder's MAUVAISE GRAINE all conform, in their own ways, to the consolidating myth of Paris as a site of cosmopolitan belonging. Where does this notion of non-Parisians coming to the French capital and being nurtured, exhilarated, and dazzled by its attractions come from? The idea of Paris itself as a spectacle for visitors to consume and admire has as one of its main antecedents the development of the physical spaces of the city under Baron Haussmann in the nineteenth century. Haussmann's redesign of Paris, with the more or less wholesale clearing and redevelopment of its central areas, effected two significant results regarding the way the city could be viewed. Firstly, in architectural, and thus also spatial terms, the strategic urban panoramic view was developed. This led to an enhanced sense of promotional civic display based on the principles of seeing and looking. As Vanessa Schwartz (1998, 2) puts it in her perceptive discussion of the inter-relationship between nineteenth century Parisian spectacular forms such as the waxwork museum or urban panorama and the development of early cinema, "visualising the city became synonymous with knowing it".

Related to this typology was the notion of the past belonging to darkness so that the example of the emergence of widely distributed all-night street lighting served an allegorical, as well as a practical, function. Christopher Prendergast (1991, 183) argues, for instance, that "the public provision of light represented a triumph over social and cultural 'darkness'; light meant *lumières* in more than one sense; the project of the illuminated city became cognate with the idea of the enlightened city" (183). The second effect of Haussmannisation, largely a result of this enhanced potential to be viewed, was a whole subsidiary set of social practices that dealt with the way the city was not just experienced by its own residents but also imagined by those from afar. These ranged from the development of window displays in department stores, aided by the introduction of sheet glass and modulated lighting features, to the spread of photographic and lithographic reproductions of sites of interest. Many of these stores or covered commercial arcades were on the *grands boulevards* which were located immediately south of three of the city's main train stations. This was at the time of the proliferation of guidebooks for the traveller to Paris and, just as importantly, the emergence of the picture postcard as a means of sending Paris as it was pictured to the provinces and overseas. The popularity of the spectacular view of the city was developed along side the running series of *Expositions Universelles*, one of which, in 1867, coincided with the first production of Offenbach's operetta *La Vie Parisienne*.[3] At such exhibitions the world came to Paris twice: first, in the physical sense of paying visitors, and secondly, in the metaphorical sense in the form of such erected displays as the "Rue des Nations" (1878) with its façade of various architectural styles from around the globe. Paris was then mailed back to the rest of the world in the form of pictorial messages; most spectacularly at the 1889 exposition when enthusiastic visitors could post images of Paris from the top of that recently erected emblem of urban modernity, the Eiffel Tower.[4]

Both the original production of LA VIE PARISIENNE and Siodmak's loose adaptation explicitly refer to this idea of Paris defining itself both *against* the world as something distinctive and unique and *within* the world as the centre for a kind of communal cosmopolitanism. It is surely not coincidental that both the theatrical and film production are the work of German émigré outsiders who found themselves producing work inside the capital about the capital.[5] In his book on Offenbach and Paris, Kracauer (1937) specifically argues that the world of the Parisian boulevards suited the composer's social status as a rootless foreigner. "They were both related in their nature", he suggests. "The boulevards were no home in the ordinary sense". Their striking characteristic was their "lack of anchorages" (75). He also goes on to suggest that the operetta was, in fact, in some ways "an émigré product" (141). These comments beg the intriguing question of whether Siodmak actually ever read Kracauer's work. It was published in German the year that the film was made, and there are certain striking descriptions throughout the text, which recall scenes from the film.

The plot of the Offenbach operetta concerns the entertaining amorous and mercenary entanglements of a visiting wealthy Brazilian baron, his wife and mistress, and two scheming Parisian fortune-hunters. A key chorus by Meilhac and Halévy (1889, 20), also reproduced in the 1935 film, gives an idea of how Paris was represented in the operetta:

Nous venons,
Arrivons,
De tous les pays du monde,
Par la terre ou bien par l'onde,
Italiens, Brésiliens, Japonais, Hollandais, Espagnols, Romagnols, Égyptians, Péruviens,
Nous venons,

Arrivons!
De tous les pays du monde,
Par la terre ou bien par l'onde,
Nous venons,
Arrivons,
La vapeur nous amène,
Nous allons envahir,
La cité souveraine,
Le séjour du plaisir,
On accourt,
On s'empresse,
Pour connaître O Paris,
Pour connaître l'ivresse,
De tes jours, de tes nuits,
Tous les étrangers ravis,
Vers toi s'élancent Paris!
Nous allons chanter,
Nous allons crier,
Nous allons souper,
Nous allons aimer,
Oh! Mon Dieu, nous allons tous,
Nous amuser comme des fous.[6]

Siodmak's film version retains the cosmopolitan narrative hinge of the visiting wealthy colonial to the capital of pleasure, but enlarges the range of entanglements by having Don Ramiro (Max Dearly) leave his mistress and Paris in 1900 and return in 1936 with his granddaughter Helenita (Conchita Montenegro). In 1936, the exuberant Brazilian is still up to his amorous indulgences and excessively energetic visits to entertainment venues. There are several key scenes set in hotel rooms and train stations to create the sense that Paris belongs not only to its residents, but to the entire world. These moments clearly underline the element of journey in the film's narrative, but they also remind one of Hamid Naficy's observation, made in another context, that exilic cinema in general often represents a range of "transitional places and spaces" (2001, 5). Train stations, hotel lobbies, the interiors of cars and the motif of the suitcase can all be used, as they are in La Vie Parisienne, to signify a sense of instability and displacement. To emphasise this point, at significant intersections in the plot of Siodmak's film, a postcard-like image is visualised in order to reinforce the idea of the dazzling spectacle of the city for the visitor. After a scene set in a drab, functional immigration office in 1936, for instance, an official moves to a open a window's left shutter and declares: "This is Paris!" The right shutter opens of its own accord and the image dissolves into a panoramic night skyline shot of the city with the illuminated Eiffel Tower on the horizon and the rooftop of apartments in the foreground. To reinforce the picture element of the city, the camera tracks back slowly to frame the image with the inclusion of the bordering element of the window. Prior to that the film opened with a tableau shot of the theatre "La Vie Parisienne" at night, again with the Eiffel Tower in the background and this time the twinkling features of the "City of Light" breaking up the darkness. The effect is of an instantly recognisable, almost iconic, display of "Parisianisme". It could also be the cover of a guidebook from the period.

Wilder's MAUVAISE GRAINE is also interested in the notion of the city on display. It frequently uses postcard-like images of urban spaces such as the Pont Alexandre III or the Bois de Boulogne and has a developed sense of the city as an open-air site of play and leisure. Scenes such as the car chase at the beginning of the film, when Pasquier (Pierre Mingand) decides to steal a parked vehicle from under the eyes of a gang of car thieves, are perfect examples of how the film turns Paris into spectacle by integrating a sense of the space and freedom of the city with the modern sensations of speed and mobility. In his deft commentary on the development of new forms of perception in Paris under Haussmannisation, Wolfgang Schivelbusch (1986, 189) has argued that the department store and railway journey developed a "panoramic" mode of viewing so that the object "was no longer experienced intensively, discretely (...) but evanescently, impressionistically". This effect is managed in the film by a range of fluid points of view. For example, as the chase begins, the camera is placed on the bonnet of the crooks' car looking in front at the speeding vehicle. We then rapidly cut across space, but in the same time continuum, to a view from the rear seat of Pasquier's car. We see him from behind but we also see his face in the rearview mirror as the city speeds by in a blur. This tightness of vision is later contrasted with alternate panoramic views which include a spectacular extreme high wide-angle shot of the two vehicles maneuvering across the space of an open square and of the moving car in relation to the mobility of the frame. This gauging of space and motion allows Wilder to integrate more fully the exhilaration of the chase with the freedom of seeing rapidly changing vistas of the city flashing by. Most "spectacular" of all is the scene when the camera is planted on the bonnet of the lead vehicle to assure a visceral sense of new forward-driven space constantly emerging into the frame to reveal the sights of a city in transit. Towards the end of MAUVAISE GRAINE another chase scene involves the Parisian police following their quarry, Jean la cravatte (Raymond Galle), by means of that iconic pictorial representation of the city, the map of the Metro system. Previous to that we witnessed Pasquier and his girlfriend Jeannette's (Danielle Darrieux) escaping from the city; their route actually mapped out on the screen with a camera moving across the map of France, mimicking the couple's "real" geographical relationship to the capital.

LA CRISE EST FINIE, Siodmak's first émigré musical, also opens with some non-Parisians – a provincial troupe of down-on-their-heels theatrical performers – taking a trip to Paris. It also entails a conflation of movement and a certain commodified or standardised imagining of the city.[7] After the umpteenth lacklustre performance of their stage number "On ne voit ça qu'à Paris" ("You Only See That in Paris"), and their being fired by their manager, the group actually decides to seek their fortunes in the capital. It is clear that for the younger troupe members Paris exists only as a representation. "Do you know Paris?" one asks. "Only as a view in a painting" another replies. "I'm afraid of Paris", one girl exclaims. The troupe shouts their denial and the girl's wail continues as the camera swish pans from the backstage area of a provincial theatre to a painted backdrop of trees. This scenery begins to rotate as a train whistle blows. We also hear the sound of the train engine picking up and the beginning of the refrain from the previous number. As the pace of the music increases in time with the rhythm of the train, the artificial scenery dissolves into a blurred vision of speed shot from a real train car window . The second, far more exuberant, version of "On ne voit ça qu'à Paris" which now follows, underlines the pleasures, delights (and dangers) of the capital that the troupe will probably encounter. The ideas that the lyrics refer to are visualised on screen by means of a witty montage of short dramatic inserts. As we see the scenery passing by, Madame Olga (Suzanne Dehelly)'s voice sings *"Aucune ville n'est aussi romantique que Paris / Montmartre et Montparnasse sont des paradis".*[8] Siodmak cuts to a shot in which the camera moves from the window pane of the carriage to rest on four seated figures: a male, Olga, Marcel (Albert Préjean) and Nicole (Danielle Darrieux). They are pictured in a state of communal imagining and anticipation. Olga, with the voice of maturity and experience, continues in full swing:

> "Les jeunes y vivent d'amour et d'eau fraîche et l'on se dit
> On se voit ça qu'à Paris".[9]

With the very youthful Nicole listening and smiling, Marcel continues spinning the myth:

> Tous les jours 100,000 taxis circulent et font du bruit
> Le soir 100,000 lumières font oublier la nuit
> Et 100,000 jolies filles font des rêves jolis
> On ne voit ça qu'à Paris[10]

He continues:

> Les apaches sont polis, leurs gestes sont précis
> Après avoir tout pris, ils vous disent merci
> Aucune ville n'est aussi romantique que Paris
> Montmartre et Montparnasse sont des paradis
> On se dit en voyant tous ces chants et ces cris
> On se voit ça qu'à Paris..."[11]

The succession of studio-bound images relating to the words of the song are very obviously artificial and thus create the impression of distance from the "real" city.

In La Crise est finie, and particularly in La Vie Parisienne, we notice a blurring between staged or imagined Paris and "real" Paris, perceived in terms of communal experience. The theatrical version of the city that "La Vie Parisienne" promises in the opening tableau is correlated with the space of the city itself as if to suggest that they constitute one seamless whole.[12] The sequence thus evokes the sense of Paris as a communal home – a place of belonging – by developing the way the theatre world and the urban world intersect. The cinema spectator is taken on a journey from "Parisian life" to "La Vie Parisienne" by the figure of a visiting male customer who descends from his carriage accompanied by a slow, romantic musical score. The camera lingers, in a medium close-up shot, on the steps outside with the doorman standing to the left and a poster announcing "La Vie Parisienne With Lianne d'Isigny" to the right. The visitor passes the ticket desk and the music begins to surge with anticipation as he climbs the stairs. The moment he exits the frame, the film cuts to a high-angle shot of the conclusion of a raucous revue number. Audience members are visible in the lower part of the frame but the energy and near chaotic spectacle of the gyrating bodies of the formally dressed performers dominates the image. This density of feeling is at odds with the quietude of the preceding sequence so that the impression is one of concentrated emotionality. The emotionality of this performance works as a bond for the diegetic audience members, one of whom, in a subsequent shot, blows a kiss to the performers. The cast raise their hands in unison, almost as if to return the affection, as the music reaches its climax. This contract with the audience and the performers is re-enacted when we cut from a backstage aerial shot of the cast preparing to bow in front of the audience to a full-frontal, proscenium shot of the curtains opening on a crowded stage from the audience's point of view. The sense of shared "Paris" created by the emotionality of the bond between audience and performers is also suggested in the final part of the introduction which takes place at the railway station. There is a long, steady tracking shot which details the many departing couples on the platform. But instead of following the di-

rection of the train, the camera moves in reverse towards the city which is being left behind. This helps us to make sense of the use of the earlier chorus as
musical accompaniment. The lightly ironic use of operetta music and accompanying visual style evoke a powerful sense of departure which is developed
in the subsequent point of view shot of the passengers gazing onto the platform and the faces of those who form the home they are leaving behind. The
emphasis, again, is on the communality of the experience. When the film shifts
to the present, we see the return to Paris of Don Ramiro after a long absence.
His arrival at the airport is preceded in the film by another musical sequence,
which is set in period costume at a railway station. This time, although the musical chorus is the same, the scene is not "real Paris" but the stage. The two
have become blurred once more.

In LA CRISE EST FINIE we never see the railway station and point of arrival,
but the transition from Paris as it is performed to Paris "as it really is" is effected during the progression of the number when we see the troupe arrive
and actually continue the song in the street. In the "real Paris" we see a succession of disappointments for the performers who have to face rejection because
theatre managers only seem to be interested in young women for their nude
revues. It is possible to read this passage from dream to brutal fact as a symptomatic commentary on the position of the émigrés in Paris. The production of
LA CRISE EST FINIE was, as we have already seen, accompanied by an orchestrated press campaign by French film professionals against the film. However,
one can also read the progression of the song in terms of one of the broader
"crises" that the film makes explicit reference to. Siodmak's obtrusive *mise-en-
scène* during the number indicates that the capital can be linked in this version
of the song not just to live theatrical performance but to the specificity of the recorded moving image. The fact that the capital is pictured through a fusion of
song and insistent cinematic devices such as the variety of wipes between
shots is an ironic foregrounding of the fact that the troupe will eventually
make their Parisian home in a disused theatre that is fatefully – for them –
eventually converted into a cinema. In this way the idea of an emotionally
shared version of mythical "Paris" sustained by the bond between the performance of the singers and the audience differs from that in LA VIE PARISIENNE.
As the song progresses, and the diegetic audience leaves the train to enter
"real" Paris, the potency of the theatricalised version of the myth of the city is
in fact undermined by a rival mode of entertainment: the cinema.

2. The theatrical troupe gather round Mme Olga (Suzanne Dehelly)
in LA CRISE EST FINIE (BIFI)

Paris and the Spectacle of Entertainment

Siodmak's émigré musical films appropriated a cluster of mythologies regarding the city of Paris. The films developed meaning in their narratives through a
journey to the capital on the part of non-Parisians. Either during the journey, or
as a result of the journey, ideas concerning the urban spectacle and display
were foregrounded in the text through the protagonists' encounter with Parisian performance and entertainment venues. The films' use of the idea of Paris
as the centre of "light" and pleasure may be read in two ways. Firstly, by placing themselves in relation to the traditions of Parisian live performance as well
as 1930s French film practice, the films sought to actively engage in the reification of certain notions of Parisianisme and thus fit in with the prevalent culture. Secondly, the negotiation between the visitor and embedded traditions of
popular pleasure in the diegesis may be read in terms of the meta-textual journey of the émigré film workers who came to Paris themselves to find employ-

ment in the French film industry. Does this suggestion undermine an attempt
to read the films as smooth adaptations to convention? To answer this question, and in order to examine the work of LA VIE PARISIENNE and LA CRISE EST
FINIE in relation to Parisian representation in more detail, I will now define
more clearly what the components of this light tradition of Parisian representation were. In so doing, I will also examine what sorts of myths were actually
proposed in these various configurations.

If I have argued that "Paris" was foregrounded in the light tradition in terms
of a sustained bond between live performance and audience, it is largely because notions of what constituted the city were, historically speaking, intricately bound up with performance and consumption in the sphere of entertainment. It is not surprising, therefore, that acts of display and acts of viewing and
communal imagining also feature in many French urban cinematic representations of the 1930s.[13] As I have already indicated, it is possible to equate this
showing and imagining of the city partly with the historical emergence of practices associated with the spectacle of "The City of Light". The very lighting up
of the city and spaces of performance by means of the use of electricity as a re-
placement for the standard gas lamp; the development of a culture of civic pro-
motion and the actual "lightening" of urban space by the removal of dense networks of medieval street complexes all relate to the concurrent emergence of a
commodified and bourgeois culture of diversion and entertainment. Clark argues the same point by stating that "the rise of commercialized entertainments
in Paris, catering to a mass public (...) cannot be understood apart from (...) the
end of old patterns of neighbourhood and the birth of a city organized round
separate unities of work, residence, and distraction" (1996, 235). This process
undoubtedly helped to propagate a master narrative of an association between
Paris, performance and pleasure which spread far outside the capital, hence the
journeying I have been referring to.[14] It also, symbolically, allowed for the en-
hancement of the equation between capital and nation – Paris *was* France.

By the 1930s and the time of the arrival of the émigrés in Paris, live city entertainment had evolved to the extent that the working class or petit bourgeois
tradition of the localised neighbourhood *café-concert* which "combined the
socialising aspect of the café with the consumer aspect of spectatorship" had
waned considerably (Vincendeau 1985, 153). It had not totally disappeared,[15]
but the more formalised *revue à grand spectacle* or the *spectacle de variétés*, which
had begun to emerge in hand with the new viewing practices of the city on display in the late-19th century, had risen to considerable prominence. These
newer types of consolidated performance offered the pleasure, as their names
suggest, of spectacle be it of the order of elaborate, and thus costly, staged music and song numbers, or a succession of variety acts consisting of wondrous
feats by acrobats, magicians, and the like. Many of the embedded notions

about the popular image of light Paris derived from a sustained relationship between performers and public which had failed to dissipate despite the shift from an intimate milieu to one of stage-bound spectacle. Indeed, it was partly because of this very heavy commercialisation of light entertainment that a mythical version of the city emerged. The idea of an image of the city being enacted in direct and quite small-scale terms by a contract between the performer and live neighbourhood audience – via song lyrics, for example – was slowly replaced by the emergence of a different entertainment complex. At the heart of this complex, which amplified the same work of staging an image of the city, was an urban-centred star system which propagated the closeness of the performer to the public in terms beyond that of the usual intimacy fostered by watching live performance. We can thus see the emergence of an extended "Parisian community" being fostered in the proliferation of sheet music, illustrated journals, posters and front-of-house publicity material. This dates back broadly to such entertainment figures as Thérésa of whom, for example, it was written at the time: "she is a woman of the people (...) she represents life as it is in the city" (Jules Vallès in Jando 1979, 20).

By the time the émigrés arrived in Paris, this correspondence between print media, performer and public had been strengthened by new forms of city-oriented communication practices. Boulevard theatre, music hall and cabaret now had to share the stage with the mass media of cinema and gramophone recordings to the extent that "the relationship between cinema and other entertainment forms [can] be seen in a multi-dimensional way rather than as a one-dimensional, linear, connection of influence or of one form's decline signalling the rise of another one" (Vincendeau 1985, 115). This multidimensionality, which also intersects with radio, was still bound up with the relationship between Paris and performance. This is not the same as saying that because so much of the entertainment industry was based in a relatively concentrated area of Paris things inevitably had a Parisian identity, though this was to a great extent true.[16] Rather, the city was performed in the sense of a, by now, *historically* calibrated collusion between public and performers. For example, through a combination of lyrics, staging and sheer charisma, the body of many music hall, cabaret or theatrical entertainers (many of whom moved in and out of film production) were now linked with the body of the city. In the case of stars like Maurice Chevalier, the performer began to personify Paris to the outside world. Large stars like Josephine Baker and Mistinguett who had performed in venues like the *Folies Bergère* (named after a Parisian 18th-century house of pleasure) or the appositely named *Casino de Paris* were intimately associated with the city in the popular imagination through song (Mistinguett's "Ça! C'est Paris!" for example), titles of revues and the commentary of both critics and fans. Performers like Albert Préjean had adopted definitive portions of their routines to include significant items of working class male Parisian iconography such as the flat cap. While in comic boulevard theatre, the delivery of precisely orchestrated witticisms in high society settings by trained actors had become emblematic of a certain metropolitan sophistication. As Vincendeau has suggested, this shift in the organisation of popular entertainment led to the subsequent reification of a mythical community which served distinctive ideological functions. By the time sound cinema in the 1930s was actually able to insert a diegetic audience into the "live" performance of music hall entertainers such as Georges Milton, Maurice Chevalier, among others, "Paris – and particularly popular Paris – had by then come to connote France, embodying the myth of a deeply-rooted community of origins" (Vincendeau 1992, 55).

These modes of performance and the subsequent notions of "community" were, of course, inflected by class in terms of the type of representations they offered and the type of audiences they attracted. The canonical films of René Clair, for example, are axiomatic when it comes to any discussion of the representation of the French capital in the period of the early 1930s. Here, Paris represented a pleasurable, detailed and inherently nostalgic evocation of a world in which the quotidian lives of urban working people are integrated into a prominent community of interests. By means of dexterously interwoven music, sound, set design and performances – by the likes of the aforementioned Albert Préjean in Sous les toits de Paris – Clair achieved a folk-based sentimental appropriation of a milieu which had come to connote a dominant notion of iconic Frenchness. Through the inscription of songs such as "À Paris dans chaque faubourg"[17] and the foregrounded motif of circularity (and thus inclusiveness) in the *mise-en-scène* in the film Quartorze juillet (1932), we can see how certain codified mythologies about the capital were sustained into the era of sound cinema.[18] The centrality of these mythologies of togetherness, resourcefulness and convivial sharing remind us of Clark's central argument regarding the relationship between performers and audience at the Parisian *café-concert*. He suggests that "the *café-concert produced* the popular, which is to say that it put on class as entertainment" (1996, 234). In Quartorze juillet, for example, we indeed *do* see the entertainment of the film fitting Clark's description of "a fiction of working-class ways of being (…) put alongside a parody of middle-class style, the one being granted imaginary dominion over the other" (1996, 238). The image of the world of warm, working class pleasure is, crucially, defined against the cold rectitude of the bourgeoisie; the circularity of the dancing, decoration, and camera movement for the symbolic community is contrasted with a diagonal linear camera movement and an emphasis on rigid straight lines in set design for the middle-class other. But it is best not to completely de-historicise Clark's argument. By making his point about the *café-concert*, Clark also wishes to demonstrate that the popular culture on offer here was generally produced for an unstable and newly emergent urban petit-bourgeoisie. Similarly Vincendeau has argued that, by the 1930s, the incorporation of the inheritance of these class-based mythologies – which stem from traditions of live performance – meant in cinematic terms an emphasis on *nostalgia*. According to Andrew (1995, 121), this emphasis on a "lost community" can be read in terms of "France's economic and international situation". As "its increasingly urban population became more alienated, the cinema conveyed the security of a former identity". The point, however, is that this "former identity" was very likely never secure in the first place – it always carried elements of myth. One can also go further to say that the element of "dropping in on a world" – made manifest in Clair's films about the *faubourg* by the gentle swooping in camera takes he frequently uses as establishing shots – is actually consistent with a certain type of class voyeurism which goes back to the inter-texts of 19th-century realist novelists like Emile Zola and Eugène Sue, painters like Gustave Courbet and the entire Parisian documentary photographic project of Charles Marville. This would suggest a paradoxical spectatorial positioning instead of one that assimilated the myth wholesale. This point may very well be underlined by the fact that directors such as Clair and Siodmak themselves came from middle-class backgrounds.

This class-based opposition, which occurs throughout the French cinema of this period, is successfully transplanted into the narrative of LA CRISE EST FINIE; particularly when the spontaneity and warmth of the theatrical ensemble is threatened by the efforts of the comically repressed piano-shop owner, M. Bernouillin (Marcel Carpentier). The audience back then would have already been cued by the coded signals provided by the Parisian performance histories of the main stars. In his revue performances, Préjean was famous for his working-class Parisian cloth cap whilst Carpentier's dress and performance style connoted a bourgeois type familiar from the boulevard stage. Suzanne Dehelly who plays Olga, the old stagehand, had a particular reputation for playing witty mature women in boulevard comedy. According to Préjean's autobiography, René Clair, who had used him to great acclaim in SOUS LES TOITS DE PARIS, said "they like you because you're just like them" (1956, 105). What is interesting in the scene where the troupe receives Bernouillin's letter, informing them that he plans to convert their theatre into a cinema, is how *well* Siodmak's *mise-en-scène* conspires to picture a performance-based urban community in opposition to its antithesis. The troupe are clearly visualised in a fluid integrated manner. In a medium close-up, we see Marcel seated at a piano on-stage with Nicole to his left and Olga to his right. Exasperated, Marcel rises and exits screen right. The camera follows him to the point when we can see Olga's reaction more fully. She then turns and moves in the same direction.

Siodmak cuts to a shot of the stage some distance ahead and the camera starts to track right in the direction of Olga as she walks across the space behind some of the cast members. The camera halts as René and the concierge enter the screen talking in the foreground. They move off and we start to follow them in the same unbroken shot. A group of girls passes in front of the couple and the camera begins to track them. As they begin to exit the stage, Marcel re-emerges screen left picking up the path they have set out on. Through this careful integration of space and movement we have a sense of how the community is linked geographically and emotionally to the environment which matters most to them: the stage. It is the actual stage that ensnares Bernouillin when the community decides to take action. Marcel hatches a plan to lure the shopkeeper to the theatre and then pull the stage trapdoor open. When Bernouillin enters with the concierge he is captured in a long-shot from way back in the aisles as if the theatre itself is watching him. The space is lit by the émigré cinematographer Eugen Schüfftan to suggest the darkened and shadowy sense of menace, which became something of a trademark of his. When Siodmak moves the camera to inter-cut between closer shots of Bernouillin and Marcel, who is hiding in the wings, we have an even stronger sense of class difference. This is managed by an effective blurring of the French and German inheritances. Marcel is shot from straight on to implicate him more persuasively with the spectator. The contours of his white tee shirt – itself a class signifier – are brightly illuminated against a background shadow. He whistles the refrain from *"On ne voit ça qu'à Paris"* as if to suggest the sense of musical Paris colluding with him in the downfall of that which threatens it. Bernouillin, by contrast, is shot from a prominent high camera angle to emphasise his isolation and malevolent intent. Schüfftan uses a minimum of identifiable light. The contours of the shopkeeper's body as he moves amongst the pools of diffuse shadow are pitch black.

There is another French urban class location that has always existed with its own set of mythologies. As Rifkin implies when he claims that "Paris can as well be typified through the society lady as the *midinette*" (1995, 108), an imaginary map of the city, composed according to co-ordinates of entertainment, must take into account more than the spaces accorded to the working-class community. It should also be read in terms of gender and sexuality.[19] Again, this version of the city works against the standards of bourgeois propriety. The mythical Paris that relates to an idea of the complex of sexuality, permissiveness and luxury moved in spatial terms from salon to theatre and opera to cabaret and night club. These representations, very often coded as feminine, in part stemmed from the 19th-century comic farce traditions of Feydeau and Labiche and the verbal wit and disruptive gender comedy of Beaumarchais in the 18th century. They were sustained by the growth of urban performance spaces in the 19th century as well as the steady commodification of the female body in relation to the material culture available in the streets of Hausmann's Paris. Through advertising and shop window displays in the city's new spaces an association between France, femininity, luxury and sexuality was consolidated and indelibly promoted. Entertainment forms such as the comic opera and the increasingly licentious spectacle of the *Belle Époque* cabaret and the world of *"gai Paris"* embodied this tradition as well as opening it to certain cross-class movements on the part of the *demi-mondaine*. The literary character of Zola's Nana,[20] for example, embodies the figure of the *courtisane*, the kept woman of wealthy married aristocrats and bourgeois bachelor society figures who were flourishing at the time of Offenbach's original production. Such figures raise the issue of what Prendergast (1995, 138) calls "an increasingly opaque and fluid urban reality, in keeping track of the identities and movements" of the unregistered prostitute. He sees the obsessive abundance of documentation – both visual and literary – regarding prostitution in the nineteenth century as evidence of an anxiety about the place of the prostitute as a metaphor for Paris. Despite the strict and hypocritical prostitution and censorship laws of the period, "the 'woman' – in particular the transgressing, adulterous woman – [was] always the site of social and sexual trouble, a trouble of classification, a problem of *identity*" (137).

We can see this blurring occurring in LA VIE PARISIENNE, for instance, through the figure of Lianne (Marcelle Praince) who is linked to both versions of Paris: the city of society and bourgeois spectacle and the city of the *petit peuple*. As the star of the "La Vie Parisienne" révue and the mistress of Don Ramiro, Lianne personifies the principal set of mythical elements that the first version of light Paris offered. In the film's prologue, set in 1900, the "world" of Paris created by the emotionality of the bond between audience and performers spills over into the subsequent dressing room party. This "world" is sustained by a good humoured and vigorous depiction of conviviality, luxury, romance and an extravagant celebration of the good life amongst the cast and theatergoers. Lianne is a figurehead of this "Paris". She represents conviviality because her sociable presence generates affection and attention. This conviviality extends to a form of cosmopolitanism by means of the inclusion of the Brazilian lover. Paris can accommodate the world. Lianne also embodies a certain blending of sexuality and romance which is a continuation of the performance on stage. There is a sense of licentiousness and permissiveness which is related to the way she displays her body; her undergarments slip down for all to see, for example. Later, when she is reunited with Don Ramiro, their relationship is far more flirtatious and physical than the sober coupling of Don Ramiro's granddaughter and Jacques (Georges Rigaud). Luxury and the good life are indicated by the spirited consumption of champagne; itself almost a meta-symbol for a certain strata of French culture. Champagne is drunk at the toast announced on occasion of Don Ramiro's impending departure to "savage Brazil". He declares that he is "leaving his heart behind" and it appears because of the wording of the toast – "*vive l'amour et la vie Parisienne*" – the object of his affection is a conflation of the city and the female.[21] This is appropriate because "Lianne" is undoubtedly a transposition of the real Lianne de Pougy, one of the "Queens of Paris" who attained fame and a certain notoriety around the turn of the century.[22] Like Caroline Otero and others, Lianne de Pougy was a dancer from the *demi-monde* who led a life of much publicised scandal. According to the 1930s Parisian social columnist Janet Flanner, "every Parisian who could afford it fell in love with her" (1988, 13). Her ambivalent class status is therefore important because it reminds us that Lianne in the film does not have the same background as Don Ramiro. In 1936, rather overweight and extravagantly adorned and clothed, she cuts a somewhat awkward figure. Her unaffected ease of manner, and inappropriate toast to the engagement of the new lovers at the sophisticated nightclub table, suggests a different social world which somehow has to lie contradictorily with the celebratory impetus of the luxury version of the Parisian myth.

LA VIE PARISIENNE succeeds in reconciling these differing elements by having Lianne literally save the day. In the montage sequence which follows Lianne's "call to arms" we see the city open up from the milieu of entertainment, and for the first time the viewer gets a glimpse of the working life of the city, as well as more detailed location footage of a "modern Paris" firmly aligned with the social world of 1936. Through a visualised bond of association with the values of Lianne's emotional appeal, the citizens of "modern Paris" – despite all the trappings of modernity – rally together to reaffirm the myth of Paris or France that Lianne adores is still alive in their hearts. In this way, the world of present-day Paris is seen in terms of a continuity rather than a separation from the past. Lianne's plot is hatched, significantly enough, backstage at "La Vie Parisienne". A despairing Don Ramiro observes that they need an army to defeat his son. "Well, I have one", she replies, "All my friends. My old friends. The friends of Lianne d'Isigny!" "That's a marvellous idea, but what are you going to call it all?" he asks. At this point, the on-stage music changes and rises in tone. The main theme of the film returns and Lianne moves her head to listen. Her eyes and face come alive with inspiration; with her finger pointing upwards she declares: "La Vie Parisienne!" We see Lianne seated at a table writing a letter. Just as the figure of a Parisian female *chanteuse* has sung earlier in the film to unite the two lovers, so Lianne speaks through the power of the memory of *her* singing to bring the couple together permanently. The camera slowly tracks closer to her as her voice can be heard: "It is necessary to remember again the France that I adore .." The shot dissolves to the earlier shot of rooftop Paris. Superimposed over this canonical representation of the city is a montage of a succession of envelopes that suggest the city is being written to, or that the spirit of the city itself is doing the "writing" as in the sense of the city "speaking" through the use of neon lettering in urban musicals of the period. Each postal destination is shown with Lianne's letters appearing on the screen coming out of the building. There is a reprise of the music which inspired her in a softer, gentler key as the occupant of the building reads the text of the letter. The same tracking in camera motif that accompanied the original composition of the plea is repeated to underscore the sense of Lianne's voice speaking.

One of the letter's recipients, a Russian prince, is interestingly enough, a fellow émigré. He is set in a redolently, almost parodic, noirish milieu, seated on the edge of a taxi in a raincoat. To underline his difference, the musical theme is now played by a more sombre oboe. Siodmak cuts to a high angle shot of the street. It is nearly dark except for a light source from the left of the frame which highlights the contours of a line of parked black cars. Four men in long, dark coats are silhouetted to the rear. The émigré gestures to the others and in the next medium close-up shot he passes the letter to one of them. Siodmak then cuts to a sudden close-up of just the envelope. The stark contrast between the blackness of the night and the whiteness of the contours suggests the heightened awareness of the object that Thomas Elsaesser has identified as a potent characteristic of German émigré cinema in general. In his article on the work of the émigré filmmakers in France, Elsaesser argues that what the German cinema inherited from the *Neue Sachlichkeit* (New Objectivity) might be characterised as "the importance given to objects (their texture, their geometrical lines) divorced from social uses and contexts, in order to bring out some vivid but unexpected qualities of abstraction and design" (1984, 282). The above is an interesting example of this tendency.

Siodmak moves on to the mass production of newspapers and a sequence which deals with the printing and distribution of an editorial in the appropriately named *Le Petit Parisien*. The editor announces to his female typists that he is changing the editorial to one entitled: "Hats Off To The People of Paris!". This is followed by a semi-modernist montage which partly through the energy and vigour of the editing and partly through the on-screen action of printing presses, photographs, motorcyclists, and so on creates a sense of the harnessed energy of the contemporary city. Stylistically this sequence does not look back to Berlin, but instead looks forward to a Hollywood-esque visualisation of the pace of urban life.[23] A prominent magazine at the kiosks is *Radio Magazine* indicating one further stage of removal from the old Parisian world of entertainment.

When the stiff and formal father tries to leave Paris with his daughter it is almost as if the city won't let them leave. The porters at the hotel plaster his suitcase with the revealing photo of him which has appeared all over the city to announce his heartlessness. He can't get a taxi, a bus stops and pretends to be full when the conductor sees Don Ramiro's son trying to get on. The couple finally hitch a lift on the back of a lorry but the drivers take them miles from the station. In a moment of visual self-reflexivity, the shot of the laughing men in the front seat is freeze-framed and then appears on the cover of a newspaper with the caption: "Bravo and Thank You!" Lianne's distinctive background enables her to access this second version of light Paris – "the Paris that I hold so dear" – and enlist its working citizens in the campaign to save the romance between Jacques and Don Ramiro's granddaughter. Though we never see Lianne directly with the ordinary citizenry, it is clear that this is the world she came from as a performer. Lianne, in fact, through her class mobility, personifies the over-arching myth of the "great Paris festival": that Paris, coded in feminine terms, is a communal home for one and all.

Parisian Journeys Across Time and Place

Thus far I have suggested that both of Siodmak's musical films are suggestive of the way the work of a prominent émigré intersected with established modes of urban representation in the sphere of Parisian entertainment during the 1930s. The films pay particular attention to the blurring of the stage and "real" Paris, depicting the city, to a great extent, in concordance with an historically and nationally specific relationship between performance and the urban public. We have seen how this collusion extends to the depiction of on-screen communities and their recognition in terms of the issue of class. But it seems apparent, in terms of both narrative and textual style, that the films also relay a certain sense of instability. This is suggested by a number of diegetic and extra-textual journeys between past and present. We have seen this in aspects of the conclusion to LA VIE PARISIENNE. To some degree, the components of Parisian mythology reduce or reconvene the instability in the films' particular hybrid nature but as I now contend, it is only through acknowledging the centrality of this hybridity to the films' history and meanings that one can fully make sense of how "light Paris" was pictured by various émigrés. This duality or two-way looking travelled outside the realm of the musical. By also examining the case of a neglected émigré urban film like MAUVAISE GRAINE, one can gain a fuller picture of Paris beyond the immediate world of performance and entertainment.

In a number of complementary contexts, LA VIE PARISIENNE is a paradigmatic example of the kind of hybrid cinema that the émigré French cinema

3. Press advertising for LA VIE PARISIENNE
(Cinématographie Française 23rd March 1935)

produced. Emeric Pressburger had initially approached Seymour Nebenzahl with the idea of a film called *French Can-Can* based on the life of Offenbach's favourite singer Juliette, but the project fell through. Interestingly, Nebenzahl had originally considered another émigré from Germany, G.W. Pabst, to direct the production of Offenbach's operetta. Family loyalty prevailed however, perhaps because the previous year, Siodmak had worked on a script based on the life of Hortenese Schneider, the celebrated lead in the original stage production. United Artists bankrolled the film and two versions were shot simultaneously with Neil Hamilton performing the Georges Rigaud part in the English-language version. It was a prestigious production in a number of ways. First, compared with the average shooting period of not more than a month for French productions at that time, the shoot stretched to five months. This was necessary because of the huge investment in set design and the subsequent requirements for shot construction. Eighty sets, designed by the prominent decorator, Jacques Colombier, were built and real locations were used, including the Café de la Paix. Secondly, as an obvious consequence of the expectations of the production company, a large-scale publicity campaign was arranged. The revealing slogan "A Piquant Cocktail of Three Generations" accompanied unusually lavish, glossy colour brochures. All of this was of little consequence, however, because the film only did modestly at the box office. In one sense, the publicity for LA VIE PARISIENNE could just as easily have read "A Piquant Cocktail of Three Cultures". This is because Siodmak's film does more than implicitly remind us of operetta's place in Parisian culture. It also looks sideways to the success, in audience and cinematic terms, of the exported Austro-German operetta such as LE CHEMIN DU PARADIS and the ongoing powerful model of Hollywood city-oriented musical entertainment.

The film, first of all, needs to be contextualised in terms of a number of various orders of urban entertainment and representation. When Offenbach died in 1880, a music critic wrote: "the sun of French operetta has set" (in Fornairon 1932, 25). This use of the light metaphor is appropriate for a man who in his work, particularly with the librettists Halévy and Meilhac, had forged a mythical association between Paris and the pleasures of spirited leisure, sharp wit and musical *joie de vivre*. LA VIE PARISIENNE was emblematic of the picture of Paris which he had propagated in his own theatre, the aptly named Les Bouffes-Parisiens in the Passage Choiseul.[24] As has often been pointed out, the operetta was rarely called just that. In most cases, terms like *opéra-comique* or *opéra-bouffe* were used to describe an increasingly loose amalgam of comic performances and scripted musical entertainments. Historically, because of the "pure" form's relative decline during the Third Republic, the heyday of French operetta is more commonly linked to the end of the Second Empire. Thus, as with so much Parisian entertainment, a certain built-in reflex of nostalgic imagining emerged with successive attempts to revivify the genre. In an ironic foreshadowing of the state of cinematic operations in the early 1930s, French operetta, always a carrier for a set of nationalistic discursive strategies, faced competition from two fronts: the Austro-German model and the American music hall tradition.[25] In the French entertainment press of the early 20th century, one can trace an ongoing sense of crisis and national resentment because this most Parisian of forms was being bowdlerised by, for example, "dancing girls and attractions which accommodate vibrantly coloured costume and décor".[26] An indignant piece published in Comédia, entitled "Where is the French Operetta Going?",[27] argued that the form was "the surest criteria for the state of a collective soul". The implication being that the state of the nation was weakening. By the late 1920s and early 1930s, the trend was for live performance venues to reinvent themselves with a mixture of film and other attractions. Operetta, as it had then developed, was seen by some in the critical press to be symptomatic of an un-Parisian modernity. Paul Achard, for example, wrote that Offenbach had been usurped. "They have replaced the spirit of words with that of legs and girls", he complained.[28] Nonetheless, sound cinema, particularly from Germany (Offenbach's native country), persisted in presenting multi-language versions which advertised the technological benefits of film such as improved sets, greater variety in decor, rhythmic editing patterns and an emphasis on performance. Productions such as LE CONGRÈS S'AMUSE, with Lilian Harvey, re-established conventional operetta as a popular form that successfully engineered references to the past in a contemporary idiom.[29] As Vincendeau has suggested (1985, 143), the costs involved in such productions because of elaborate sets and large casts meant that, on the whole, Parisian audiences only saw the French versions of German films like LE BAL (Wilhelm Thiele, 1931). The popularity of these films must also be seen compared to the competition of large budget American musicals like 42ND STREET (Lloyd Bacon, 1933). It is therefore interesting to note that the operetta returned to Paris via the German cinema at the same time as a revival of Offenbach's production took place in a Parisian theatre. Jane Marnac took the lead with Max Dearly at the Mogador in 1931, the same year she starred in Augusto Genina's PARIS-BÉGUIN. According to some, she had a hand in the revival of Second Empire headgear on the streets of Paris. Marnac also went on to appear in a play based on the life of Hortense Schneider. In the popular press, her star persona was based on her paradoxical ability to unite the appeal of the past with the frenetic world of modern-day France. Siodmak's film, in its casting, also attempts to incorporate this paradox by emphasising the appeal of such performers as Max Dearly and Marcelle Praince who were intimately associated with the more contemporary aspects of Parisian pleasure and could thus straddle the worlds of Paris 1900 and 1935. Dearly and Praince had worked together previously in theatre and vaudeville and, in the same year as the film was produced, they could be seen at the Théâtre des Bouffes-Parisiens in *Les Popinod*. Whilst Dearly also specialised in comedies of Parisian manners (he created the notorious *valse chaloupée* with Mistinguett), Praince made her name as a "Parisienne" in boulevard roles. Siodmak's version of LA VIE PARISI-ENNE thus contains a multiple history. It is a film made by a German, financed by Americans, and set in Paris with a Parisian cast. It is the work of an émigré on his way to Hollywood but it makes explicit reference to Parisian entertainment like the "French Can-Can". Finally, it looks back to a distinctively French genre which had evolved to include Viennese and American-influenced off-shoots and had been recently reborn in Germany and re-exported back to Paris to ward off American competition.

LA VIE PARISIENNE not only offers a sense of hybridity in terms of its production history and its eventual place in Parisian entertainment. By looking at the film's formal workings we can also discern a sense of journeying between the practices and values of more than one place and time. It is appropriate, therefore, that a key instance of this takes place in the intermediary space of the international hotel. After a farcical sequence involving the raffish gadabouts, Georges and Helenita, and a scene involving mistaken bedrooms, which could have come from a Claudette Colbert vehicle, Jacques has returned to his proper quarters. He observes Helenita through the net curtain in his room as she gazes out over the city from her balcony. The idea of a character viewed through the separating surface of a screen or curtain is in fact a recurrent visual trope of the film. In "le Grand Noir" nightclub, for example, we see the arrival of Jacques and Simone (Germaine Aussey) – Lianne's successor at "La Vie Parisienne" – by means of a camera track in front of a dividing black chiffon curtain. This trope suggests the material doubling or splitting of the story world that Elsaesser has also noticed, in parallel with the attention to the object, as a frequent motif in Weimar exile cinema (2000, 89). For Elsaesser, this "hesitation or doubleness" constitutes a clear "investment in something other than, or apart from, narrative as the depiction of character-centred action" (92). I think this is true, especially since the film continues to appropriate this form of *mise-en-scène* by developing the notion of spatial separation in the way Jacques appears to join Helenita. The point must be, however, that the *mise-en-scène* does more than serve a formalistic argument; it also works to distinguish space and light in gendered terms and thus here, it not only separates two bodies, but two distinctive ways of seeing the city.

Jacques tiptoes out to the balcony, which is followed by an echo of the previous shot, which seems to confirm that he has joined Helenita screen right. Siodmak then cuts to an overhead shot which dramatically realigns our spatial perception by revealing that, although they indeed occupy a similar horizontal plane, they are, in fact, separated because Helenita's balcony is foregrounded in a diagonal relationship to Jacques's. Siodmak goes to a closer shot in which the distinctive geometry of the hotel architecture underscores the spatial relationship of the couple. In his early work on the émigrés Elsaesser, argued that "light and lighting (its intensity or distribution across the frame) [became] through the precise outline it throws on objects, almost a substitute for editing" (1984, 282). This is echoed in how the characters are subsequently pictured. Having established the lack of equilibrium between the two people, Siodmak goes on to demonstrate a distinctive example of how the Parisian male privilege to view women as objects – amplified in a different way by Don Ramiro's philanderings – can be further underlined by cinematic style. The mythical component of light and somewhat frivolous Parisian (male) pleasure indicated in the preceding farce is temporarily given a darker hue. A very diffuse light source to the rear of Jacques reduces him to a near silhouette with only the left-hand side of his facial features illuminated by a strong side light source. Helenita is more obviously lit but strong light contrasts make her appearance to the right of the frame equally distinctive and spatially at odds with the figure, which occupies the rear left of the image. Siodmak cuts to a powerful medium close-up of the shadowed facial features of Jacques. Only the contours of the left edge of his physiognomy are apparent. He is smoking and as he slowly raises his hand and draws on his cigarette, the features of his face, which is gazing intently rightwards, are softly but dramatically illuminated. When he lowers his hand, the shadow of the initial shot returns. If the masculine gaze is coded as dark, the object of his obviously eroticised attention is coded with a profusion of distinctive whiteness. In the subsequent shot, Helenita is shown looking down at the street with the details of her hair and the luxuriant, fair-toned wrap around her shoulders illuminated by a light source from above. Now comes the rub, for Helenita is shown to have her own active relationship with the city. In this sense, *her* Paris of 1936 is a different place from the city her grandfather knows and insists still exists. According to the boundaries of the myth of "light Paris" her relationship to the city is pictured in terms of a blurring between musical performance and "real life". In a subsequent point-of-view shot in the balcony scene, we see that the object of her attention is a group of swirling, singing figures who emerge from the shadows of the street, screen right. Siodmak cuts to a medium close-up tracking shot of the musical ensemble temporarily stopped by the outstretched arm of an authority figure. But because this is Paris, they are, of course, allowed to continue performing and they are led along their way into the rear left hand shadows of the screen. "La Vie Parisienne" is part of the life of the street as well as the stage. When we return to the granddaughter's face, she is gazing to the right, which confirms that all of what we have seen has been through her eyes. Significantly, what follows is an exact duplication of the image of Jacques, which enables the cinematic spectator to understand that the relationship between the performance on the street and the female protagonist has excluded the male.

Later in the film, when the romance between the couple is in full bloom, the two are seated together and a similar exchange of feeling between city dweller and city performer takes place, this time at a specifically coded site of entertainment: the nightclub. Because of Jacques's impecunious state he is forced to tell Helenita that he is leaving her but the way he puts it is that he is leaving *Paris*. "It is good-bye to walking in the Bois every morning, strolling around museums without looking at anything", he says. As the music strikes up another song, he moves in closer to her. She motions to him to be quiet and then turns away from him; her gaze screen left is distracted by the anticipation of another performance by the *chanteuse* we saw earlier. This is *her* version of the city, and it is the profoundly emotional power of the sung version of city-based feeling that unites the lovers on screen. That this coupling is guided by the seeming inter-relationship of subjectivities between the singer and the female viewer marks the moment as distinctive. The granddaughter turns back to look at Jacques. "I love you", he says. A song begins as the camera slowly glides in closer to the couple. Helenita's eyes turn down as she turns again toward the *chanteuse*. We cut to a shot of the *chanteuse* centre stage to match her gaze. The emotional momentum of the musical performance overwhelms the scene and in the following shots, the granddaughter gets up from the table and leads her lover to the dance floor where she begins to sing the song to Jacques. It is as if, enabled by this moment, she can lure Paris back to him through song.

Elsaesser has also suggested (1984, 283) that the split between this cinema of charged *mise-en scène* and particular French performance traditions produced a "sense of unease and disorientation" in a number of the French films made by émigré filmmakers. Like Vincendeau (1988, 49), he claims, that "trained mainly in the theatre or coming from the music-hall revue and the Paris cabaret, the French actor [brought] to a role not only the carefully distilled observation of social types and the body language of an immediately recognisable milieu, but the sense of an established rapport with an audience" (283). Elsaesser's implication is that this performance tradition worked against the visual style of the émigré filmmaker in which "the decor and the objects become the mirror and repository of reaction and response" (283). This case is not as strong in the émigré Parisian musicals for two inter-related reasons.

Firstly, if one looks at other French film versions of popular operettas such as MAM'ZELLE NITOUCHE (Marc Allégret, 1931)[30] and CHACUN SA CHANCE (Steinhoff and Pujol, 1930), one finds the same emphasis on visual doubling, illusion and play inherent in the diegesis and consequent visual style. It was part of the genre's form. There is a scene in MAM'ZELLE NITOUCHE, for instance, which is set backstage at a theatre. Floridor (Raimu) has to continue sweet-talking Corinne (Edith Mera) despite the fact that she has heard of Nitouche's (Janie Marèse) arrival. The comic conversation is shot from an oblique angle, the "other side" of the mirror, so that the spectator sees the two guiding the dialogue whilst simultaneously looking at their reflection in a mirror that we, in fact, do not see. Much of the *mise-en scène* emphasises, in spatial terms, the film's narrative obsession with what one character or set of characters knows at the expense of the ignorance of the rest. In CHACUN SA CHANCE, another key film from the period, the whole narrative hinges on disguise and duplicity from the transposition of roles between an aristocratic Baron (André Urban) and the shop worker Marcel (Jean Gabin), the emphasis on performance, and on the blurring of the worlds of illusion and reality. This is heralded by the intriguing opening of the film. After a silent production credit sequence, an unseen "host" introduces the film's cast who emerge in couples from behind a stage curtain. This gives us a cue that the film is going to concern itself with shifting roles and an unreliable fluidity between two types of acting: that of the film star and that of the character the film star plays. The "host" gives the command for "the show" to begin and we witness a musical prelude with a concluding medium close-up of a conductor waving his baton looking up at the closed stage curtains. The curtains then part and instead of the expected artifice of a designed set, we see a location shot of a busy Paris street at night. The city as it is performed and the city as it really is – something that only the camera can capture – are inextricably fused. What both of these examples reveal is that the film operetta was indeed "a matter of knowingly accepting deception and self-deception as the 'normal' state of existence" (Elsaesser, 2000, 351). What I believe is most telling are the ways in which Siodmak, as a Weimar émigré, was able to bring an eminently suitable "ironic self-awareness" to his own interpretation of the genre during his stay in France.

The second way in which the émigré musical actually fitted in with French norms was in the way it showcased a meaningful hybridity regarding performance. Instead of disrupting the "established rapport with an audience", Siodmak's *mise-en-scène* may actually have actively complemented the idea of disparity already present in the use of stars. As Vincendeau (1988) suggests, part of the "rapport" Parisian audiences of the era had with the screen's performers was the ways in which they were able to recognise their range of generic acting registers. The disparity between the extravagant comic performance of Max Dearly and the mild matinée manner of Georges Rigaud in LA VIE PARISIENNE, for example, actually enhances the utopian aspect of the film's narrative which finally reconciles the past and present versions of Paris.

Indeed, the mythical world of the "La Vie Parisienne", that both Dearly and Don Ramiro represent, can only really be made sense of in the present through the contrast with the more modern-day, less theatrical, and perhaps, therefore, "American" style that Rigaud represents. Elsaesser's argument "that a mode of divided perception, and awareness of a double focus in narrative and representation [was] one of the principles that the German cinema of the late Weimar period seems to have carried into exile" (1984, 280) does make sense in relation to the film, but only if one applies it to the deliberate division in the way the city is pictured.

We can see this division during a key musical number in the film which features Georges and Don Ramiro and explores the intermingling between reality and spectacle and, in turn, the intermingling of past and present. The sequence begins in the transitory space of the contemporary hotel which, as we have already seen, is depicted using a modernist, linear design scheme. The two men have returned with Helenita after a night out on the town. After leaving his female charge in her hotel room, Don Ramiro takes Jacques by the arm and suggests they go out for more entertainment. "Ah (...) to return to Paris!", he declares. The camera tracks the two men as they move down the corridor. It stops and the men exit the image screen left. There is a rapid wipe cut to the nightclub and the two reappear with their arms linked, as if by magic, screen right from behind a pillar. It is as though they have transcended time and space, which in a sense they have since the sophisticated luxury of the nightclub's ambiance and entertainment promises a world embedded in a sense of the city far removed from the exclusive geometric features of the facade of the modern hotel.[31]

As Don Ramiro moves through the various social spaces of the hotel and the nightclub, Paris of the past, which he embodies, is seen coming back to life. What is interesting is how the returnee, dressing the part in top hat and tails, commands the venue's space. Modern-day Jacques is left to look on passively. As the camera follows Don Ramiro across the floor and up the stairs he gesticulates and dances as if he is in control of the spectacle. The film makes it clear here, as it does in other instances throughout the narrative, that it is only largely via the exuberance of music and performance that the past can be actively remembered. Don Ramiro seems to embrace the world around him and because he is in constant motion, space is continuously being revealed to the spectator. He continues to dance his way to the top of the stairway while a trail of amused, mainly female, participants are led around the contours of a bar in front of which he comes to a halt. This emphasis on circularity – the antithesis of the hotel's modernist rectilinear style – is reinforced in Colombier's extravagantly swirling decor. In a medium close-up he is pictured singing "Paris, Paris, Paris, Paris!", a glass and bottle of champagne in respective hands. We cut to a sudden overhead view of the action from which Don Ramiro can be seen with arms outstretched overlooking the stage-like space below on the ground floor. On the final "Paris", the stage figures start to move and the "show" begins as if, through his agency, past Paris has been brought into the present.

Siodmak's earlier musical, LA CRISE EST FINIE, also reveals its hybrid nature in a number of ways and points again to how the émigré picturing of Paris casts the city of the present as a staging area for a journey across time. The film explicitly recalls earlier Parisian entertainments through the characters Madame Olga and the actress Suzanne Dehelly and through the setting of the Elysée Clichy theatre. When the troupe arrives in Paris, Olga is recognised by a waiter who used to work with her at the venue. She alludes to a past sexual scandal involving the then director and when she arrives at the stage door she recalls passing through the entrance garlanded with flowers. This instant of nostalgia works in two ways. Firstly, it posits a continuum of stardom and performance that involves the city. As with Lianne in LA VIE PARISIENNE, the Paris of live spectacle and glamourous entertainment is kept alive by an inter-relationship between the female body and memory. But secondly, this version of worldly, metropolitan and sexually experienced femininity accentuates the portrayal of provincial and optimistic innocence that Nicole represents. Nicole's difference is also one of stardom. Danielle Darrieux was in the process of becoming one of France's leading female film stars. Unlike her co-star in the film Albert Préjean who had already had a career in silent cinema and live entertainment, Darrieux, because she was still very young, was completely identified with the new. With her debut in LE BAL, she began being promoted in specifically French and cinematic terms so as to rival her Hollywood counterparts. This strategy is important, for although the film abounds with references to the specificity of Paris and Parisian musicality, it also looks sideways to the model of the contemporary Hollywood musical and its typical rendition of the virtuous and dynamic young female seeking romance in the big city. In fact, during and after its production history, LA CRISE EST FINIE was consistently compared to the Warner Brothers musicals of the time. "M. Siodmak makes 'La Crise est finie', a French '42nd Street'" was the headline for a vivid on-the-set report of the filming.[32]

The film alludes to the scale and tenor of the American musicals of the time in a manner unlike other French titles with similar music hall backgrounds such as PARIS-BÉGUIN (Augusto Genina, 1931) and ZOUZOU (Marc Allégret, 1934). The journal Candide even went so far as to say that "in ten minutes, one can see on the screen more original ideas than one can find in two hours of spectacle in one of our large music halls".[33] In PARIS-BÉGUIN, the social life, back-stage interaction, and actual "live" stage numbers are centred around the star of the show, Jane Diamond, a more or less direct transposition of the star persona of the performer Jane Marnac. Even the curtains of the revue bear her face. The film is thus a star vehicle that deals with the encounter between the glamorous world of the stage and the semi-underworld milieu with which Parisian theatre was then geographically related in the areas around Pigalle and Montmartre in the 18th *arrondisement*. The encounter is anticipated by the constant use of posters that advertise Diamond's revue appearing in the background of street conversations. Marnac is constantly pictured centre frame and her mainly white and sparkling attire is boldly lit to contrast with the darker clothing of the people around her. This patterning is reinforced more broadly by the contrast between well-lit interiors and more nocturnal street scenes. The bourgeois milieu of the theatre itself, which is demarcated by the dress and demeanour of the audience, indicates the evolving status of the revue-spectacle in Parisian society and its alterity to the world of the *apaches* inhabited by Dédé (Jean Gabin). With LA CRISE EST FINIE, however, Siodmak integrates the star performers into a narrative model that involves putting on a show from scratch. Instead of inherent plenitude, a display of vigour and an energetic spirit of resourcefulness is used to suggest the effort involved in achieving a utopian outcome for all concerned. This allows Siodmak to combine Parisian communality with the generic Hollywood musical's triumph against all odds à la 42ND STREET.

Light is foregrounded by the theft of some light bulbs from the home of a young aristocrat. One of the girls from the troupe lures the man to his apartment and we see each window being lit from an exterior long-shot as the couple enters each room. There is a close-up of hands unscrewing and removing several light bulbs and then Siodmak cuts to a comic reversal of the previous long-shot with the light in each window going out in time to a musical motif. Rather than contrasting the street with the stage, Schüfftan uses light to highlight the disparity in attitude and degree of optimism among the members of the troupe. At a critical moment in the film, for example, Marcel gesticulates in an impassioned manner: "be full of life, enthusiasm, colour, and light!" His raised arms are bathed in a strong, intense glow from above. Siodmak cuts with irony to a *lighting* technician standing nearby whose body creases up in sarcastic applause. As his body descends (in antithesis to Marcel's) his crumpled features are defined against a pool of shadow. On his knees, now bathed in real gloom, he says: "we don't even have one light bulb!" We return to Marcel who declares: "Now there is the crisis. He personifies it". The troupe succeeds but, in turn, so does the world of live spectacle for the disused theatre is saved from being turned into a cinema and is returned to the city audience whom it used to delight.[34] In the film's conclusion when the homonymic relationship between the title of the revue (and film) – "La Crise est finie" – and the name of the theatre – L'Elysée Clichy – is most clearly underscored, the movie spectator is incorporated within the point of view of the Parisians who are themselves in the process of re-becoming a theatrical audience. The paradox is, of course, that the film is part of the spirit of crisis and displacement which the film's narrative seeks to obliterate.

The spectacular finale fuses the optimistic energy of the performance (and the Parisian public) with a highly developed cinematic *mise-en-scène*. Like PARIS BÉGUIN the musical number begins with a parade of Busby Berkeley-esque revue girls pictured on top of a sequence of individual podiums. At this moment both films seem to be simply recording the nature of the increasingly "Americanised" French music hall tradition. But whereas Genina's film stays with the stage and opts for an evermore elaborate choreography of multitudinous chorus numbers, Siodmak breaks into the realm of cinematic invention. In one sense these sequences serve as a kind of calling card from an émigré versed in a film culture "preoccupied with (...) a fetishism of technique" (Elsaesser, 1984, 282), but they also underline the twin paradoxes of making films about theatre, and of German personnel making films about an "alien" culture with one eye, perhaps, on the future filmmaking destination of Hollywood. We see Marcel alone, playing the piano, in front of what appears to be a world map. The superimposed words "LA CRISE EST FINIE" emerge screen right and curl around the space of the frame. Eventually, after some inter-cutting with the chorus-girls, the camera tracks out and reveals a blackened globe, lit in a swirling strobe-like fashion, with a number of girls in various national costumes on top. The crisis is global but as Siodmak goes on to show, in the milieu of this film, so are its resolutions. In the subsequent series of bizarre national tableaux set in France, the United States, Russia and Great Britain we see money falling from the sky like snow or confetti. Each country is introduced by an iconic image of a major city so that we have a fascinating on-screen foretelling of one of Siodmak's eventual fictional destinations: the crime-ridden world of noir New York. This montage of the nations is immediately followed by Siodmak's cut to the diegetic audience as if they have been watching this bravura display. The theatre stalls are packed to the rafters with laughing Parisians. In this way, the film has its urban cake and can eat it too. It pays attention to the Parisian past and to the American future by integrating them both into the present. The sequence ends with a close-up embrace of the romantic couple.

We have seen in LA CRISE EST FINIE how the improvised community of theatrical performers plays with the artifacts of Paris for its own ends. In one comic sequence we even see the troupe appropriate letters from a bank sign "Crédit Parisien" to create the word "Crise" for their revue. The "crisis", emphasised in the title, represents the poverty and homelessness of the performers and serves as a metonym for the external economic crisis that is besetting France. This financial situation is also alluded to in Billy Wilder's only

French émigré feature MAUVAISE GRAINE, but in this case it probably also refers to the personal legal and financial predicaments of many of its creators.[35] Wilder, for example, left Berlin immediately after the Reichstag fire on 27 February 1933 and had arrived in Paris with his girlfriend without a visa. Without a work permit, he was forced to earn money from hand to mouth. He had, in fact, been given the job of directing the film because the project's independent producer was unable to pay for an established professional. The film depicts a comical but effective community of thieves who also "play" in the city for their own gain, stealing cars from the well off. The gang then refashion these vehicles to disguise their origins and then resell them. Much of the film was shot on location on the streets of Paris around Vincennes and the Bois de Boulogne, preceding the *Nouvelle Vague* by several decades. The production had its own peculiar set of hybridities and perspectives. It looks back to Berlin and it looks forward to the United States, but it does so by incorporating a vivid and rhythmic sense of the spaces of the Paris of that moment.

In Berlin, Wilder had worked as a writer with a keen interest in the sensibilities of the modern city. As well as writing for the leading journals of the day such as *Tempo* and *Querschnitt*, he helped on the bizarre sounding operetta DAS BLAUE VOM HIMMEL (Victor Janson, 1932) that was set in the Berlin U-Bahn with singing and dancing commuters. He also had script credits on two important Berlin films which heralded the pace and tone of MAUVAISE GRAINE. In MENSCHEN AM SONNTAG (Siodmak et al., 1929) we see a *plein-air* version of the city in which quotidian reality is presented in a form not unlike a photo spread in a typical photo magazine of the period. German critics of the film had actually made reference to its Parisian-like light touch by comparing it positively to the negative intensity of typical Berlin representation. According to *Der Abend*, "once Paris was shown to us in an impressive, simple manner; now, we see Berlin without the shine of advertisements in lights and the crazy nightlife of bars" (in Lally 1996, 33-34). In MAUVAISE GRAINE, there is an extended sequence set around an open-air swimming pool on a Sunday afternoon which like MENSCHEN AM SONNTAG, Marcel Carné's NOGENT, ELDORADO DU DIMANCHE (1930) and Augusto Genina's PRIX DE BEAUTÉ portrays a space made for movement and release in contrast to the tensions of the weekday workplace. The film recalls, as many have observed, the caper movie qualities of the location-driven EMIL UND DIE DETEKTIVE (Gerhard Lamprecht, 1931) for which Wilder also wrote the screenplay. Indeed, some of the Paris reviews picked up on the relation between the soundtracks of the two films. Both features involved a fellow émigré of Wilder's, Franz Wachsmann (de-Germanised to Waxman). In MAUVAISE GRAINE he matched the spirit of the fast moving images of urban modernity to the speed of an American syncopated jazz score.[36] The music also works to underline the consistent references to the recently

4. Duplicity and Performance. Jean-la Cravatte (Raymond Galle, left)
in Mauvaise graine (BIFI)

vanished world of the silent cinema. The chase sequences between police and
criminals and the use of sight gags alludes to the American tradition of fast-
paced urban visual comedy exemplified by Mack Sennett and Harold Lloyd.
We can see this when the Zèbre (Jean Wall) attempts to park his car by trying to
tie it to a lamppost. We see a close-up of a "No Parking" sign. The Zèbre looks
at the sign to the explicit rhythm of the jazz with a succession of jump-cuts
bringing the sign closer and closer to the viewer and him. Thinking, he digs his
hands into his pockets, then approaches the sign and peels it away to reveal a
second message – "sens interdit" – which can be translated either as: "this way
prohibited" or, just as likely, as "sense forbidden". This interest in modern visual humour is combined with a number of wipes, dissolves, and superimpositions to break up time and space. More than one critic at the time noted that the
camera work and the music produced a sense of modernity to match the subject matter of the automobile in the city. One critic, in particular, saw it as a re-
freshing antidote to filmed theatre. In an approving tone, typical of the "real
cinema" debate mentioned in Chapter Two, he called Mauvaise graine a "reaction against the 'Pagnolisation' of cinema".[37]

It would be wrong to simply portray MAUVAISE GRAINE as a project of expediency made in transit. What makes it especially interesting is how, like the émigré French musical, Wilder's film can be seen simultaneously as both a typical French and a typical émigré production. References to Parisian culture abound within the diegesis as well as the various performance registers which stem from the Parisian music hall. Jean Wall plays the kind of comic buffoon that was familiar to stage audiences of the period while Pierre Mingand, playing the rogue doctor's son Pasquier, was known for his impersonations of Maurice Chevalier at the Folies-Bergère. Trying to pick up a young girl at a garage Mingand challenges her to identify him. "You don't know me?", he says. "Wait! Look!" He picks up a boater which magically appears from screen-right. "Do you recognise me now? Do you know who I am? I'm Maurice Chevalier!" Mingand starts to sing and then adds: "as for Josephine Baker – well!" Later, in the narrative when Jeannette leads an unsuspecting gentleman away from his car so that it can be stolen by the gang, the "fake couple" go to see Dranem perform in a live show. In many ways, the entire film is about performance and disguise and the key to this is the concurrent Weimar cinema interest in visual doubling. This visual doubling allows Wilder to work another visual field onto the conventional surface trappings of a "French film". MAUVAISE GRAINE may remind us of a film like Jean Renoir's LE CRIME DE M. LANGE (1936) in that it also concerns a "little community (...) the chance product of urban geography" (Bazin 1974, 45) battling against larger forces, but in MAUVAISE GRAINE we have the city community resorting to disguise, not the villain, thus rendering the group's status in the narrative more ambivalent. It is not surprising that one of the main gang members is actually visibly split in that he wears zebra-like, striped attire. Even the space of the community – the garage – is divided by a hidden sliding wall. Renoir's *mise-en scène* accentuated the mythical stability of the world of the *faubourg* by portraying the court-yard bound together either by the circularity of the camera movement and significant decorative features or by the complex staging in-depth of key scenes. In the case of MAUVAISE GRAINE, there is an inherent instability that is suggested most forcefully by the constant framing in motion of the city passing by from the vantage point of the motor car.

Wilder's visual doubling in relation to the city of Paris takes on a number of additional aspects. Firstly, there is the visualisation of the split in the character of Pasquier who, deprived of his car, is forced to join the ordinary world of the streets. It is this separation from the object of his social status that enables him to play with the hitherto unknown milieu of the city criminal and transgress class boundaries. As Païni (1992, 61) has pointed out, many of the film's city images recall a different spatio-temporal aesthetic, one that is more reminiscent of central European photographers of that time like Laszlo Moholy-Nagy.

He argues that the Constructivist interest in the plasticity of the image and the near-abstract attention to the details of form in Wilder's film at times compete with the more traditional space in the frame that is usually reserved for the action of the French stars and the subsequent advancement of the diegesis. We can see this jostling of viewing practices in relation to the city when we watch Pasquier walking along the pavement after the loss of his treasured possession. His head and shoulders are superimposed over the forward motion of the figure so there are in effect two patterns of movement. This duality is reinforced by the way the head and shoulders are shown in the style of a photographic negative to produce an ethereal, psychological impression over the darkness of the main image. We then see his car being taken away in a split-screen effect so that the action is repeated in the form of a mirror image on both sides of the frame. The central character of Pasquier walking down the street is superimposed onto two succeeding abstract shots: one of a close-up of a car wheel spinning and the second, a close-up of the rapidly rotating hands of a clock. After a cut-away shot, we return to Pasquier who is now gazing into car showroom windows. Instead of simply making the shot a further example of the viewing practices embodied in the idea of the city as spectacle, Wilder complicates the *mise-en-scène* by re-employing the motif of visual doubling. Pasquier is shot at an angle to the frame of the store window and, as he looks longingly at the new car inside, he and the viewer see the reflection of a car identical to his own pull up and "super-impose" itself onto the original object of his attention. It is as if it is only when Pasquier sees his car "come back to life" that he becomes a "whole" character again and Mingand is simultaneously allowed to re-establish his position as the star.

The second aspect of Wilder's visual doubling lies in the motif of disguise or an instability regarding appearance and reality. This is particularly true in the case of Jeannette who performs the same kind of role of an available Parisian woman in the street that Don Ramiro is seen watching from the vantage point of an outdoor café seat at the end of LA VIE PARISIENNE. It is her job to attract male car-owners so that they can then become the victims of the waiting thieves. Much of the film's rather skimpy narrative hinges on this sort of trickery and deception, but it does lead to the third kind of visual doubling: the relationship between Paris and the rest of France (and the world). When Pasquier and Jeannette's boss become irritated by the complaints of gang members about their cut of the take, he sends the couple on a mission to Marseilles with a set of forged papers. It is at this point in the film that the narrative itself literally splits in two. The couple's journey south is shot as a sequence of dissolving maps, emphasising the provincial towns they pass along the way to Marseilles. They become embroiled in a high-speed car chase when the police notice the smudged ink on their fake identity cards. Their passage across the space of non-metropolitan France is represented by an evolving sense of liber-ation. We see them on the back of a haytruck before they arrive in Marseilles, gazing out across a sparkling expanse of ocean and sky. Meanwhile, the rest of the gang is left behind in Paris as the police use the iconography of the Métro map as they attempt to trap the men. This contrast between entrapment and release simultaneously places the film outside and inside the French cinematic tradition. The escape into a world beyond the city, typically the colonies, was a recurring motif of 1930s French cinema. Pasquier and Jeannette's decision to leave France is therefore, in some ways, expected. But one can't help reading this narrative progression as something symptomatic of the émigré filmmak-ers' own need to escape to a world beyond Europe, to America and the oppor-tunity to make films in a more Hollywood-influenced style. The final signifi-cance of "light" here is that of a Paris as the springboard to the greater "light" of cultural freedom.

4 City of Darkness

The Camera Goes Down the Streets:
'The Hidden Spirit Under the Familiar Façade'

The Paris cinema auditorium of the 1930s was a place city dwellers largely entered at night, attracted by the building façade's display lights. Off the street, the audience found themselves in darkness again for the duration of the evening's main entertainment whilst images of the city were projected via light onto the screen. Discussing the work of the novelist Emile Zola in relation to the historical depiction of social experience in the French capital, Louis Chevalier wrote: 'paradoxically (...) the triumph of light, for him, far from eradicated the shadow and the past which it concealed. It actually accorded it a new form of life as if light was a dazzling container for shadow' (1980, 23). To unravel exactly what the legacy of this sense of urban "darkness" meant in relation to the émigrés' interpretation of Paris, we first need to consider the depiction of the street and the emphasis on authenticity and social concern found in strains of French realist cinema of the period. In a key polemical article *"Quand le cinéma descendra-t-il dans la rue?"* (When Will the Cinema Go Down the Street?), published in *Cinémagazine* in November 1933, Marcel Carné anticipated the fascination that the streets of Paris would hold for filmmakers and filmgoers alike throughout the decade.[1] Carné called Paris "the two-faced city". By this he meant that according to established tropes of representation, Paris had been divided in terms of place and class between the frivolous high life and the "real world" of the ordinary urban dweller. Carné thought there had been too much of "the murky and inflated ambiance of night clubs, dancing couples, and a non-existent nobility" at the expense of "the simple life of humble people (...) the atmosphere of hard-working humanity" (in Abel 1993, 129). Since the development of Haussmanisation in the nineteenth century, "the simple life of humble people" had, to a large extent, become associated with darkness in the medical and socio-scientific writings of the day. Writers frequently stressed the association between the proliferation of disease and the darkness of the typical Parisian overcrowded *faubourg*. "Tuberculosis is the disease of darkness" the Commission d'Extension de Paris wrote in 1913, for example. "To combat it effectively, one must first of all oppose it with its natural enemy, the sun" (in Evenson 1979, 211). How did the Parisian cinema of the émigrés fit into this equation? Did the traditions of visualising Berlin's urban space, and the narrative possibilities that space contained, spill over into films made about the French capital? When he implored that the camera go into the streets, Carné was thinking of the reality of location footage as opposed to the constructed verisimilitude of people like Lazarre Meerson who designed the sets for René Clair's SOUS LES TOITS DE PARIS and QUARTORZE JUILLET. For him the urban picture needed a frame which contained "a decor of factories, garages, slender footbridges, and unloading carts" (in Abel, 129). What did this difference between Paris as a place to be captured on film, and Paris as a theatrical set, actually mean in terms of the émigrés' own relation to urban set design and location cinematography?

It is surprising that Carné's article did not mention Victor Trivas's pivotal émigré film DANS LES RUES, which began filming in April 1933 and was released in July of that same year. Its very title seems to manifest Carné's contentions regarding the relationship between cinema and the French capital. Although the film also reveals traces of a different cultural heritage. Trivas was an émigré twice over in the sense that he came to Paris from Russia via Berlin. He had worked as a set designer for Pabst on DIE LIEBE DER JEANNE NEY/THE LOVE OF JEANNE NEY (1927). In Germany, he also co-wrote the script for MIRAGES DE PARIS (1932) with fellow Russian émigré Fédor Ozep (Fyodor A. Otsep). This was subsequently filmed in French and German by Ozep in 1932 after he too had made the move to France. In an interview published in *Paris Midi*, Trivas confirmed that his real métier in cinema had been work related to his architectural design training.[2] This education is certainly apparent in the way he shaped the visual organisation of urban space in the film. In the same interview, Trivas also stressed how his outsider status informed the way he represented the French capital. Like many of his fellow émigrés, however, he was also keen to demonstrate how he would be able to fit in. "Paris for me is the great unknown", he commented. "First of all, I sense here an ideal atmosphere for the collective work that is cinema. The Paris that I will describe to you, and that will be the protagonist of my film, isn't that of the Champs Elysées or the Stock Exchange, but the Paris that René Clair so admirably showed us in his most human and seductive film QUARTORZE JUILLET. (...) [My film will be] the homage to Paris of a stranger who believes he can uncover its everyday, moving beauty".[3]

As Trivas's remarks suggest, it would be a mistake to read DANS LES RUES solely in terms of directorial authorship. The list of credits for the film reveals many other fascinating contributions which clearly point to its particular historical status as a hybrid production. Alexandre Arnoux, the founder of *Pour Vous* and the author of a previous particularly favourable and perceptive review of Litvak's COEUR DE LILAS, co-wrote the screenplay which was mentioned by many film critics including Paul Souillac. In his review, Souillac noted that Arnoux was a "possessor of a sense of Paris and the souls of its citizens".[4] The lead cinematographer was Rudolph Maté who had worked previously with Carl Dreyer and was also to become involved in Fritz Lang's French émigré film LILIOM. The sets were by André Andréjew who had also worked with Pabst, on L'OPÉRA DE QUAT'SOUS (1931), and the distinctive edgy melancholia of the score was written by Bertolt Brecht's former collaborator, Hanns Eisler.[5] At an important preliminary press reception for the film, even fellow émigrés Joe May and G.W. Pabst were on hand to lend support. The story of the film concerns a war widow and her two sons who live in an impoverished *quartier* of the capital. Jacques (Jean-Pierre Aumont) refuses the path of steady employment taken by his brother and falls in with a band of small-time street criminals. A romance develops between him and Rosalie (Madeleine Ozeray), the niece of a local second-hand goods dealer. Jacques becomes involved in a local burglary and after the accidental death of the elderly victim he goes on the run from the law. After days spent in the streets and on the riverbanks of Paris the police catch him but he is saved from prison by his mother (Marcelle-Jean Worms) who makes a special plea by arguing that her son is a victim of social circumstances.

DANS LES RUES was based on a novel by the populist novelist Joseph-Henri Rosnay *aîné*. The term *populisme* signified an interest in the lives of ordinary Parisian people and was a matter of contemporary interest amongst the city's intelligentsia. It had been made the subject of a polemical manifesto by Léon Lemonnier in *L'Oeuvre* in 1929 and in 1930, a populist literature prize was created and won by Eugène Dabit's *Hôtel du nord*. The following year, the journal *Monde* sponsored a written debate on the topic which included contributions from Lemonnier as well as Henri Poulaille. Poulaille, the author of *Populisme* (1930), then wrote his own manifesto in 1932 which was co-signed by a number of film-related figures such as Georges Altman and Marcel Lapierre.[6] It was this trend in literature that Marcel Carné had turned to as a model for the kind of cinematic representation of the city that he envisaged. Indeed, he was, of course, to direct his own version of the Dabit novel in 1937, starring Jean-Pierre Aumont.[7] In Carné's clarion call he praised the "number of novelists [who] have not been afraid to study certain quarters of Paris and seize the hidden spirit under the familiar facade of their streets" (in Abel, 129). This conflation of novelistic intention and the idea of uncovering a hitherto unexplored social reality is a key element in the set of inter-textual cultural practices concerning the discussion of "dark" Paris which go back, as in the case of "spectacular" Paris, to the nineteenth century.

With the growth of the city due to the pressures of industrialisation, came an increased anxiety on the part of the Parisian authorities about the *classes dangereuses* and their perceived "natural" milieu – the darkened streets in the working class urban areas untouched by the brightness of modernity. This anxiety led to an ever-widening social division, especially in the way the capital was imagined by its citizens. As Schlör (1998, 123) points out, "on the one hand, it [was] a matter of keeping the areas and regions thought of as *potentially dangerous* under perpetual surveillance (...) [whilst] on the other hand, the areas of the city regarded as *potentially endangered* [had] to be saved and protected from the penetration of 'crime'." Darkness thus meant more than just the natural correlation to illumination (be it from daylight or artificial sources), it also suggested an ill-focused combination of danger and immorality. Above all, for the city's bourgeoisie, it suggested the perilous seduction of the unknown. Narratives such as Eugène Sue's hugely successful *Les Mystères de Paris*, serialised between 1843-44, capitalised on these themes to represent a city which needed to be investigated because of this profusion of darkness. The contemporaneous expansion of the police's functions and its methodologies of detection was paralleled by a culture of revelation. In the fiction of writers like Sue, Hugo and Zola, this process often meant an exploration of the city at night. Similarly, in the musical tradition of the *chanson réaliste*, the feeling and suffering of those who came from the darkened streets was actually relayed to an audience as nighttime pleasure. In the visual arts, Courbet's "Realist Manifesto" of 1855 proclaimed the painterly desire "to know, in order (...) to translate the customs, the ideas [and] the appearance of my epoch" (in Rubin 1997, 158), and the early Parisian photographic work of Gaspard-Félix Nadar and Charles Marville also specialised in seeing the streets of ordinary Paris in new ways.

We can summarise these sources by claiming that what they had in common was a set of assumptions which played on two inter-related variables: firstly, a sense of ethnographic curiosity about the social "other" and, secondly, an interest in urban marginality and the equation between class and darkness. To show how clearly DANS LES RUES assimilated these codes of Parisian representation, there is an introduction to both of these tropes in the film's trailer. It commences with a high-angled close-up view of the cobblestones of a Parisian street. The edges of the silhouettes of residents are visible crossing the top part of the screen and as the camera begins to track backwards, moving vehicles enter the frame in the reverse direction. The effect is of an almost voyeuristic opening up of a detailed social world based on the motif of the everyday or typical in motion. An introduction to the cast follows which begins with the musical and emotional register of the *chanson réaliste*. Charlotte Dauvia is seen knitting and singing in a medium close-up shot of her behind a café bar. Her figure is linked to the world of the *quartier* in two ways. Firstly, through visual repetition as the camera tracks back in the same revelatory motion as the preceding shot and then, secondly, in the lyrics of her song about the Paris working class milieu of Belleville and the Parc des Buttes-Chaumont. The song continues as the following shots of the film's leading characters convey the impoverished milieu that the narrative inhabits. The greys and dark areas of the ordinary interiors frame the set of predominately melancholic faces to suggest a naturalism committed to revealing "life as it is led".

This notion of revealing "life as it is led" is furthered by the integrated use of more documentary type footage of horse racetracks and crowds, children playing and couples dancing. These kinds of images that convey the leisure and pleasures of typical Parisians were also found in the pages of the numerous urban photo albums of the period and the new photo-journalistic periodicals such as Lucien Vogel's *Vu* (established 1928) and the highly successful illustrated city newspaper *Paris-Soir* (established 1931). In the words of the editors of the latter: "the image has become the queen of our time. We are no longer satisfied to know, we want to see (in Warehime 1996, 6-7). The development of photographic publishing had in part been based on the success of German Weimar counterparts such as *Berliner Illustrite Zeitung*. Indeed, DANS LES RUES can also usefully be compared with the realist impulses of a "Zille film" such as MUTTER KRAUSEN'S FAHRT INS GLUCK (Piel Jutzi, 1929) which in sections of its narration re-presented, in cinematic terms, print documentary photo-spreads of the modern city.[8] Both films do incorporate moments of politically guided vérité footage, but there is a vital difference. The harshness of the Berlin in MUTTER KRAUSEN is largely seen as the brutal consequence of an uncaring and failed economic project that must be opposed by organised resistance. The Paris of DANS LES RUES, on the other hand, whilst still a place of social hardship, is also a site of collaborative play, communal pleasure, and improvised satire.

The trailer of Trivas's film also makes direct reference to the visual codes of expressive darkness which had surfaced throughout the heyday of the Berlin late silent cinema in features like M (Fritz Lang, 1931) and ASPHALT (Joe May, 1929). To a large extent, it does this by using night in relation to notions of desire and criminality. In a close up of two lovers embracing at night against a backdrop of inky darkness, the edges of the male's cap and jacket are illuminated by a strong, direct light source. Later, a dramatically lit nighttime gang fight is pictured in medium-long shot to utilise the expressive inter-relationship between the shadowy architectural space of the street and the criminal sub-culture. This is a move away from the naturalistic model of ordinary city life to a stylised form of visual commentary which is designed to evoke sensations of danger and hitherto hidden feeling. This patterning of the city at night, it must be said, is also evident in the work of a number of prominent photographers of the time including Marcel Bovis, René Jacques and especially the fellow émigré from Hungary, Brassaï. In his photos of nighttime Paris taken in the 1930s, and published either in popular photographic journals or deluxe art books for the connoisseur, Brassaï skillfully examined the congruence of night and secrecy. Paul Morand, in his introduction to the photographer's first book

Paris de nuit, (published the same year as Dans les rues), wrote that "night [in Brassaï's work] is not the negative of day; black surfaces and white ones are not merely transposed, as on a photographic plate, but another picture altogether emerges at nightfall" (in Warehime, 1996, 63). In Brassaï's own essay "Techniques de la photographie de nuit", republished in 1933 in the annual photography issue of *Arts et Métiers Graphiques*, he actually equated "the city at night with a darkened studio set" (in Warehime, 35). These themes clearly occur in Trivas's film, which used a significant amount of nighttime location footage. Indeed, in one production report, Trivas's distinctive use of Paris at night was highlighted by the journalist concerned. "All last week Victor Trivas has been shooting location scenes for his film Dans les rues around the quays of the Seine and Paris's distant *quartiers*", the author commented. "It has been a veritable peaceful revolution in the quiet streets around Ivry where a number of dramatic scenes have been directed during nighttime shoots".[9]

Mention of Brassaï's name returns one to the French literary inter-text for Dans les rues in that Brassaï illustrated articles by two leading writers who made their own contributions to the visualisation of 1930s Paris in the dark. The detective novelist Georges Simenon and poet-essayist Pierre Mac Orlan were similarly fascinated by the ambiguities of the after-hours intersection of light and shadow on the streets of the city. Simenon, himself an émigré of sorts because of his Belgian origins, actually wrote many years later that he equated learning about Paris in terms of night. "You really get to know Paris, silhouette by silhouette", he argued (in Ford and Jeanne, 1969, 77). The popularity of his fiction and that of other detective writers such as Léo Malet is indicative of the general proliferation of crime-related fiction during the period that had been fostered as much by the success of recent American urban crime writing in translation as the popularity of pre-established local narrative traditions.[10] This phenomenon very quickly spilled over into French film culture. Three of Simenon's early Maigret novels were filmed and made into important French dark city productions: La Tête d'un homme (Julien Duvivier, 1932), Le Chien jaune (Jean Tarride, 1932) and La Nuit du carrefour (Jean Renoir, 1932). Mac Orlan also referred to Paris as the city of darkness in his revealing text *Le Fantastique* (1926). It is important to note that he had proposed a new way of looking at urban reality which linked the emergent mass medium of the cinema with the privileged gaze of a certain kind of urban spectator. "[Y]ou could say that the cinema has made us notice the social fantastic of our times", he wrote. "All you have to do is wander the night to understand that new lighting has created new shadows" (quoted in Ford and Jeanne, 122). Furthermore, in 1932, the year before the release of Dans les rues, Mac Orlan had written a revealing article on Piel Jützi's film adaptation of *Berlin Alexanderplatz*[11] entitled "Le Réalisme de certains films évoque le fantastique social". In this fascinating piece, he explicitly linked his idea of the inter-relationship between cinema spectatorship and city viewing to the streets of the German and French capitals.[12]

It is clear that Mac Orlan was proposing more than a suggestive curiosity about the hidden surfaces of Paris. He also wanted to infer a sense of urban poetry which would have surely appealed to a particular educated metropolitan sensibility far removed from the very lives of the many ordinary Parisians it sought to detail. In this sense, like many of the prominent city photographers of the era, he can be seen as the inheritor of the largely male tradition of the urban literary *flâneur* – the man in the crowd who self-consciously moved across the spaces of the modern city relating his exterior observations to an interior narrative. This is the perceptual mode discussed by Walter Benjamin who considered that Paris taught him "the art of straying" (1997, 298). It is a mode of looking and being that suits the visual-minded outsider and it is captured well in Kracauer's formulation of the "aimless saunterer who sought to conceal the gaping void around him and within him by imbibing a thousand casual impressions. Shop windows, window displays, prints, new buildings, smart clothes, elegant equipages, newspaper sellers – he indiscriminately absorbed the spectacle of life that went on around him" (1937, 88).

For Benjamin, the world of the city street meant that "signboards and street names, passers-by, roofs, kiosks, or bars [could] speak to the wanderer like a cracking twig under his feet in the forest [or] like the startling call of a bittern in the distance" (1997, 298). This startlingly evocative phrasing both points to an abiding fascination with the city poetry of Baudelaire and a fascinating collusion between the mind of the *flâneur* and a proto-cinematic practice relevant to at least one part of the film culture of this period. As Anke Gleber has perceptively remarked, by seizing on the "phenomena of modern street life and the effects they have on the experience of movement …[Benjamin turned spaces] into objects of scopophilia that [could] be experienced either by walking in the street or by tracking extended lines of serial images [in the mind] (1999, 53). This heightened appreciation of the synergy between the material environment of the modern city and a highly nuanced private perception spills over into the ways in which dark Paris was depicted as a central narrative component in contemporary print and cinematic culture. Like the Maigret novels, many dark city films clearly relied on their readership's awareness of the city as a kind of circuit map in which journeys of detection relied on precise topographical coordinates. Having said all of this, however, it is well to also remember that a film like DANS LES RUES would not have been made purely with the sophisticated literary thinking spectator in mind. Alexandre Arnoux, wrote presciently in relation to COEUR DE LILAS that this particular vein of Parisian cinema also had the potential to appeal to "both the adolescent and the rather more mature bourgeois".[13]

This complex inter-textual equation between popular cinema, nighttime shadow, and social voyeurism is certainly evident in Trivas's DANS LES RUES – particularly in its depiction of Paris locations at night. In a key section of the narrative, following a police raid of the fight between two rival gangs, Jacques and his accomplice plot the burglary on a nearby street. The sequence begins with a close-up of a particular element of the social decor. This type of sequence occurs throughout the film. Interestingly, in this case it is a movie poster depicting a masked criminal figure. This degree of self-consciousness underscores the equation drawn so far between nighttime Paris and the cinematic, but it also reminds us of Elsaesser's argument regarding the Parisian work of the German émigrés. Elsaesser, we may remember, suggested that Weimar cinema was, to a great extent, a cinema pre-occupied with technique and visual brio to the extent that the delineation of the processes of narration often overtook the simple rendering of action. This degree of fetishism had been continued after "German" filmmakers left Berlin so that in their French films, and later in Hollywood, one can still see "a persistent discrepancy between narrated time and action time" (1984, 282). It is certainly true that we can partly see this in the way the camera pans swiftly downwards to reveal the two young men at street level with their eyes fixed firmly on the ground. Jacques's face is markedly divided between shadow and light. As they talk and move, the camera tracks the figures to reveal a subsidiary set of movie posters on a back wall which Jacques is gazing at, as his friend outlines details of the planned crime. There is a cut to a full-shot revealing the main source of light – a lamppost. The direction and strength of this light produces a strongly defined shadow of the men on the illuminated section of the wall behind them. In the next shot these two figures are squeezed pictorially into the left-hand corner of the frame while two girls stop and chat about the images on the wall. They discuss the sex appeal of one of the female stars and comment on the luxurious fabric of her dress. This sequence of images does two things almost simultaneously. On the one hand, it draws attention in a self-reflexive manner to the inter-relationship between cinema, the city, and modernity. One could even suggest that in another characteristic of much Weimar filmmaking, it foregrounds the instability or "duplicity" (Elsaesser, 2000, 339) behind the cinematic representation of material reality. But on the other hand, it also reveals a particularly gendered dimension of Parisian cinematic representation where codes of glamour and criminality neatly fit in with notions of femininity or masculinity. Paradoxically, because both are founded on a certain level of identification which foregrounds the *artifice* of cinema, the presumed *ordinariness* of the character drama of DANS LES RUES may actually also thus be underscored. The idea of a humourous collusion between image and reality is again produced at the end of this section when after further plot developments, in conjunction with a surge of music, there is a return close-up of the poster-image of a masked male figure in a dinner suit and a couple embracing with emphasis on the subjectivity of the female. This masked criminal is probably the hugely successful character in Marcel Allain and Pierre Souvestre's *Fantômas* who in Dudley Andrew's evocative words inhabited a "dangerous topography of streets, alleys, department stores, warehouses, railroads, and townhouses ... [amid an] atmosphere of mystery and alienation hovering above modern city life" (1995, 27). The novel was, of course, filmed by Louis Feuillade between 1913 and 1915 and had recently been recaptured on film by fellow émigré Paul Féjos in 1932.

To illustrate the singularity of Trivas's film, we can turn to Jean Renoir's LA CHIENNE (1931) which also works on this same conjugation of reality and representation regarding the city at night. It explicitly differs from DANS LES RUES in that it establishes a more naturalistic vein less heavily coded by the processes of cinematic narration. As Janice Morgan (1996) has noted in her own discussion of LA CHIENNE's relationship to the Weimar aesthetics of the street film such as DIE STRASSE, Renoir also offers an "audacious ironic tone and sharp sense of social realism"(35) in place of an "intense preoccupation with the shifting, and potentially dangerous social terrain of the urban environment" (34). There is a sequence in LA CHIENNE which begins after Legrand (Michel Simon) has met Lulu (Janie Marèse) on a street in Montmartre. Lulu's pimp Dédé (Georges Flamant) has been dispatched to a hotel and Legrand has agreed to accompany Lulu to Barbès, where she lives.[14] As opposed to the close-up framing device of DANS LES RUES, the city is first visible from the vantage point of a long-shot. The couple emerges from off-screen left onto the pavement and begins walking in the darkness in the direction of the camera. The city was there first. The sense of an emphasis on an authentic social milieu is developed by the incorporation of off-screen street noises like the traffic and the naturalistic diction of the ensuing conversation which conveys "the solidity of a world that [resonates] with (...) distinctive accents and timbres" (Andrew, 104). As they walk forward, the camera tilts slightly rightwards and we see Legrand and Lulu move out of the darkness and into the light. They now occupy most of the frame and the two bodies are kept centred as the camera continues to track their movement. As they walk in and out of naturalistic pools of shadow and the illumination of the streetlamps they come across a number of passers-by which heightens the sense of the seizing of a typical moment. It is obvious, however, that at key moments in their dialogue, for example when they stop in front of a wall covered with theatrical posters, that Renoir is also using key and fill lighting. Legrand's face is fully lit when he stands in front of an illustration for a musical revue and announces that he is a painter. Similarly, Lulu is brightly lit when she jokes about how well Dédé imitates

Maurice Chevalier. The surface irony of both of these moments and the explicit appeal to conceptions of Parisian performance and lightness are the reverse of DANS LES RUES in which darkness takes over and the references to cinematic form and appearance are so insistent.

One of the continuing traits of French realist cinema's depiction of the world of the Parisian *quartier* of the early 1930s was an almost ethnographic concern for the listing, portraying and recording of the ordinary world of the city. Anatole Litvak and Victor Trivas appear to have for the most part shared this project. We know that one of Litvak's avowed intentions was indeed to make what he termed "real cinema". This concern was manifested not just in terms of the possibilities of the cinematic image, but also in terms of an interest in sound and its descriptive properties. Urban sounds form, for example, a key mode of expression in French films like FAUBOURG MONTMARTRE (Raymond Bernard, 1931) and LA PETITE LISE (Jean Gremillon, 1930). At the end of the former, the world of the city is specifically recalled as one of the main characters listens to the noise and clamour of Paris from the other end of a telephone line. Geneviève Sellier (1989, 89) has noted that LA PETITE LISE deserves attention because of the very fact that as "an attempt to break with the sheer plasticity of the film image [it uses] the counterpoint of sound chosen for its realism". This subject of recording the city has a complex genealogy. Rifkin (1995, 103) has persuasively related the taxonomic interest of such pivotal figures as Pierre Mac Orlan in urban aural and visual ephemera to the "overlapping language of guidebooks [and] urban tourism", and the nineteenth century tradition of "Parisian *Physiognomies* or *Typologies*".[15] He draws attention to the interest Mac Orlan had in radio and recorded Parisian music – he authored several radio documentaries during the period including a series on the accordion. Interestingly, DANS LES RUES and COEUR DE LILAS directly feature several close-ups of radios and gramophones in communal moments, either in the Legrand family home or in the "family" space of the café. Similarly, they both gain in effect from the use of natural recorded Parisian noise. In the opening of COEUR DE LILAS, Litvak choreographs an expressive and evocative inter-relationship between the sounds of local non-professional Parisians, the whistling of a passing train and the uneasy melancholia of a typical Parisian street organ-grinder.

The attempt to capture "real" Paris pictorially, as well as aurally, is evident in the early work of the French director Pierre Chenal.[16] Chenal worked on several documentary short films about Parisian architecture and city life such as LES PETITS MÉTIERS DE PARIS (1931-32) which had actually contained a commentary spoken and written by Mac Orlan. The film was praised by the critic A. Bourgoin for its ability to "know how to find the picturesque in places where one would imagine coming across nothing more than the most unimaginative banality".[17] Bourgoin's notion of the combination of the urban commonplace

5. Framing the urban decor in DANS LES RUES (BIFI)

and the picturesque is a key point; not least of all because it also reoccurred in several émigré features. It is there explicitly in DANS LES RUES, for example, when Jacques takes to the streets on the run from the law and we see a wistful analogy drawn between his social isolation and the ongoing lives of river workers hauling bricks onto the banks of the Seine. The predominance of images captured in documentary-like long-shot contrasts effectively with the tightly-knit claustrophobia of the previously foregrounded set design of the *quartier*. It is also there in the depiction of the detailed open spaces of the Parisian *zone* at the beginning of COEUR DE LILAS which features an iconography of factory-scapes, railway lines, wastelands and marginal lives. These picturesque but everyday visual motifs, along with the atmospheric banks of the urban canal networks, were found in a significant number of other 1930s' French films such as Marcel Carné's JENNY, LA GOUALEUSE (Fernand Rivers, 1938) and LA MATERNELLE (Marie Epstein and Jean Benoit-Lévy, 1934). They have come to be seen as a distinguishing component of the term "poetic realism".

Framing the Urban Decor – The Emigrés and Poetic Realism

The phrase "poetic realism" was actually coined by Jean Paulhan, the editor of *La Nouvelle Revue française*, in a 1929 review of Marcel Aymé's populist novel *La Rue sans nom*. The novel was adapted by Pierre Chenal in 1932 in a feature of the same name. The critical reception of an early, totally French poetic realist film such as LA RUE SANS NOM is of crucial interest regarding any discussion of the Paris of the German émigrés. It becomes evident that such films coincided with an attentiveness in French film culture towards the depiction of the French capital that, in fact, had as much to do with national cultural prestige as social concern. Therefore, it was important that being for or against the tendency to "go down the streets" meant more than just "uncovering the hidden spirit under the familiar façade" of the city. It also meant the possibility of taking of sides on the issue of the creation of a French sound cinema that could be as worthy of international esteem as that of the German cinema of the silent period.

For the writer Michel Gorel, for example, LA RUE SANS NOM merited a return to the terms "poetic" and "realist" largely because of the way it constructed a distinctively *French* vision of tenement life: "I've said 'realism' and I've also said 'poetic' because even in treating such a hard and brutal subject, Chenal never renounces poetry. The most beautiful scenes of the film are perhaps those where the characters, who have been gradually worn down by the stones of the hovels where they are imprisoned, try to escape, some by love, others by wine, adventure, revolt".[18] One simply cannot imagine a German critic making the same references to wine, romance, and revolution. Another reviewer noted that Chenal had made "a powerful and sober film which immediately catapults him to the premier league of German directors".[19] For many French critics of the period, this allusion to the sophisticated and crafted style of the German street films of the 1920s such as Pabst's DIE FREUDLOSSE GASSE, also meant an occasion to come down on one side of the debate over whether cinema should turn to the theatre or to the social world of "real Paris" for its point of reference. Jean Fayard in *Candide* saw LA RUE SANS NOM in terms of another chance "to condemn that execrable genre: the 'slice of life'"[20] whilst *Gringoire*'s critic argued that the film was far superior to not just the uncinematic form of filmed operetta but also German Expressionist cinema. Implying that Chenal's film transcended the Germanic for something distinctively Parisian, he claimed that "what's even better [in the film] is the impression left that [the modelling] has nothing to do with morbidity".[21] As we have already seen, this reference to "morbidity" must be taken simply as racially motivated shorthand for "Jewishness".

The debate over the turn to realist depictions of life in the French capital should be seen in the context of the competition which early French sound cinema also faced from the United States. If commentators of the period frequently referred to German city cinema's heavy and sombre concerns, the consensus was that Hollywood's version of urban life also had its own particularities. In an article commenting on the contemporary popularity of the city crime drama in French, German and Hollywood film releases, the journalist and script-writer Paul Bringuier noted how films such as CITY STREETS and SCARFACE (Howard Hawks, 1932) relied on a conjugation of violent narratives taken from the headlines and a visceral *mise-en-scène* which "sacrifices everything for gesture and movement".[22] This tendency to categorise different versions of cinematic urban realism had a wider significance beyond the French film industry's need to compete on an international level with its German and American counterparts. It also fed into the growing tide of cultural xenophobia involving differing notions of where the direction of France's modernity actually lay. In this sense, the dark city film became, in part, a staging ground for a wider set of cultural anxieties. Here, the entertainment and economic model of the United States was not just applauded for its energetic dynamism, invention and brightness, it was also denigrated for its vulgarity and excesses. Writers such as Paul Achard may have praised the efficiency, standardisation, and comfort of the American system in glowing texts such as *A New Slant On America*, but for Paul Morand, in *Champions du monde*, the United States was a society "weak in the head, infantile, lacking natural curbs or morality" (in Weber, 95). Again and again, these anxieties surfaced in moralistic discourses about the cinematic representation of urban life. American cities were seen as too violent and corrupt compared to place like Paris. Films like CITY STREETS showed the dark criminal excesses of modern urban life which had resulted from a society that favoured the individual over the warmer pleasures of community.

This emphasis on the fixities of national identity makes for an interesting, even almost contradictory situation when it comes to looking at the world of the Parisian *quartier* depicted by the Berlin émigrés. I would like to therefore now turn to COEUR DE LILAS as an example of the complexities involved when talking of the representation of Paris in émigré poetic realist cinema. The film derives its title from the name of Lilas (Marcelle Romée), a local girl whose glove is found near the corpse of Novian, a murdered industrialist, on the wasteland of the *fortifications* in the northeastern part of Paris.[23] Following what he believes to have been the wrongful arrest of one of Novian's employees, Detective Lucot (André Luguet) adopts the disguise of an unemployed mechanic to penetrate Lilas's milieu and comes into conflict with a former lover of Lilas –

the louche *apache* Martousse (Jean Gabin).[24] There is a police raid and now in love with the object of his search, Lucot makes off with Lilas to the centre of Paris. The couple ends up on the banks of the River Marne but the law catches up with Lilas and eventually she turns herself into the police.

Unlike many later successful poetic realist films such as LA BÊTE HUMAINE and QUAI DES BRUMES, COEUR DE LILAS was based on an original stage production. The film went into production in August 1931. Looking at the full credits for COEUR DE LILAS, apart from the name of Litvak, one sees the names of other Russians such as the set designer Serge Pimenoff and assistant director Dimitri Dragomir. Prominent French personnel were also involved such as the composer Maurice Yvain who was later the co-writer of the famous song "*Quand on s'promène au bord de l'eau* in Julien Duvivier's LA BELLE ÉQUIPE (1936). In the words of Alexandre Arnoux, COEUR DE LILAS "is at once a detective story, a sentimental comedy and a picturesque portrait of the underworld. (...) It is also a slice of life by Charles-Henry Hirsch, seasoned, perhaps with some underground irony by Tristan Bernard, as a Cornellian tragedy, a debate between passion and duty in the soul of a police agent".[25]

Despite the number of non-French personnel working on the production, COEUR DE LILAS, like LA RUE SANS NOM, was received in the French press as an example of national cultural specificity. The reason for this may be two-fold. Firstly, there was the aforementioned critical interest in building up a distinctly French sound film output to match the critical prestige of German urban cinema and Hollywood's own dark city features such as CITY STREETS and the frequently referred to UNDERWORLD (Joseph von Sternberg, 1927). Many of the film's critics saw COEUR DE LILAS as a specifically *Parisian* crime film because it was not as driven by violence and sensation. The film depended on a sense of urban communality at the expense of individualistic action. "The Americans have 'gangster films'; we have films of the *milieu*", wrote *Avenir*.[26] Georges Champeux in *Gringoire* also noted that the film "isn't about the gangsters of Broadway. Because it is set in Ménilmontant, it is in another style. First of all, there are fewer corpses (...) and then material concerns give way to higher things. Thugs, girls, police officers, the *milieu* and all that surrounds them have only one thing on their mind: love".[27] Secondly, it was perceived as French because of the way that nationally specific locations and acting styles were then being prioritised in French critical discourse. Writing in *Ciné Miroir*, in a later interview with André Luguet, Claude Doré, in referring to COEUR DE LILAS, noted that "it is impossible to find the atmosphere of a Parisian street, a *bal musette*, or a restaurant on the banks of the Marne anywhere else than in our home country and with French 'Parisian' actors. The success of films of this kind shows that it is possible to make films which, instead of being interna-

6. Fréhel (La Douleur, left) and Martousse (Jean Gabin, right):
crime and community in COEUR DE LILAS (BIFI)

tional, express the character of a particular country town or determining milieu".[28]

The central paradox of poetic realism was that, as the phrase indicates, it meant more than one thing at the same time. It suggested a broad naturalism and interest in ordinary urban lives whilst also simultaneously presenting a concentrated aestheticising of film form which lent itself to poetic effect and commentary. This notion of a tension regarding the representation of Paris – the predominant, but not exclusive, geographical locus of poetic realism – is evident in the way in which COEUR DE LILAS specifically deals with the picturing of the world of the *quartier*. On the one hand, there is the difference between the use of outside locations and inside studio decors that was typical of French film production of the period. In COEUR DE LILAS, for instance, the pressures on the individual within the social family of the *quartier* are cast in terms of criminality and the film portrays an escape from the physical and affective confines of this enclosed and constructed environment to the wider embrace of the heart of the city through the split between studio and location interpretations of Paris. On the other hand, there is another crucial distinction between inside and outside that emerges because COEUR DE LILAS was made partly by non-Parisians. The film may display a sophisticated awareness of the iconography and popular culture of a typical French urban milieu, but it does so by utilising the faculties of the outsider.

By looking at the preliminary section of the film, we can see that it does more than introduce a number of motifs which will reoccur throughout the course of the narrative. There is also evidence of the co-existence of a conventional urban realism and the same modernist visual aesthetic that we have noticed previously in émigré Paris films like Wilder's MAUVAISE GRAINE. The film begins in the *zone* – the ring of wasteland which surrounded Paris as a barrier of sorts between the walled defences of the *fortifications* and the industrialised inner suburbs spreading out from the official borders of the capital. The *fortifications* themselves were built between 1841 and 1845 under Prime Minister Adolphe Thiers in order to stave off a Prussian military invasion. In 1860, Thiers had extended the capital's boundaries to include the string of suburban villages such as Belleville, La Chapelle and Montmartre into the orbit of official Parisian culture. Because the *fortifications* had failed as a defence, it was decided to demolish them after the First World War, although the intact gates continued to serve a financial purpose until 1930 through the levying of city-related taxes. At the time of the making of COEUR DE LILAS, the geographical margins of the *zone* clearly represented a topographical notion of Parisian-ness in rapid transition. In fact, these areas were already included in a cultural mythology of Parisian marginality. Indeed, as Rifkin (1995) suggests, it was precisely "because these margins were already the myth materials of a literary treatment of city spaces and social differences, and were already signifiers of nostalgia, [that] the threat to their actual existence could only elevate their status in systems of representation" (28).

The first visual motif that is introduced is that of the world of male social authority which eventually presides over Lilas's fate. This is prefigured in the opening depiction of the military troops marching. Throughout the film, each part of the city is accompanied by a different register of music and in this instance the regimented rhythm of the refrain matches the image of coordinated control which the framing of the line of figures represents. The camera moves, in a clockwise pan, away from the soldiers disappearing across a bridge to a gang of boys who are following their elders' example. The youths are kept mainly in the middle distance of the image and we are able to see the expansive industrial wasteland all around them. Their role play comes to a halt when a younger member of the troupe approaches the "Major" to tell him that he doesn't want any more "war". The gang switches to "cops and robbers" and they make off to an open area where in the course of their game a *real* police investigation is instigated when a real corpse is discovered. This switching of roles and the playing around with disguises is another trope that will reoccur throughout the film. The change to "cops and robbers" is echoed by a new, more informal, musical register. The film at this point cuts to a medium close-up of a blind organ grinder whose haunting and repeated melody continues as we see the children spill over the rubble and forlorn open space of the *fortifications*.

As news of the crime spreads, another aspect emerges: that of the communality of the working class milieu in which the film is mainly set. People appear to enter the frame from all sides and in a rapid succession of shots, mainly composed of fleeting low-angled impressions of figures, the sense emerges of a social world being pulled together. (The opposite effect is produced later in the film when the police raid the street. Here, Litvak portrays this subsequent dispersal of figures into the crevices of the built environment through a montage of *high-angled* shots to underline the fragmentation of something previously whole and seemingly integrated). As the people gather near the site of the crime, we see the first of many shots which begin with a static image of a character or two from the crowd. This kind of shot then typically starts to track or pan across several other faces to produce a unifying sense of inclusion and shared values. In this case, the camera moves in a gentle circular motion away from two figures conversing to pick up snatches of commentary from other individuals. A sense of a specific social world is enhanced by the uniform dress codes and the way the characters, as they enter the frame, seem to continue the conversation of the witnesses that have preceded them. The sequence is also distinguished by the fact that it is the only time the community beyond the main characters speaks on screen. Partly because of the use of real city locations, which adds a dimension of *vérité*, and partly because of this sense of audible and visual eavesdropping on a pre-existing milieu, this moment has a peculiarly semi-documentary edge which is absent from the stylisation of the later studio sequences. In one of the film's production reports it is mentioned how locals from the Porte de Clichy area were recruited to appear in this scene.[29]

This sense of social documentation is furthered by the inclusion of details of the subsequent police operation. Foregrounding the work of the police photographer through a striking close-up of a camera lens opening – to the sound of an off-screen train whistle – achieves two things. Firstly, it draws attention to the recording or documenting of a verifiable reality as if to underline the authenticity of the film's visual narrative. But, secondly, as a moment of striking visual intensity, it seems to call particular attention to the pictorial and material nature of the cinematic image. After the close-up of the lens, the screen fades to black. We then see a shot of the corpse itself surrounded by the feet of the crowd. This image dissolves into a printed, still photographic version on the cover of the

Parisian newspaper, *L'Intransigeant*, with accompanying headlines. This sequence reminds one of the use of the self-conscious conjugation of the frozen image and the newspaper front page in the montage sequence of Siodmak's LA VIE PARISIENNE. Litvak then uses a close-up of another newspaper, *Le Petit Parisien*, to furnish further details of the inquiry. As the camera moves down the page one sees, for the first time, a full-frame shot of Lilas's face. She has already been fixed as an image to be looked at. A synchronicity is thus established between the look of the film itself and the journalistic look that is being constructed within the narrative. The resulting images remind one of the vivid layouts in *Détective*, the voyeuristic crime periodical of the time.[30]

Both COEUR DE LILAS and DANS LES RUES actually suggest a contradictory perception of the Parisian *quartier* in relation to the depiction of social space. The milieu of the *quartier* is a snapshot of the city, a typical fragment of a greater whole, but it must also be seen as something separate and distinctive with its own modes of representation. To some extent this gets played out, in cinematic terms, in the transition from a recorded location reality to the crafted visualisation of the Paris produced in the studios. Crisp (1993, 372) has argued that "given the supreme creative task of designing and building a world, [set designers working in France] found themselves restricted to building one that would be a credible replica of the real world. The décor must pass unnoticed, yet determine the mood and atmosphere of the film". Yet, in both of these émigré films there is evidence to suggest that the latter part of the equation gained the upper-hand. Whilst not presenting an overtly ultra-stylised version of Paris, the films do both, nonetheless, point to what André Bazin (quoted in Crisp, 374), in talking about LE JOUR SE LÈVE, called "a formal and poetic transposition" of urban life. Alexandre Trauner's actual dictum that "an interior setting must flow into the street setting which we see through a window" (in Crisp, 371) remains unrealised in COEUR DE LILAS. The film's Russian émigré set designer Serge Pimenoff had bemoaned the constraints of working in film over theatre by saying that "We might as well note that the scope available for a film decorator's imagination is fairly limited. In the studio it's always a question (…) of a *realistic* décor (…) of a naturalistic setting, a more or less faithful copy of reality. It's pretty well out of the question for a film decorator to have a spiritual conception of the décor, as is possible in the theater" (in Crisp, 369). Yet the transition from the wide spaces and broad daylight of the opening location footage of the *zone* to the portrayal of the street *is* abrupt and this heightens the sense of an enclosed world of criminality and pleasure.[31] This is a social world which rather than looking *out* from à la Trauner, one looks *into*, as if through a viewing glass darkened by the grime of the locale. Indeed, this immediate textual difference enhances the sense of separation and enclosure which the progression of the narrative elucidates. Unlike Lazarre Meerson's set in René Clair's QUARTORZE JUILLET, for example, it is noticeable that there is no identifiable exit to the design of the street. The world beyond the top of the stairs at one end or beyond the corner of the alleyway at the other is never glimpsed. This makes the milieu immediately darker. Whilst the wasteland and railway scenes evoke space through the use of a wide-angle lens and the inclusion of significant tracts of sky and clouds, there is a strong tight-knit aspect to the way the street is framed.

This concentration of effect is underscored by the reliance on artificial light sources and the frequent dramatic and pointed contrasts between darkness and light in Courant's distinctive photography. Indeed, this collusion between émigré cinematography and set design was commented upon in another production report which appeared in the film press. The designer and the camera operator "appear to be in the middle of developing a strange world which under the harsh light of the projectors is confounding the separation between fiction and reality" wrote a journalist from Le Courrier.[32] As in the relationship between Andréjew and the cinematographer Rudolph Maté in DANS LES RUES, the correlation here between the modulated light of Courant and the distinctive space of Pimenoff's street set is particularly noticeable in the treatment of the city at night.

The mise-en-scène, as a whole, exemplifies a non-naturalistic novelistic or theatrical approach to the depiction of social space. This is seen in the technically virtuosic introduction to the world of the street which, because of its integration of song and mobile camera, exemplifies a kind of consciously staged display. The sequence begins with a close-up of a hand turning the crank of some window shutters. The sound of the organ grinder can be heard again. It is almost as if the turn of the crank and the off-screen turn of the organ become one, creating an intense correlation between music and the physical space of the street. As the camera begins to track left, the window begins to fill the frame to suggest the opening up of the world to the spectator's gaze. The light from the interior of the bal musette illuminates the darkness outside. As the tracking shot continues, the figure turning the crank reverts to a shadow and the details of the milieu – the familiar tropes of net curtains and drink logos – are seen more clearly. Other figures enter the frame, including the organ grinder himself, before the camera begins to tilt upwards and the words of a song begin. The silhouette of a street lamp fills the right-hand part of the frame and in the rear of the image some of the street's occupants exit round the corner of a hidden alley. The strength of the artificial light source emerging from this out of view path also reduces these figures to silhouettes. The camera comes down to street level again and begins to rotate leftwards until a stone public stairway fills the frame. A man is seen lighting a cigarette for a girl and as the camera begins to ascend the stairs in conjunction with a passing couple, a pair of women come into view perched on the railings. The female voice is singing about her life as a prostitute and the lives of the people that we are watching. The lyrics of the song, *Dans la rue* (Serge Veber, Maurice Yvain), refer to the ending of the day and her work on the street at night.[33] The silence of the locals, the hovering sense of gloom and the watchful circumscription of the mobile camera produce a distinctive tone of voyeurism, of examining something ordinarily hidden. Finally, the shot dissolves into a medium close-up of a large middle-aged woman, La Douleur (Fréhel), singing and washing her tights on a balcony. At this point in the song she refers to the appeal that her silk stockings have for male customers. La Douleur's gaze is turned downwards to the world that has just been explored. It is as if she is both singing to herself and singing to the street. The camera now turns to track leftwards and through the dramatic perspective of the upper ironwork of the gateway, which borders the street and the apartment block from where she is singing, the street which we have come from reappears. The camera tilts down slightly so we can see people descending the steps. From this aerial vantage point the camera moves leftwards, further across in space and beyond the gate, to gaze down at the entire street as if from a bird's eye view. The coordinates of the whole set have now been made sense of in a complex inclusive fashion which has linked the movement of the residents and the probing camera to the spatial arrangement of the buildings. There is one last cutaway shot to the world beyond – a night-sky view of a factory – before we return to the milieu where the action will now unfold.

André Andréjew's set design for DANS LES RUES also privileges certain viewing relations regarding the world of the street. For example, the film features a number of high-angle shots looking down from the rooftops at the integrated milieu below. What is even more significant, however, is the way that the relationships between domestic space and external street space are managed through the prominent incorporation of the staircase which acts both as a dramatic device and an iconographical element. In his perceptive review of the film, Souillac argues that the staircases in DANS LES RUES are "unforgettable"; for him the staircase is the soul of the humble milieu the film represents.[34] Souillac is undoubtedly thinking of the way the film acknowledges the centrality of this communal area in the everyday experience of the Parisian tenement dweller but Trivas's film appropriates Andréjew's designs in more ways than one. Firstly, the staircase is used to link the individual to the community. This is evident in the opening sequence which takes place in the living room of Jacques's family. As with COEUR DE LILAS, the film begins with military marching music, this time on the radio. The music's connotations of patriarchal order and stability underscore a sense of absence that is represented by the image on the wall of Jacques's dead father in a military uniform. Just as

Coeur de lilas moves from the soldiers to the freedom of the street children playing, Dans les rues moves from this settled domesticity to the allure of the street below. There is a cut to a shot from the window of a boy calling from the pavement. When Jacques leaves his home the camera does not move directly to the street. Instead, he is first seen on the landing outside and only afterwards does the camera follow him all the way down. As he descends, a whole world of local residents opens up before us from a cleaner, children at play, figures at a window sill to the sounds of people in their homes. Jacques is portrayed as part of all this. A high-angle shot of him sliding down the banister dissolves into a high-angle shot of the cobblestones to emphasise his descent from the integrated world of the tenement block onto the world of the street.

The staircase, on the other hand, is also used to connote tension and menace in the Germanic sense of a psychological rendering of ordinary space. One scene, in particular, recalls the many Weimar films including Pabst's Die Büchse der Pandora, which used the motif of the staircase to suggest a disruptive intensity and feeling of foreboding.[35] It is night and Rosalie, Jacques's girlfriend, has rushed back from the *bal musette* to warn her father, *père* Schlamp, that she believes Jacques is getting himself into trouble. There is a high-angle shot of *père* Schlamp walking up the shadowy stairway to the apartment where Jacques's brother and mother live. Instead of a communal space of clearly delineated spatial codes of intimacy, there is now a heightened sense of disequilibrium caused by the decision to position the camera at a distorted angle to the regular contours of the staircase and the low level of lighting. Père Schlamp is drunk and this adds to the disorientation. When Jacques's family opens the door, his mother gasps his name and there is a sudden cut to an intensely lit close-up of the troubled criminal on the street.

Spaces of Crime and Pleasure in the City of Darkness

The representation of dark Paris in several émigré films reveals the same degree of textual and narrative instability that can be found in various other émigrés' depictions of the City of Light. Films like Coeur de lilas and Dans les rues worked within popular realist traditions of representing the city by relaying an attentive sense of the marginal world of the working class Parisian *quartier*. They thus participated in a depiction of the urban commonplace that had its historical antecedents in French city representations of the nineteenth century. But they did more than that; these dark Paris films by the German émigrés also showed an interest in the visual codes of expressive shadow by foregrounding the ways in which film form can manifest feelings of danger, entrapment, or unease. At certain moments these shadows fractured a visual continuum of depicting "life as it is" by drawing attention to the processes of film technique or narration. In so doing, they helped to unsettle the debate in French film culture about how to counteract the prestigious and economically powerful examples of the German and Hollywood film industries by depicting the city of Paris in a distinctively French way. Somewhat ironically, it was by largely working within pre-existing traditions of Parisian cultural representation that the émigrés were able to participate in the development of the poetic realist cinema that was to hold so much sway in critical (and export) terms in the latter part of the decade. DANS LES RUES and COEUR DE LILAS were "poetic", as well as simply "realist" exactly because of the central contribution of non-French personnel who delivered a distinctive congruence between aesthetic effect and social commentary. Crucial to these depictions of social life in the "city of darkness" were the intersecting worlds of crime and entertainment. Unlike the case of the dark and dangerous streets of cinematic Berlin, which connoted a *contemporary* unease with the modern city, Parisian cinematic crime often became fused with a safer and less confrontational perspective which looked back at *past* imaginings of the city. One of the ways this perspective worked was by frequently inter-relating the depiction of criminality in French city films of the 1930s with aspects of popular community pleasure. If we therefore look once more at key "dark" émigré texts such as COEUR DE LILAS and DANS LES RUES in relation to these notions, we can see again how the émigrés produced something distinctive by, at the same, fitting in.

To uncover the genealogy of the conflation of crime and entertainment in cinematic representations of the French capital in the 1930s, we need to return to nineteenth century discourses of the city which depicted the Parisian *quartier* as marginal. As Donald Reid argues, in his introduction to Jacques Rancière's *The Nights of Labour* (1989, xxiii), nineteenth century knowledge of the Parisian working class was always mediated "in conversation and confrontation with an apparent bourgeois 'other'. The identifications and representations that resulted, in turn, became the sites of ceaseless rounds of exclusion, inclusion, and differentiation that periodically produced confident assertions about *the* proletariat, *the* people". The world of "*the* people" thus became the subject of a series of mediated cultural representations which ranged from Aristide Bruant's cabaret songs to the poeticised urban tourism of Francis Carco. Carco's own interest in the *quartier* was based on the specific allure of "the dark streets, the small tobacconists, the cold, the fine rain on the roofs, the bars, the chance meetings, and in the bedrooms, an air of abandoned distress which shook [him] to [his] core" (in Chevalier, 1980, 187). His words suggest as did Brassaï's photographs, that "the otherness of the city" relied on a litera

and imaginative transposition of values. The city literally turned from daylight to darkness and this meant that, figuratively speaking, "the social codes
of nocturnal life [could] contrast with those of ordinary bourgeois society"
(Warehime 1996,103). The appeal of the correspondence between crime and
entertainment in popular film's depiction of the *quartier* can therefore, on the
one hand, be explained by the socially privileged view of the allure of the city
at night for the bourgeois spectator. On the other hand, however, it is important to recognise the role that popular entertainment itself played in mediating
the dangers and pleasures of the world of the *quartier* to the film audience. As
Vincendeau has pointed out in her discussion of the tradition of the *chanson
réaliste* – directly incorporated into both COEUR DE LILAS and DANS LES RUES –
singers such as Fréhel did more than just sing about the world of prostitution
and petty thieves. They also came from that world in real life, and because of
this and the visible record of that life on the appearance of their bodies, they
sang with the "testimony of authenticity" (1987, 124).[36] French film of the
1930s, by incorporating self-referential forms of Parisian entertainment into its
narratives, therefore described a new collusion between on-screen urban visual space and urban representational mythologies previously contained in literature, song, and music. In one sense, this was a progressive accumulation of
motifs of meaning but it was also, in a very real sense, a pleasurable recaptur-
ing of a version of the city already long gone. What is more, the representational mythologies often contained in Parisian song and music, were themselves, as Vincendeau (112) also points out, describing a French capital on the
point of transition.

   The space of the café was central to the construction of the popular community of the *quartier*. In a key sequence in DANS LES RUES, it is used in conjunction
with the mediating element of Parisian song to delineate both the growing affection between the two romantic leads of the narrative and a sense of communal interaction. Andréjew's set design is meticulous – right down to the details
of the posters and furniture – but yet again the *mise-en-scène* also self-
consciously foregrounds the process of visual narration to suggest a secondary
level of mediation: that of the émigré with the established tropes of Parisian
representation. The sequence begins with a tightly framed shot of Rosalie. Her
face is boldly lit. As the camera slowly pulls away, the viewer realises that this
image is actually only a reflection. The "real" Rosalie seems to emerge from the
mirror as she is pictured at a bar table between Jacques to her left and a sleeping boy to her right. Jacques is carefully lit by Rudolph Maté so that the
left-hand side of his face is in shadow. The edges of his side of the image blur
into an atmospheric darkness; just the contours of his hand and the glass that it
holds are illuminated. The camera begins to track in again on the face of
Rosalie at which point a pianola starts up and, off-screen, a bar lady begins to

sing a *chanson réaliste* about two lovers and the cinema. This self-referentiality recalls the sequence previously described involving the layered conjugation of the street, the male and female locals of the *quartier* and a cinema poster advertising a Paris crime film. The shot gradually ends with a second close-up of the girl. There is then a cut to a new perspective on the play between reflection and reality. The "real" Rosalie is now framed at an angle on the left-hand edge of the shot, whilst to her right, we see her reflection in the mirror and the edges of the figure of Jacques. The rest of the café is slowly assembled into this interaction between visual space and song as the camera starts to track rightwards, as if through the mirror, to include other figures in its circular motion. We pass an elderly bearded man at a table and another seated figure at the bar before ultimately stopping in front of the singer who is behind the counter knitting and singing. The sombreness in her voice is matched by the heaviness of Maté's dark, low-key lighting. Eventually, the camera begins to track back to Rosalie and Jacques. There is an obvious correlation between them while the music is underscored by the way the camera now bypasses the other figures and moves in a direct sideways, rather than circular, fashion back to the seated couple. The song finally fades as the couple dissolves into the darkness of the shadows in an embrace.

The introduction to the space of the hotel in COEUR DE LILAS similarly sets up a certain visual detachment before integrating the decor of the social setting with the action of its inhabitants. After the introductory song by Fréhel, the camera comes to a halt at the exterior of the local hotel. Inside, a petit-bourgeois businessman is audibly remonstrating with the owners about his bill off-screen. His provincial accent marks his difference as an outsider. The camera is initially interested in setting the scene from a slightly detached vantage point. The drama in the ground floor café is viewed from the landing above in a wide-angle shot through the banisters of a staircase. This emphasises the dimensions of the social milieu at the expense of depicting any one individual protagonist. The camera descends to ground level following the steps of one of the female prostitutes who evidently works in the hotel. The man, dressed in a formal suit and straw boater, is obviously out of place in this locale. The point of the episode is to set up the social authority of Martousse, the local gang leader, who physically ejects him onto the street. Martousse is differentiated from the psychologically disturbed criminal loners seen in Berlin films such as M. He is introduced in a particular way which enables him to be seen as both an emblematic member of the class-based community and a distinctively charismatic and separate figure. This trait which must serve as *the* defining characteristic of the French, rather than German, cinematic criminal, is later carried over in the representation of entertainment at the local *bal musette*. We see in a

7. A face divided by darkness and light: Rosalie (Madeleine Ozeray, centre) in the café in DANS LES RUES (BIFI)

leftwards tracking shot a procession of local faces, both seated and standing, on a level picture plane at an angle to the off-screen argument. The shot comes to a halt with the image of a louche *apache* slouched in a corner. Martousse is differentiated on two counts. Firstly, in spatial terms, he is separated from the line of figures by the fact that he is seated *behind* the table which occupies the same plane as the group. He is also neatly framed by the corners of the seating. Secondly, his costume connotes glamourous difference. Throughout the film there is steady attention paid to the hat that Martousse wears. He tilts it down to affect a dandyish insouciance when a policeman stops him from running to the cellar during the raid and he later tilts it *up* to allow a particularly menacing lighting effect to fall over his facial features. This sartorial attention, which extends to the distinctive white scarf – used again in key lit sequences for dramatic purpose – works in relation to the prim propriety of the misplaced boater.[37]

Kurt Courant's distinctive, finely graded lighting maximises the potential of the inter-relationship between Martousse and his milieu. This can be seen in two key instances, each of which signify a different aspect of Gabin's powerful dramatic persona. Firstly, there is the scene when Lilas has come down to the café. She wants to be alone but Martousse comes over to her table. There is a disturbing low-angled two-shot with a fully lit Lilas to the left of the frame looking intently toward Martousse who is gripping her hand. His body is turned at such an angle that his face is caught in almost total shadow except for the marked outline of the edges of his facial features. Lucot tells Martousse to let the girl go, which he does eventually. Martousse begins to walk away from Lilas and as he moves forward, the camera tracks back so that the figure of Gabin is kept in the centre of the frame. The figure of Lilas begins to dissolve into a background blur but Martousse is kept in the foreground of the image and he passes through a dense pool of shadow which momentarily washes over his face. It is as if the room has become the personification of his state of mind. By the time he emerges from this pool, Lucot has entered the frame and the two square up to face each other. Martousse now occupies the left side of the image and his menacing and tensed face is fully and boldly lit by a new light source. In the second moment, belonging to the end of the *quartier* sequence when he is on the run from the police, the figure of Martousse becomes a roguish denizen of the underworld whose guile is quite charming. He is chased by the police across the rooftops above the street. This time he strives to remain in the shadows but his body is constantly caught between the boundaries of light and darkness. When he is caught he returns to ground level and the bright full lighting of the *bal de musette* where the music of his previously performed number is still playing. A policeman has his arm on Martousse's shoulder as they walk through the room. With one swift glance, Martousse comically effects the removal of the hand and in so doing, he doffs his hat one last time to return his face to a zone of darkness more befitting of a local *apache*.

From the moment that Lucot penetrates the world of the street, COEUR DE LILAS begins to elaborate on the pattern of disguise and transgression set up by the police officer's appropriation of the social codes of the milieu. The figure of Lucot is employed to further the narrative of detection but also, because of his disguise and the mobility this allows, he can be perceived as colluding with the degree of social voyeurism that the *mise-en-scène* itself appears to perpetuate. Thus, although Lucot does break the law, his real transgression is not just a matter of professional misconduct. It is a departure from a stable class identity which is perilously complicated when the object of his pursuit also becomes a figure of desire. This tension may appear to conform to the pattern of the conventional Weimar street film such as ASPHALT, but it is also rendered equivocal by two factors: the unsettling appeal of the character of Martousse and the ambivalent status of Lilas in the film. Martousse is so troubling to the convolutions of the detective narrative because he simply represents an allure that Lucot, as a bourgeois in disguise, cannot muster. The Paris that Lucot, and via him, the spectator has penetrated is not only represented as a dangerous world of illicit criminality; it is also something that is portrayed as subversively attractive. This instability is foregrounded by the frequent play of light and darkness on both the surfaces of the *quartier* – the pavement, the alleyway, or rooftop – and the actual body of its principal agent. It is furthered by the differences signified by the modes of performance of the two male stars. Gabin's success as Martousse stems from the degree of Parisian proletarian authenticity he is able to deliver. Marcel Carné had noted, in relation to Gabin's performance style of this period, that he showed "a marked taste for a people on the margins and a use of slang dialect embellished with picturesque images. Like all Parisian kids he [liked] to give himself an air of freedom, of permanent revolt".[38] The suggestion here is that Gabin (unlike Luguet playing Lucot playing an unemployed mechanic) *was* the person he was playing. As Vincendeau has convincingly argued "the proletarian register in which Gabin [operated], defined by his voice, his gestures, his clothes, and the decors in which he [moved], [designated] him as more authentic than a bourgeois character, since French proletarian culture distinguishes itself from bourgeois culture (...) by its desire to get at the substance of things rather than concentrate on appearances" (1993, 28).

Central also to the criminal conception of the Parisian *quartier* was the figure of the female prostitute. Although absent in DANS LES RUES, she lies, as the title of the film suggests, at the heart of COEUR DE LILAS. Crucially, the prostitute is represented twice: through Lilas and then through her older counterpart, La Douleur. Whilst Marcelle Romée is almost silent throughout the film, Fréhel is distinguished by her earthy physicality and voice. The two embody separate performance traditions and, in turn, separate relationships to the film's conceptions of Parisian space. As already noted, Lilas occupies an ambiguous place regarding the central concerns of the narrative. On the one hand, as the chief murder suspect, she is the focus of the investigation of the male protagonist. This is exemplified by the way she is fixed by the gaze of Lucot in her introduction. But on the other hand, she relays a sense of indeterminate fragility which comes across not only in her positioning within the frame of the image but also in how these images relate to the surrounding world of masculine subordination. Lilas thus comes to represent a particular aspect of the social entrapment that the film constantly alludes to. Just as the setting of Lilas is pictured as separate from the heart of Paris, so the person of Lilas is pictured as separate from the conviviality and communality of the *quartier*. She is frequently shown upstairs, spatially separated from the rest of the community. When she is downstairs, she is normally shown in one-shots. Her eyes are usually fixed off-screen at some unspecified object of attention and the stillness of her body language not only contrasts with the fluidity of many of the central male characters but it also suggests an internalised sense of containment and isolation. What is more, there are brief moments when an aspect of her subjectivity is allowed to highlight the difficulty of the space that she occupies socially. When the group get ready to playfully re-enact the police investigation in the café, the camera looks up to the banister and landing. This shot is from no one's point of view, it simply shows Lilas emerging from the gloom upstairs. We then cut to a shot from Lilas's point of view. The group below is shown through the banister. The film intercuts between this image and a disturbing medium close-up of a nervous looking Lilas. A medium close-up pan shows the main figures laughing downstairs to further emphasise Lilas's separation. Martousse stops laughing, aware of being looked at, and his eyes turn left. We cut to Lilas's reaction and then back to the group staring upwards. Finally, Litvak cuts to the full-length point of view shot of Lilas standing at the top of the stairs. The fact that this return of the gaze has been so delayed only reinforces its intensity.

This tenuous inter-relation between a momentary feminine subjectivity and the objectification of the powerful male look is absent in the depiction of the older prostitute, La Douleur. As the emblematic title of the opening song *Dans la rue* suggests, her identity is based on an almost physical embodiment of a certain kind of Parisian-ness which relies on the now recognisable alliance between nighttime crime and entertainment. The fact that she is older and bulkier gives her a subtle kind of physical liberty in relation to the space of the *quartier*. She is pictured sitting and joking with the other *apaches* and her body is linked to a bawdiness and vulgarity which can only come with the accumulation of life's experiences. In the words of André Maugé: " she manages to seduce you with her good-natured brusqueness and the populist verve that doesn't flinch from the overtly obscene gesture; the direct brilliance of her make-up laden eyes and the magnificent strength of her low-pitched voice which rumbles and rolls like a storm holds you in her sway".[39] What is more, Fréhel's experience denotes a secondary layer of pastness to further underscore the current of nostalgic imagining. Fréhel's relationship to the mythical milieu of the Parisian *quartier* was not only given a loaded degree of authenticity because of her own origins, but through the chronology of her career she would have provided an built-in reflexive sense of the past for the French audience of the 1930s. As Vincendeau points out, Fréhel had two careers. Following an initial spell of stardom in the Parisian music hall and a tumultuous series of personal tragedies, including a broken romance with Maurice Chevalier, she left France. Upon her return "prematurely aged, fat and sick", she began the second phase of her popularity. "Thus her life, like most of her songs [which] displayed dialectics of joy and misery, beauty and destitution (...) had a similar built-in structure of nostalgia" (1987, 117). This structure is signaled in COEUR DE LILAS by the way Fréhel is constantly pictured close to a gramophone in the hotel, even to the point of putting a new record on.

As Chevalier (1980, 196) argues in his study of crime and entertainment in Montmartre, the way different Parisian neighbourhoods were distinguished in terms of criminality was through the formation of gangs. Geographical space was gendered in masculine terms through a particular form of male-centred local patriotism which grew out of distinguishing characteristics such as dialect slang, dress, song, and even hairstyle. The way that this can be seen in DANS LES RUES and COEUR DE LILAS suggests, again, the degree to which the émigrés were able to draw upon standards of Parisian representation. In both films, the *bal musette* becomes a staging ground for both male display and male control and exchange of the female lead. The *bal musettes* were typical spaces to congregate for popular Paris with their emphasis on communal singing, drinking and dancing. In the cinema of this period, their main representational function was to "draw the neighbourhood *visibly* together" (Vincendeau 1992, 57). Chevalier (409) suggests that in the city itself, they were the main meeting point for the exchange of information among those in the local underworld: "it was the place you had to go to be seen". DANS LES RUES portrays the *bal* in a sequence of tableau-like images with the emphasis on the communality of the space. The location is introduced with an establishing aerial view of the decorations and the interweaving figures on the dancefloor before moving on to a series of static shots in which the rotating dancers move in and out of the frame. The human warmth of the setting is underscored by the introduction of bright, electric lighting on the set which is in marked contrast to Maté's chiaroscuro palette for the surrounding streets. The spontaneity of the moment is captured by the contrast between the live band and the previously depicted café pianola. In terms of the narrative, the *bal* is the place where Jacques "trades" Rosalie for another girl. This other woman will unwittingly lead Jacques and his partner in crime to the mansion where the robbery will take place.

In COEUR DE LILAS the depiction of the *bal* is constructed around a series of visual opposites. Firstly, there is the distinctive "soulful inwardness" or "perverse eroticisation" (Elsaesser 2000, 44) of Courant's émigré cinematography which consists here of the vivid descriptive alternation between darkness and light. Then, secondly, there is also the difference between the rotating long-shots which manipulate the degrees of space perceived and the brief static shots which punctuate this motion to dramatic effect. The main song number, *La môme caoutchouc*, commences in unsettling fashion with a full shot of the reflection of the gathering on the angular mirror wall. We see the refracted couples begin to rotate, before the camera itself begins to circle around the room, picking up the balcony band and the circular motifs of the spot lighting, the whirling wall fan, and the rounded caps of the dancing male partners.

The camera alights on the immobile, seated Lilas and Lucot and eavesdrops on their conversation until, on the cue of the girl's distracted gaze rightwards, it finishes its rotation across almost the entire space of the room to focus on the spectacularly portrayal of Martousse. Thanks to Courant's sophisticated cinematography, his body is literally split into zones of darkness and light with his face being the clear battleground between these two elements. In a fit of temper, he flings a glass to the floor and we see Martousse emerge from behind the edges of the bar wall as if he's treading onto his own territorial stage. Two shadowy criminal types glance at him admiringly in the background. Martousse thus combines a mastery of the room's dimensions and a mastery of the community's gaze. He briefly comes to a halt, standing next to his burly male companion before breaking through the shadows to stroll across the room. His body is simultaneously integrated and separated from the procession of dancing figures. He belongs spatially to the flow since he occupies an intermediary plane between two lines of dancers who move behind and in front of him but, significantly, he is moving against the crowd in the opposite direction. He briefly comes to a halt again to totally occupy the centre of the frame. His face is now fully lit by a new and brighter source of light. Martousse's relationship to the frame alters and he is highlighted in near close-up. After La Douleur's singing retort to his performance, Martousse returns to the couple to confront them. He tells Lucot to leave. The detective stands up and there is a cut to a dramatically lit medium close-up of Martousse. Martousse is motionless whilst a posse of men moves in behind him to crowd the frame. In the return shot, Lucot, as in the café, is isolated within an empty space. The pair of shots is repeated but this time when Lucot glances off-screen we cut to an extraordinary close-up pan of a sea of menacingly lit local faces, all denizens of the world to which Lucot is now insistently made to feel that he's an interloper. It is as if he has been defeated twice: firstly by the charisma of performance and then by the congregation of now darkened faces from the underworld that the performance has unleashed.

COEUR DE LILAS and DANS LES RUES both clearly demonstrate the powerful allure of a particularly Parisian mode of integrating crime and entertainment with the depiction of the values of the popular street community. As Rifkin has argued though in his observations on the multi-layered depiction of the French capital in *Détective*, Parisian crime was also "a relationship of social classes, strata, and sexes" (1993, 123). To this extent, one also needs to consider the other key site of the period where urban danger and pleasure intersected: the "murky ambience" of the Parisian nightclub. By looking at Kurt Bernhardt's émigré film CARREFOUR – interestingly enough originally entitled L'HOMME DE LA NUIT – it is possible to see how the topography of the criminal *quartier* coincided with the more luxurious glamour of the Montmartre nighttime venue.

8. Michèle (Suzy Prim, left) and Lucien (Jules Berry, right) in CARREFOUR (BFI)

The film, in fact, recalls Rifkin's description of the representational mode of *Détective*. Like the pages of this sensational journal, it suggests "the interrelatedness of different kinds of history and political and social presents [in which] narratives of crime or vice are (...) part of the coming to know and handle the urban (124)". During the course of the narrative of CARREFOUR, de Vetheuil (Charles Vanel), a prominent bourgeois industrialist from an exclusive *arrondissement* on the west side of Paris, discovers that his identity might not be what it seems. A war wound from the First World War has induced amnesia to the extent that he is uncertain whether a Parisian newspaper's claim that he is Jean Pettier, a one-time city criminal, is the truth or not.[40] At de Vetheuil's trial, a mysterious stranger, Lucien (Jules Berry), provides evidence to clear his name but shortly thereafter Lucien attempts to blackmail de Vetheuil by claiming that he had lied on his behalf. Gradually, it is revealed that the blackmailer *is* telling the truth and de Vetheuil rediscovers his past by meeting Michèle (Suzy Prim), a nightclub hostess, who is not only Lucien's current mistress and accomplice but is Pettier's former lover. De Vetheuil comes to a psychological and emotional crossroads, but is saved from deciding which identity to choose by Michèle's actions. Michèle shoots Lucien in an argument backstage at her Montmartre club. She then commits suicide to save de Vetheuil from recriminations.

CARREFOUR was lauded in the French entertainment press as a model of national prestige. Suzy Prim, for example, was often referred to in the press as "the French Marlène [Dietrich]"[41] and *Le Matin* heralded it as "a French Film Made in France".[42] But like COEUR DE LILAS and DANS LES RUES, the film was very much an émigré production; a product, in fact, of the distinctive crossroads of French and German personnel. Bernhardt had just returned to Paris after making a multi-language version with Maurice Chevalier in England (THE BELOVED VAGABOND/LE VAGABOND BIEN AIMÉ (1936), and the script was written by the émigré journalist Hans Kafka. It was edited by Adolf Lantz and produced by Eugene Tuscherer, Bernhardt's brother-in-law. (Tuscherer was one of the six German émigré producers who was able to set up an independent production company in Paris. The others were Seymour Nebenzahl, Max Glass, Hermann Milkowski, Arnold Pressburger, and Gregor Rabinowitsch (Horak 1996, 376-377)). In interviews just after his arrival in France in 1933, Bernhardt had expressed his hopes for the development of Franco-German filmmaking collaborations, arguing that the arrival of foreign film personnel in Paris was actually a moment of opportunity. "We should intensify the points of contact between the French and German film worlds", he commented. "Together, they could reveal a considerable amount of useful information".[43] CARREFOUR can be seen, to some extent, as the outcome of his wishes.

The introductory scene to Michèle's venue indicates how the nightclub was a place of cosmopolitan allure in Parisian cinematic representations of the 1930s. Here the wealthy, generally male, bourgeois visitor was entertained in a lavish, often feminised space of performance and illicit temptation. Temptation was identified with prostitution as the names of the establishments run by Françoise Rosay in JENNY – *Chez Jenny* – or Michèle Morgan in L'ENTRAÎNEUSE – *La Dame de Coeur* – suggest. The venues were often signaled as feminised in two ways. Firstly, they were usually contrasted with a formal, heavily masculinised commercial or residential space. In L'ENTRAÎNEUSE, for example, the narrative begins with an all-male business dinner. We move from a dreary, elderly speaker to a shot of the butler opening a window. In a style similar to that of LA VIE PARISIENNE, when we glide through the customs' window to the splendour of spectacular Paris, the camera lunges into the new space of the street and the lights of the club beyond. In the case of CARREFOUR, the first view of the *Michèle* nightclub is preceded by a tightly framed two-shot of the interior of a taxi carrying the stiff, dinner-suited figures of de Vetheuil and his assistant through the city. The second cue, before the camera as per custom moves inside, is the postcard image of Paris at night with illuminated neon lettering of the nightclub shining in the city's darkness. In CARREFOUR, there is a beautifully composed image of the club's exterior. One part of the frame is taken up by an external view of the building with a line of descending letters spelling out the name "Michèle". The other part of the frame is a shot of a view over the rooftops of the city at night to the distant Sacré-Coeur on top of Montmartre. As the pianola music in the club plays, the letters appear, one by one, until the name "Michèle" is integrated with its surroundings. There is a neat touch at the end of Bernhardt's film when, after Michèle's death, this process is reversed and the letters are systematically extinguished.

When we move inside the nightclub, the motif of crossing – already signaled spatially in the narrative by the various journeys across the city – is reinforced in a material sense by the construction of the *mise-en-scène*. Elsaesser's suggestive notion of German émigré cinema's "preoccupation with disjuncture, space and light" (1984, 282) is evident here in the way Bernhardt depicts the coherence of the identity of the protagonists becoming distorted as their bodies fragment with the criss-cross patterning of shadows across their skin and clothing. This is unlike the general whiteness and depth of the space of the club in Marcel Carné's JENNY, for example, where the characters are also momentarily fixed or hemmed in by the collusion of the decor and the camera placement. Michèle thus leads de Vetheuil and his companion from *behind* the lattices of the doorway into the space of the club. Nonetheless, the emphasis on luxury and glamour in CARREFOUR remains consistent with other established tropes of Parisian representation. A visit to Michèle's clearly entails a certain class privilege. Each surface of the interior of the club connotes excess and glistening luxury. When the male couple enter we see Michèle telling an assistant who has remarked on the *eighth* bottle of champagne a customer has ordered: "Well he knows the superior way to live!".

Montmartre itself can be read as a crossroads. By the 1930s this northern part of the city had become a meeting point for various Parisian social types. Whilst the nightclubs, cabarets and entertainment venues of the area played host to performances of Parisian-ness for visiting upper-class and bourgeois audiences, the streets were populated with the hoodlums and prostitutes beloved by the likes of Pierre Mac Orlan and Francis Carco. Montmartre also signalled a meeting point between French and international entertainment cultures in that here the non-French were offered some degree of cultural assimilation not provided elsewhere. In her opening number at the nightclub, for example, a black jazz singer sings a romantic number in a hybrid mixture of English and French. The alterity of the language and musical form that she offers can be read in more ways than one. Firstly, it works to simultaneously produce a sense of both exoticism and Frenchness.[44] The crossing of French with English by the *chanteuse* may finally define her in relation to the local onlookers, but this performance of two cultures *in Paris* is actually curiously much like the performance of Parisian-ness undertaken by the German émigrés. Both could be said to have staged an aural or visual negotiation between two specific points of reference. This ambiguity takes us back to the cultural representations of the city in Siodmak's LA VIE PARISIENNE where Paris was defined as both uniquely French, and as belonging to the world. The second way in which the alterity of the music works in the film lies clearly in the context of the direction of international cinematic culture. The perhaps crude association between jazz and the nighttime's dangerous desire in Bernhardt's French thriller still nicely anticipates the American noir city that he was to portray upon his arrival in the United States and Hollywood.

Having said this, however, the representation of the nightclub in CARREFOUR does works suggestively within parameters set by other French films of the period, and this is particularly noticeable in the inter-relationship between space and performance. When we see Michèle lead the two men to their seats it is done through a complexly staged tracking shot which simultaneously depicts the details of the social milieu and presents the partnership between de Vetheuil and his former mistress. At the moment that Charles Vanel says he wants to see Suzy Prim alone, their figures almost fill the frame, momentarily erasing the space of the heightened *mise-en-scène*. It is almost as if they are speaking exclusively for the benefit of the spectator – which is, of course, what they *are* doing in their simultaneous roles as renowned stars of Parisian film and theatre. This partnering of two character types is typical of the film. It is as evident in the repartee between Prim and Jules Berry – who were married to each other at the time – as it is in the contrast between the fixity and sobriety of Vanel and the fluid, constantly mobile, gestural performance of Berry. Without any editing, the couple move back into the middle distance of this visually intoxicating spectacle and the men sit down. Elsaesser's argument that "the difference between an actor's cinema such as prevailed in France and the German cinema of *mise-en-scène* and space may well have been the biggest obstacle to critical success for the émigrés films" (1984, 283), does not really appear to be true in the case of CARREFOUR. Throughout the film, the collusion between the known actorly styles of the lead performers and an aspect of the *mise-en-scène*, be it stronger lighting, the decor or the space, works to produce distinctive meanings. As was the case of Gabin in COEUR DE LILAS, Vanel seems to literally emerge from expressive pools of shadow during key dramatic moments. The tension produced by the German characteristic use of psychologically motivated lighting works *with* the particular narrative's focus on unreliable identity as it destabilises the spectator's own perception of the ordinary figure of Vanel's taciturn but reliable persona. In the previously mentioned 1933 interview, Bernhardt had referred to the commonly perceived difference in performance styles between French and German film actors. "German actors put more research into psychological motivation but they tend to be heavier and slower [than the French]", he remarked. "French actors are lighter, less deep but, at the same time, they have a greater degree of naturalness. The ideal would be halfway between one and the other".[45] One way of looking at CARRE-FOUR, therefore, is to suggest that this ideal was achieved in terms of viewing the film itself as a crossroads – a meeting between the brio of French performance and the narrative possibilities of Germanic visual style.

Parisian Journeys Between the Past and the Present

Just as LA VIE PARISIENNE, LA CRISE EST FINIE and MAUVAISE GRAINE partly functioned as émigré texts by including the depiction of travel across Paris, COEUR DE LILAS, DANS LES RUES and CARREFOUR similarly made sense of the city by a set of journeys. In so doing, they produced new perspectives on the centrality of the *quartier* and the worlds of crime and entertainment to the representation of the French capital as a site of darkness. They also suggested, in a number of different ways, that one must relate these narrative journeys to broader textual and historical questions about the travelling inter-relationship between the past and the present in French cinematic representation of the 1930s.

It is clear that a complex layering of nostalgia has to be acknowledged in relation to the portrayal of Paris in the decade's cinematic output. This is certainly true in the way that a sense of the past informs the links between urban crime and entertainment in the films I have already mentioned. As we have noted, Parisian crime films of the period differed from those found in the dark and dangerous streets of cinematic Berlin. Instead of connoting a *contemporary* unease with the modern city, they often became infused with a safer and less confrontational perspective that looked back at *past* imaginings of the city. By the 1930s, for instance, the pre-First World War figure of the Parisian *apache* was already being widely mythologised within French cultural discourse. We can see émigré examples of this in the song *"On ne voit ça qu'à Paris"* in Siodmak's LA CRISE EST FINIE and in Litvak and Courant's use of the figure of Martousse and the milieu of the criminal *quartier* in COEUR DE LILAS. Here, shadow was linked to notions of the past in a complex manner. In one sense, darkness could be simply read as all that signified a lack of progress – the old Paris of densely woven, badly lit streets that was not considered spectacle. But we may also find contained in this idea an element of social criticism or reproach which suggests that the unnecessary consequence of urban modernity was the suffering and impoverishment of those excluded – those who remained in the shadows. The narrative movement *away* from the mythologised darkness of this environment in Coeur de lilas provides one specific example of this particular journeying between past and present. If we examine this key sequence closely, it becomes apparent that a different, more contemporary Paris also emerges in the light of day. Furthermore we can see, once again, how the émigrés' sophisticated handling of light helped, both in a technical and aesthetic sense, to bring a past prowess in picturing Berlin forward to the present of picturing Paris.

The fact that the *quartier* in Coeur de lilas is seen as a world apart from the modern everyday city is developed, first of all, by the narrative transition back to the use of Parisian location footage. This happens soon after Lucot and Lilas leave the intimacy and complex spatial design of Pimenoff's set, following the police raid. The couple are pictured in a long-shot of a darkened and deserted rainy street which recalls the potent atmospherics of the empty city at night in La Chienne. The intense light from a streetlight on a corner breaks up the blackness. The two fugitives hail a bus and ask to be taken to the end of the line. The idea of the end of the line is a practical reality enabling the couple to go backwards and forwards along the route of the bus until dawn, but it also suggests a metaphorical dimension – there is nowhere else to go. The heightened atmosphere in this scene is derived partly from an almost surreal juxtaposition between the excessive noise and commotion of the raid and the quietude and isolation of this section of the city. It is also produced by Courant and Litvak's delicately staged inter-relationship between space, light and the object of the camera's attention. At one point, the couple are framed in a medium close-up. Lucot has his arm around Lilas who is again gazing off-screen. As she speaks, the city passes by behind them in the bus window. The contrast between this flow of framed motion (akin to the progression of a reel of film) and their stillness works not so much to separate the couple from the city. Rather, instead, the city also passes *through* them in the form of light which illuminates their features.

The limpidity of this extraordinary sequence is accented by the preponderance of soft dissolves. After a succession of close-up images of an increasingly over-stuffed breast pocket of bus tickets, there is a dissolve to a view of the city during daytime taken from inside the bus as it turns a street corner. Again, the city comes inside the bus. At the moment the bus swings around the corner, the camera swings rightwards "into" the carriage and we see the conductor make his way down to the sleeping couple. Paris is pictured full of life in daylight. As the bus pulls away and the passengers spill into the crowded public space of Les Halles, the screen fills up with traffic and shouting street vendors. The sense of a shift to a new and more immediate social reality is effected. It is as if the bus has been a temporal and spatial border-zone between the *quartier* and the city centre. The progression from night to day underlines the fact that the *quartier* is only seen in the film as a nighttime space but the destination of the bus is also significant. Les Halles is itself a blurred location, caught between night and day because of its nature as a late night as well as early morning market with its own set of cultural mythologies.[46]

The *quartier*'s version of urban representation relied on the inter-related components of song and music, costume, and the careful choreography of performance and set design, but Paris is now pictured here by means of a succession of documentary style shots of present-day social reality. The density of auditory and visual signifiers is signaled as distinct from the *quartier* by the integration of Lilas's individual reaction to this new version of city life. It is as if we are now being invited to view the city through her eyes. The close-up of her feet on the pavement which dissolves to a close-up of her eyes flashing rightwards and leftwards invites a reading based on her momentary subjectivity. This is sustained by a succession of tightly framed shots which presents her sense of her own self in this stimulating landscape. We cut from a shot of bunches of flowers to Lilas looking mutely off-screen to the right. Her gaze turns down to the floor and her head appears to bow. The blaring interruption of the sound of a car horn breaks this interiority and the camera cuts to another close-up of Lilas's body. This time she appears to remove a handkerchief from the belt around her waist. We then cut to a shot of Lilas fervently sniffing the flowers. Litvak has briefly shown the newness and sensory impact of the heart of the city on one individual through a cinematic monitoring of optical, auditory and orafactory-related responses. The sense of release from the past class and gender restraints of the *fortifications* is furthered by Lilas's makeover at the modern boutique. When she exits the shop onto the Parisian street she declares: "Call me madame now!" The showroom dummy, foregrounded at the end of the previous shot, remains in frame throughout the slow dissolve and only disappears at the moment when Lilas steps out the door onto the pavement. This neatly visualises the transition between aspiration and realisation regarding a different model of urban femininity. Lilas's new look removes her from the old marginal codes of the *quartier* and provides her with a tentative foothold in the social currency of the present-day urban female consumer.

If the modern city is a place of liberation for Lilas, her past nevertheless comes back to haunt and imprison her. The past literally catches up with the present with the near simultaneous arrival of Martousse and Lucot's police superior at the *guingette* where she is hiding with Lucot. The revelation of Lucot's deception and the threat of entrapment prompt Lilas to attempt an escape. We see her running in a long shot away from the camera towards the direction of an overhead railway bridge, across which a train is moving. At this point, the fast-paced reprise of a wedding party song heard at the *guingette* is under-scored by unsettling drumming on the soundtrack. Litvak then cuts to a long series of forward tracking shots which show Lilas constantly running into for-ward space, her body held relatively constant in the middle of the frame. The effect of this is giddying as she seems to be running back into her inescapable past. This notion is further suggested by the expressionsitic superimpositions of grotesque and distorted spectral faces – first the people at the wedding re-ception then various male police officers. At the moment the policemen's faces appear, the music returns to the theme of *Dans la rue*. In her head, it seems, she is back in the dark world of the streets.

The question that arises from this extended sequence in COEUR DE LILAS is why the "dark" world of the Parisian back streets – in obvious contrast to the modern city centre – was so frequently represented through the gauze of the past? What was the precise allure of seeing cinematic images of Paris framed by a sense of their own real or imagined history? We have already noted that one way of understanding the representational difference between Berlin and Paris lies in the distinctive inter-relationships between place and memory in the two cities. In the case of the French capital, there was a naturally "accumu-lated sense of social inheritance" which related to the complex "modulated temporal layerings of Parisian existence". In other words, unlike Berlin, Paris had always had a more sedimented set of representational mythologies to draw upon. Another way of reading this recourse to Paris's urban past in the 1930s might be to briefly return to the example of Walter Benjamin's contem-poraneous reading of Baudelaire and his subsequent discussion of the ques-tion of subjective experience in relation to the city environment.

In his overall discussion of the impact of modernity on the urban individ-ual, Benjamin reinterpreted Baudelaire's perceptual distinction between the eternal and the transitory. He examined the notion of memory and private ex-perience in relation to traditional and modern forms of knowledge produc-tion. Taking his cue from the work of Bergson, Benjamin claimed that "experi-ence is indeed a matter of tradition, in collective existence as well as private life. It is less the product of facts firmly anchored in memory than of a conver-gence in memory of accumulated and frequently unconscious data" (1992 ed., 153-4). Benjamin differed from Bergson, however, by arguing that one could not voluntarily activate the re-emergence of this sensory data through the act of contemplation. Instead, he quoted Proust who wrote that the past is "some-where beyond the reach of the intellect, and unmistakably present in some ma-terial object (or in the sensation which an object arouses in us)" (in Benjamin 1992 ed., 155). What Benjamin went on to suggest was that by the 1920s, the im-pact of modern European city life was such that the traditional contract be-tween subjective experience and the processes of memory accumulation had been broken. Modernity could be distinguished instead by a particular *disruption* in subjectivity which rendered the "isolation of information from experience" (155). The oral tradition of storytelling, with its emphasis on the experiential contract between teller and listener, had been broken by the emergence of abbreviated and unrelated data in mass circulation. Benjamin, for example, believed that the sensory shocks of modern urban experience even served the purpose of preparing the modern individual for the stimuli of the recorded moving image. He went so far as to suggest that in the movie spectator's experience, "perception in the form of shocks [was actually] established as a formal principle" (171).

Whilst retaining a certain measure of agreement with Benjamin's overall validation of the increasing pressures of contemporary city life, it appears that in the case of the Parisian-related French cinema of the 1930s he may have been wrong. Film spectatorship was clearly less a matter of continuous perceptual shocks than a pleasurable social activity which, through various acts of storytelling and modes of performance, actively *engaged* the urban audience with notions of an apparent collective past. Rather than being a way of forgetting, the cinema was in fact a social environment in which to practice remembering. The images of Paris on the screen could even be seen, in one sense, as the Proustian mechanisms for the retrieval of a world which was now in transition. Pierre Nora has argued that the 1930s was a crucial decade in the development of French culture in that it saw a loosening of the grandiose unity between state and nation in favour of a plural notion of memory formation concerned, instead, with the relations between state and society. History became transformed "into a laboratory of past mentalities" (1989, 11). Film culture clearly played a significant role in this. This can be seen not only in the narrative qualities of various film texts, but also in the flowering of a memorialising film culture, which included the first publication of Maurice Bardèche and Robert Brasillach's *Histoire du cinéma* in 1935 and the founding of the Cinémathèque Française in 1936.

Despite the general tangible sensations of change in the material quality of the European urban experience, it is still necessary to account for the particularities of 1930s French cinema's relationship with the city and its representational past. An account of the work of the émigrés in the industry can shed some useful light on this process. In the early years after their arrival in Paris, the German émigrés were perceived negatively by some as representatives of a disruptive urban order, at odds with local Parisian tradition. This anxiety about destabilisation also had economic as well as cultural roots. It has almost become a truism that France in the 1930s was a nation in economic and political upheaval, but this sense of insecurity must have played a significant role in the popularity of "safer" depictions of Parisian life in popular entertainment

culture. The delayed effects of the Great Depression had hit France hard and
urban unemployment soared amidst the backdrop of a succession of short-
lived governments. Since the end of the First World War, national revenue per
capita had grown by an average of five per cent. But in the 1930s, this figure fell
twice as rapidly as it had once risen (Weber 1995, 42). The material nature of
the constructed environment of Paris was emblematic of the overall stasis in
society. In the French capital, building industry contracts, even as late as 1938,
were down by 40 per cent from their level a decade earlier (Weber 1995, 48).
Added to all this was an important demographic shift between the populations of the country's urban and rural areas. With the urban population now
greater than the rural one, the role of Paris, as the depository of the nation's
central mythologies, arguably became intensified.

What still remains under-recognised regarding French cinematic production during this period, however, is the sheer material and psychological impact that the First World War had on France. One of the longest legacies of its
devastation was the introduction of a deeply felt need for recuperation combined with a longing for the reassurances of past notions of national belonging. The impact was clearly enormous – not least of all because of the scale of
the nation's suffering. Most of the men killed would have actually seen their
lives come to fruition in the 1930s and everyone was surrounded by surviving
veterans – they comprised almost fifty per cent of the male population (Weber
1995, 12). The war remainned a constant topic in political and cultural discourse in the 1930s. Many native French film personnel such as Charles Vanel
had actually fought in the trenches. Others had lost their lives and thus deprived the post-war film industry of their talents. Eugène Dabit was but one of
the many close to the film world in the 1930s who laid claim to the powerful effects of memory in relation to his war experiences. He wrote in his diary that
"almost every night since my demobilisation, images of the front came back to
haunt me, and – a still worse nightmare – I dreamed that hostilities were starting again" (in Weber, 12).

How did the war affect the émigrés' representation of Paris in the French
cinema of the period? Did it play a similar role as with native personnel, in that
it contributed to the sense of creating a safe distance from the problems of the
present? For many of these émigrés, the impact of the First World War helped
shape both the welcomes they received and the hostilities they experienced.
On the one hand, their skills and training served a compensatory purpose,
making up for perceived native weaknesses due to war-related economic un-
der-development. On the other hand, there were constant reminders of an enemy from the past. For some, this even forewarned of a potential enemy in the
future. In terms of the relationship between memory and the portrayal of Paris
as the city of darkness we can discern two trends. One was largely concerned

with uncovering the dark city and still representing it as it was once thought to be. This is largely the mode of DANS LES RUES and COEUR DE LILAS although, as we have also seen, there were other signs of a complex interchange between notions of the urban past and the present. The second trend was that the war's past literally caught up with the present so that the battleground was transferred to the individual mind. Here, the past literally *was* dark because it remained unknown. This is the case in CARREFOUR.

It has not been sufficiently recognised that Bernhardt's film was actually based on a real-life war-time incident. According to an interview with CARREFOUR's scriptwriter, Hans Kafka, the film was inspired by the Bruneri-Canella case which had shocked Italian society in the 1920s. At the end of the First World War, two physically similar Italian soldiers had disappeared in Macedonia – a Paduan professor (Bruneri) and a wanted Roman street criminal (Canella). A derelict, unidentified man was found and claimed respectively by Bruneri's widow and the crook's father. Both cities campaigned for the identity of "their own man" until Canella's old fingerprints were accidentally discovered by the police in Rome. The match was made and the case solved; the amnesiac had indeed had a criminal past. Despite all of this however, Bruneri's widow refused to accept the verdict and after Canella was released from prison he eventually went on to live as "Bruneri" with his "wife" in Padua. Hans Kafka, perhaps because of his German cultural heritage, was fascinated by this *Doppelgänger* narrative and went to visit "Bruneri" while he was preparing the script for CARREFOUR. He likened it to other examples in Germany and France. What fascinated him, "was how an individual is impregnated by his milieu".[47] Kafka's comments remain forceful, not least of all because of the subtle awareness of his own situation as a German émigré still working in a largely alien environment and having to contribute to the production of an ostensibly "French film".

In CARREFOUR, the mingling of past and present is achieved through the central figure of Vetheuil. When the war veteran first appears at Michèle's nightclub, it is clear that he is not so much entering a novel world of danger and cosmopolitan allure, but returning to his past – to the world he came from. It is not surprising that this mingling of past and present takes place in Montmartre. As we have seen, much Parisian music hall entertainment that took place in this section of Paris explicitly projected an interpretation of past pleasure for a contemporary audience. Vetheuil is, in one sense, emblematic of the way Parisian film culture of the period also made use of past city mythologies by reconstituting them in contemporary cinematic contexts.

If we focus on the conclusion of the cabaret sequence in CARREFOUR, we can see how the film draws meaning from a sense of the past that comes back to unsettle the spectacle of contemporary Parisian pleasure. When de Vetheuil walks

through the separating curtain to visit Michèle in her living quarters above the
cabaret, he initially enters the transitional, empty space at the foot of a stairway.
Unlike the *quartier* staircase that integrates the various levels of the community,
this passageway separates the past from the present and the public from the
private. Because of the shot's carefully constructed lighting, the spectator is
treated to the shadow of de Vetheuil's former self literally catching up with him
on the wall as he mounts the stairs. By the time de Vetheuil enters Michèle's
room, he has also become Pettier, the Parisian criminal. The worlds of crime
and entertainment are fused yet again. Like Jenny's quarters in JENNY (also designed by Jean d'Eaubonne), Michèle's room is decorated in a range of lightly
coloured, soft and luxurious fabrics. The zebra skin print on the floor connotes
a different class reading of luxury from the more sensible and discrete fabric
found in de Vetheuil's bourgeois mansion. As Michèle recalls her romance with
Pettier off-screen, the room's space is detailed in an extraordinarily rich, slow
circular pan. We pass a large window that reveals the nighttime cityscape. An
illuminated cinema sign breaks up the darkness outside. The camera also fo-
cuses on a prominent photograph from Michèle's younger days before resting
on a medium long-shot of the couple with de Vetheuil/ Pettier seated on the
sofa and Michèle reclined on the floor. Dance music filters in from downstairs
and the camera tracks in as Michèle reminiscences about a *bistrot* they used to
frequent and about living together in an apartment in the emblematic working
class district of Belleville. The sequence's powerful emphasis on visuality and
remembering comes to the fore at the moment when this portrait of shared nostalgia is punctuated by a fierce close-up of Vanel. Suddenly the dance music is
interrupted by the sound of an interiorised soundtrack of music from Pettier's
past. Or to put it another way, Belleville collides with Montmartre and the dark
Parisian past enters the light Parisian present.

5 Divided City

The Divided City in Context

The critic Georges Champeaux noted that PIÈGES (1939), Robert Siodmak's final film made in France before departing for the United States, seemed to be
like a dark Parisian police drama but indeed it was something else. "PIÈGES
has neither the cut nor the rhythm of a police film," he stated. "What it seems
like is a succession of sketches destined to bring its comical or bizarre characters to life in front of us. The slowness and, it has to be said, the talent with
which the director Robert Siodmak describes the social milieu of each of his
characters scarcely contributes to strengthening the film's illusion".[1] Fritz
Lang's only film made in France, LILIOM, was given similarly contradictory reviews at the time, no doubt in part because halfway through the film, the eponymous lead, a Parisian *mauvais garçon* played by Charles Boyer, leaves the Parisian *zone* for a fantastic journey to heaven. Many of LILIOM's critics also
pointed out the national hybridity of the film, which was based on a play by
the Hungarian playwright Frederic Molnar, produced by the renowned U.F.A.
producer Erich Pommer, and directed by Germany's most famous director,
Fritz Lang. To the right-wing cultural press, for example, LILIOM was a prime
example of the dangers of having a multi-cultural film culture in France. The
virulently anti-Semitic François Vinneuil saw "this French-Jewish-Hungarian
collaboration" as a return to "that bizarre and boring cinematic country produced by U.F.A.'s French-German dramas [which was] a 'no man's land', a Babel emptied of all character lying a lot closer to the Sprée than to the Seine".[2]

   PIÈGES and LILIOM are further examples of how different groups of émigrés
portrayed the French capital. In part, they consolidate the ideas discussed in
the preceding chapters. Yet at the same time, they also express a more fragmented notion of the conventions of Parisian representation, and in this sense,
they are both divided on a textual and representational level. To understand
this sense of division we should examine the films in relation to three overlapping contexts. Firstly, we need to consider the way the two productions actually frame the period in question. Fritz Lang's LILIOM follows along the lines of
the work produced by the émigrés who came to Paris for economically or technically related reasons in the 1930s and in this sense, LILIOM may be seen as a
snapshot of the opening wave of the primarily politically minded emigration of
Berlin film personnel after the Nazi consolidation of power in 1933. It was the
first film produced by the French subsidiary of the American Fox Film Corporation headed by fellow émigré Erich Pommer, former production chief at

U.F.A. in Berlin. Robert Siodmak's PIÈGES, on the other hand, was completed just before his departure for Hollywood and did not even receive a Parisian release until December 1939, by which time Siodmak was already in the United States. In one sense, it was really a passport film with one eye firmly on the future and one on the present.[3] If we look at the production histories of the two films, we can begin to redefine the work of the émigrés in terms of how these features relate to the apparent division between the idea of Paris as the centre of domestic film production and the idea of Paris as the place of temporary exile. Secondly, we need to return to the issues of performance and identity. Both films starred lead actors with international careers who were, at the same time, closely connected in the public sphere to specific notions of Frenchness and Parisian culture. Both Maurice Chevalier and Charles Boyer were used in these two features because of their relationships to the specific question of the representation of Paris. Their own "divided status" informs an understanding of the way the French capital was portrayed. A third frame of reference is based on these two points. Here I would like to address the question of travel and return again to the notion of journeying, which has been a principal metaphor for this book. How does the evident mobility in the films' narratives relate to the representation of place and location? In other words, if one is to characterise the Paris of PIÈGES and LILIOM as divided, in what ways was the city itself split, and how was this division informed by the matter of emigration?

When Josef Goebbels called for a boycott of all Jewish businesses, soon after Adolf Hitler became Chancellor on 30 January 1933, it became clear that the Nazis were targeting the widespread popularity of the national film industry for immediate political and ideological reorientation. On March 29, two days after the Hotel Kaiserhof meeting between Goebbels and a group of film industry professionals, Fritz Lang's most recent German film, DAS TESTAMENT DER DOCTOR MABUSE (1933), was formally banned from German cinemas by the German Board of Film Censors. U.F.A.'s board not only fired all Jewish employees, it further authorised that two films of "purely German character" be given immediate production priority over previously scheduled French-language versions (Hardt 1996, 138). It is ironic then that LILIOM, Pommer and Lang's first émigré film project in France, notably played up its sense of national hybridity to the point where the formal qualities of the film's depiction of Paris were criticised in the French press for being too "German". For example, Jean Laury even commented that "the concern of the director might have been to make a French film, but in fact, LILIOM is a German film par excellence".[4]

According to the legend, repeated not least by Lang himself, Germany's most celebrated film director fled Berlin on the night train to Paris after being asked by Goebbels to head a new Nazi film agency in early April 1933. However, it has recently been ascertained that Lang's movements prior to his final stay in Paris were more fluid and less dramatic than the scenario hitherto painted (McGilligan 1997, 173). As an elite member of the German film industry, like his friend Erich Pommer, he was able to make extensive preparations for his departure from an increasingly anti-Semitic and xenophobic Berlin. He already knew Paris well from having studied there as an art student in 1913 and 1914. He departed for the French capital in late June 1933, but actually returned to Germany before finally leaving for good on 21 July 1933. Unlike the case with many of his exiled compatriots who stayed in poorer Paris lodgings like the Hotel Ansonia, 8 rue de Saigon, Lang's luxurious room at the Hotel George V was proof of his status and economic mobility.[5] Curt Riess, in fact, was to call him "an emigrant deluxe" (in McGilligan, 191). Pommer had in early 1933 made detailed financial arrangements in the United States with Sidney Kent, president of the Fox Film Corporation, to set up a film production division based in Europe. This enabled him to leave Germany for France with the knowledge that he had an established business to come to. Originally, of course, Fox Film Europa was to be based in Germany. By August, however, announcements were made in the French film press that Pommer had established a *modus operandi* which would stimulate French film production by producing French- and English-language films in Paris.[6] One of the directors he wished to work with was his compatriot, Fritz Lang.

It is also ironic that Pommer should choose such a determinedly cosmopolitan project for Fox Europa's first French venture. LILIOM was closely based on Frederic Molnar's successful play which had been performed with Georges Pitoëff at the Comédie des Champs-Elysées in Paris in 1923. Interestingly, the stage production had been set in the context of the dark tradition of urban representation. One critic observed that it was reminiscent of the work of Francis Carco, while another anonymous writer thought that the *mise-en-scène* was heavily influenced by the Berlin cinema "with an accumulation of heavy and clumsy details in the German style".[7] Lang had actually seen the Berlin production with Hans Albers in the 1920s. An earlier, rather unremarkable, film adaptation was produced by Frank Borzage for Fox in 1930 starring Charles Farrel in the lead role. The national origins of the production crew were heterogeneous: Lang's assistant, Gilbert Mandelik, was a German-Jewish film professional; the cinematographer was Rudolph Maté (who had completed DANS LES RUES that same year); the composer was Franz Waxman (who had arranged the score for DER BLAUE ENGEL and was to work on LA CRISE EST FINIE and MAUVAISE GRAINE) and the script was co-written by former-U.F.A. employee Robert Liebmann. Liebmann's Berlin credits included Robert Siodmak's VORUNTER-SUCHUNG (1931) and STÜRME DER LEIDENSCHAFT (1931). LILIOM was nonetheless a project specifically designed for Lang. The director's credentials were heavily signalled in Nino Frank's contemporaneous interview where he described Lang as having "a German build" combined with "the elegance of a Parisian *bon viveur* (...) in short, a curious mixture on first sight of a man of the North and a man of the South – of German and Latin culture".[8]

Lang began shooting LILIOM in November 1933 at the Studios des Réservoirs at Joinville and it was released in Paris the following spring. The film's plot concerns the life and death of Liliom (Charles Boyer), a *mauvais garçon* who lives in the *zone* on the outskirts of Paris. Liliom works as a hawker at a local fairground for Mme Moscat (Florelle), the owner of a merry-go-round. One evening he decides to approach two girls who have been coming to the fair regularly. He begins a love affair with one of them. Julie (Madeleine Ozeray) and Liliom set up house with Julie's aunt Madame Menoux (Maximilienne) and they establish a photography business together. Liliom is often moody and short-tempered at home. Julie becomes pregnant and, because he's short of money, Liliom plans a robbery with his former criminal cohort, Alfred (Pierre Alcover). The plans go awry and in desperation Liliom kills himself. Liliom is taken to the judicial courts of heaven to watch a film recording of his earthly activities and numerous temper tantrums before being placed into purgatory. Many years later he is briefly allowed to return to earth where he meets his daughter. Liliom's tears of regret back in heaven restore the scales of justice so that he is ultimately absolved of his crime.

Numerous production reports in the French film press took a two-fold interest in the film. Many writers noted the contribution of a particularly German aesthetic in the way that Lang depicted life in the French capital. Paul Reboux's comments were typical at the time when he wrote about LILIOM's "rather dark cinematography" and the "habitual slowness in the rhythm often found in German films".[9] However, interestingly enough, at the same time as recognising difference, commentators were also keen to evoke the verisimilitude of the production's depiction of Paris. Reporting in *Paris-Midi*, Claude Jahni thought that the film's atmosphere captured the exact "sentiments of anguish and melancholy" that he felt at a *fête foraine de quartier* (local fairground). "All that was missing for the illusion to be perfect was the smell of chips. (...) Fritz Lang has masterfully reconstructed an ambience so French that down to the finest detail one is left confounded".[10]

As we saw in Chapter Two, Robert Siodmak's French career was more extended and uneven than Lang's. He actually worked as an émigré in France from 1933 to 1939 without a work permit (Dumont 1981, 122-128), and was undoubtedly relieved to discover by chance during the shooting of PIÈGES that he had not in fact lost his original American nationality. After years of professional insecurity and anxiety, caused by, among other factors, the sometimes hostile resentment of his presence in the French film industry, he seized the opportunity and moved to the United States. He left Europe on 31 August 1939, sailing aboard the French liner, the Champlain, with a copy of Pièges packed in his luggage. He had originally had plans to return briefly to France the following year and complete a proposed project in Holland, but war broke out the next day on 1 September 1939.

Siodmak's last French film was a heterogeneous one in more than one sense. To the film historian, it looks backwards and forwards at the same time. Dumont, for instance, insists that "Pièges at times returns to the climate of Siodmak's early U.F.A. films with their fascination for sordid details and their pitiless lighting, whereas certain harrowing parts (...) already foretell his American works like The Spiral Staircase" (125). Elsaesser even suggests that the film "should really have been made in Hollywood, and by Lubitsch (...) because it illustrates to perfection the 'miscognition' factor of Austro-Germans as directors of Hapsburg decadence or Parisian operetta, given the prominent presence in Pièges of both Erich von Stroheim *and* Maurice Chevalier" (1996, 140). These points may be true, but it is also useful to position Pièges within the hitherto relatively ignored historical context of Siodmak's own French work.

The film's narrative and aesthetic framework relies on the motif of detection to knit together a varied series of sequences and episodes set in Paris. This particular instance of disparity is in fact indicative of the variety of Siodmak's entire period of exile in France during which he made films in various genres. What is more, despite the fact that Pièges was seen as a Siodmak film at the time of its Paris release at the end of 1939, it was also an "international" production in the sense that it was, like so many émigré films made in France, a joint creative venture by film people of various nationalities. The numerous sets by the Russian émigré Georges Wakhévitch not only let everyone know that this was a prestigious production, they also represented an geographical scope to the way in which Paris was portrayed. Wakhévitch had already been working in Paris since 1921. He designed the noirish Montparnasse interiors for Julien Duvivier's version of Simenon's La Tête d'un homme, as well as the sets for Pierre Chenal's James L. Cain adaptation Le Dernier tournant which also appeared in 1939. The complex lighting ranged from depicting extensive scenes of Parisian high life to the nocturnal shadows of city streets and back rooms. It was organised by Michel Kelber and Ted Pahle who had worked together on other French productions in the 1930s. Neither were French natives; Pahle was an American of German origin and Kelber, though educated in France, was a Russian. Ernest Neuville, one of the screenwriters, was also a Berliner. He had worked with Siodmak on Der Mann der Seinen Mörder Sucht (1930) under the name Ernst Neubach.

Pièges was based on a Norbert Garay stage play, but it had its origins in the sensational Eugen Weidman affair that had gripped the attention of Parisians in 1937. Weidman was a linguistically gifted German intellectual living in Paris who turned out to be a serial killer who had committed a series of widely publicised murders of tourists in Paris. The aunt of one of his victims was forced to place contact messages in the Paris edition of the *Herald Tribune* – hence the use of the newspaper motif in the film. His trial was covered in the press by the likes of Colette and even attended, according to Dumont, by Maurice Chevalier – the film's star. Weidman's was the last public beheading in France (Flanner 1988, 206-217). When the film was released, it was reviewed in the French press as a *policier*. It is, indeed, a detective mystery in the sense that it concerns the efforts of the Parisian police to apprehend a mysterious murderer of young women tourists in Paris. The police commissioner Ténier (André Brunot) is confounded by the killer's teasing letters and is forced to enlist the assistance a young "taxi-girl"[11], Adrienne Charpentier (Marie Déa), who worked with the most recent victim. Adrienne is sent in disguise to answer a number of personal announcements in the city newspapers where the police believe the killer finds his victims. She meets Pears (Erich von Stroheim), an insane former celebrated Parisian fashion designer, who invites her to his "latest collection" in his empty mansion. Adrienne escapes when Pears in despair sets fire to his own home. A mysterious music lover invites her to a classical concert where she meets Robert Fleury (Maurice Chevalier), a suave nightclub owner and his assistant Brémontière (Pierre Renoir). Adrienne works as a maid in a large house run by the sinister head butler Maxime (Jacques Varennes). One evening she meets Fleury again as one of the houseguests. He invites her out but she declines as she has a date to go to the "Cordon Bleu" dance with the housekeeper. At the dance, Adrienne is surprised by Fleury who arrives in disguise. The same evening, she discovers the female white-slave racket run by Maxime and the housekeeper, which explains the mysterious number of young girls who had "left" the house in the past. Adrienne and Fleury eventually marry. The case appears solved except for the subsequent discovery of a number of incriminating photographs and mementos in Fleury's house. Fleury is arrested, and is only saved from the death penalty when at the last minute proof surfaces that Brémontière was the true killer after all.

PIÈGES was advertised as an investigative police drama, but according to interviews with the director, it was conceived more as an "episode film" in line with the internationally successful UN CARNET DE BAL (Julien Duvivier, 1937). In an interview with *Le Jour*, Siodmak described how he actually saw the detective theme as the framework for an exploration of the many milieux of Parisian society. "Circumstances lead us into lifting the curtain which masks the private life of individuals (...) who belong to very different social backgrounds", he noted. This framework also meant a looser generic structure for the film.

9. Adrienne (Marie Déa, left) and Fleury (Maurice Chevalier, right) in Pièges (BFI)

"There is a chance of not being strictly locked into one kind of film. On the contrary, one can touch on the differing rhythms of comedy, drama, adventure comedy and develop sketches with either happy, sad or humourous ambiences".[12] In a later interview, the director went on to argue that Pièges was a psychological film, claiming that he had chosen his cast for reasons of psychological and physical authenticity. These are clearly the words of an experienced professional who had, by now, formed an intimate knowledge of the repertoire of French film and stage acting talents, but Siodmak's comments also point to the central contradiction of the film. Whilst the surface of the text presents a gallery of distinctly recognisable Parisian character types and locales, the narrative also draws attention to the unreliability of such appearances. In fact, most of the central characters are engaged in some form of duplicitous performance and these performances are cues for an exploration of another kind of Paris, another kind of reality. Just as Liliom hovers between a minutely detailed, if somewhat stylised, realist drama of "dark Paris" and a "lighter", more fanciful and metaphysical version of the city, so Pièges similarly plays with the Paris "we know". A mysterious and shadowy encounter on a Parisian street corner between Adrienne and an unnamed stranger turns from a conventionally noir-like encounter to the revelation that the stranger is

Batol (Jean Temerson), the buffoonish police inspector and bodyguard who lives with his mother in an ordinary Paris apartment. The constrained and ordered world of a bourgeois Parisian mansion is the setting for an intricately structured international prostitution ring. Central to these sets of interlocking parallels is the way the virtuous duplicity of the female lead is seemingly mirrored by the shocking and murderous duplicities of the *male* lead played by Chevalier. And so because of the way Siodmak cast Chevalier against type, we come to the greatest play on the question of performance that the film contends with.

Divided Characters, Divided City

An understanding of the inter-relationship of stardom, identity and the performances of Maurice Chevalier and Charles Boyer in PIÈGES and LILIOM is crucial to the broader issue of how the two films depict Paris. At home or abroad, on stage or on screen, both stars in the 1920s and 1930s were associated with particular versions of Parisian-ness and this, in turn, meant the expression of various forms of French masculinity. The two men were friends whose careers dovetailed in the realm of international film stardom. They had both become known in Hollywood in the early years of the sound era when French speaking actors were required in the numerous French language versions that were being shot in the United States. Boyer, for example, starred in the hugely successful French-language version of BIG HOUSE (Paul Fejos, 1930) as well as English-language version films such as THE MAGNIFICENT LIE (Berthold Viertel, 1931).[13] Chevalier starred in both the English- and French-language versions of films like PARAMOUNT ON PARADE (Arzner, Goulding, Lubitsch et al., 1928).[14] Chevalier's part in FOLIES BERGÈRE / L'HOMME DES FOLIES BERGÈRE (Roy Del Ruth, 1935) was even originally intended for Boyer.

According to his memoirs (1946, 198), Chevalier looked to Boyer for intellectual guidance in their friendship. This biographical detail points to the main cultural difference between the Parisian personas of the two men – one of class and location. Boyer came from a highbrow tradition of theatrical training combined with a formal university education at the Sorbonne. His smooth, rounded facial features suggest a polished and groomed version of the French male, which in his overseas persona became inflected, notoriously, with stereotypical notions of the allure of the French Latin lover. Writing in *Cinémagazine*, Jean Vidal noted that "French cinema possessed in Charles Boyer one of its finest actors or rather it would possess him if it had known how to keep him...[Boyer] has a bright and vivacious sensibility but one that is subject to a willful and penetrating intelligence".[15] If Boyer represented a more timeless, cultivated tradition of Parisian culture, Chevalier, fashioned a complex identity in relation to the French capital that had its origins in the working class milieux of the 19th and 20th *arrondisements*. Chevalier was born in Ménilmontant, on the edge of Belleville and so, according to his own mythology, his character was informed, from the beginning, by a sense of geographical and cultural division. Belleville, he wrote, was "a swarming rabble [which] made it seem like the capital of the *faubourgs* of Paris. (...) Brave and honest lads were used to rubbing shoulders with the pimp suspected of the most awful deeds. Ménilmontant, by comparison, was a bit like a calm parent; gentle and in some way, poetic" (198). Chevalier's first stage performances, at local *café-concerts*, were as an earthy comic singer in the tradition of Dranem. Only after the First World War, when he learned English in a German prisoner-of-war camp, did he begin to play on his origins and appear as the archetypal Parisian *gavroche* for the bourgeois, grand music-hall venue audience. His persona became a complex negotiation between nostalgia and modernity, between a past and a contemporary urban identity. On the one hand, Chevalier "acknowledged the image of the cheeky Parisian (...) with his *gouaille* (cocky Parisian banter), his accent and his gestural arsenal: the swaying gait, the putting on for show, the shrugging of the shoulders, the raising of his hat with his hands in his pockets or the armholes of his waistcoat" (Vincendeau 1996, 95); yet, on the other hand, he also signalled something more contemporary. By also adopting the recognisable trademarks of the bow tie and boater and a looser, more syncopated orchestration to his melodies, he embodied the more metropolitan sophistication of the urban dandy who was just as at home among the upscale modern milieux – the casino or the luxurious art deco music hall – as the working class streets. Central to this modernity are two other inter-related factors which also contributed to Chevalier's subsequent success as a film star – technology and international travel. Through the developments of gramophone recordings and radio, the star's rendition of Paris was performed and circulated for audiences beyond the contours of the city's geographical boundaries. In the printed fan magazines, Chevalier became associated with other signifiers of modern life like the automobile and jazz and this accelerated his integration into an internationalised discourse of Parisian identity which was then reinserted into popular on-stage performances for tourists at leading French venues.

Charles Boyer and Maurice Chevalier were both, therefore, conventionally cast in the light Parisian tradition of representation. They shared a double cinematic appeal which meant something identifiably Parisian, and thus French, to both the national *and* the international film audience. For the domestic spectator, this appeal could mean a sense of intimate recognition and pride – Chevalier was called *"notre Maurice national"*.[16] To the international public, Boyer and Chevalier were the signifiers of an exportable version of national identity. Boyer, for instance, was called "the ambassador of French film to the United States".[17] In LILIOM and PIÈGES the two stars were, however, seemingly cast against type. In Lang's film, Boyer is a rough but somewhat lovable Parisian former petty criminal whereas, in the Siodmak vehicle, Chevalier, is cast as a raffish and well-connected night-club owner who actually spends a good deal of the film suspected of being the serial killer. These reversals foreground the means by which the two films, as émigré productions, stage a sense of division between the city of darkness and the city of light.

Vincendeau (1996, 95) has argued that Chevalier's French films of the 1930s reconcile the dichotomy between the world of luxury and the world of popular Paris in his star persona by situating the narratives within the sphere of urban spectacle or performance. This is true if we look at AVEC LE SOURIRE (Maurice Tourneur, 1936), for example. At the beginning of the film, we see Chevalier strike a Chaplin-esque pose on a road to Paris to seek his fortune. He is dressed in conventional workingman's clothes including a proletarian cloth cap. By the end of the film, by dint of his élan and natural cheek, he has worked his way up from doorman to theatrical revue performer to the position of director of the Paris Opéra. Although Chevalier is now habitually found wearing a dinner suit, the fluidity and ease of his body language and character still mark him as separate from the dour, stiff bourgeois male he has replaced as director. In PIÈGES, Robert Fleury is already a man at the top but, as with AVEC LE SOURIRE, one who is not readily identified with urban high culture. He is introduced at a classical concert, where he is seen complaining to his friend that there are no pretty women around. "Be quiet and listen to the music!", his companion retorts. "Aren't there any lyrics?", a surprised Chevalier wants to know. Later, during the interval, Fleury is called "our ambassador to Parisian night life". These remarks are the hallmark of the conflation of a man of spectacle with that of the archetypal Parisian dandy/lover that Vincendeau argues ultimately leaves Fleury positioned in the narrative as an "empty shell" (97). In a film in which the motifs of disguise and transgression are paramount, Fleury's "tragedy", she points out, "is not that of a judicial error but that of the myth of the Parisian seducer" (97).

The core of Vincendeau's argument rests in the way that PIÈGES manages to integrate the luxury-popular dichotomy into Chevalier's persona via the two songs he performs and the milieux in which they are set. The first song, *Mon amour*, is sung in Fleury's flagship nightclub, whilst the second, *Il pleurait comme une madeleine*, takes place at the more modest Bal du Cordon Bleu with a decor of muralled trellises, chains of bobbing lights and decorations reminiscent of the popular milieu of a *guinguette*. At the nightclub, Fleury sings as "himself" – even though we are, of course, cued to recognise this as "a Chevalier moment" – but at the Bal, he plays a singing working-class chauffeur in disguise. In a neat twist on the play between appearance and reality that the film constantly perpetuates, Fleury the "chauffeur" is matched here with Adrienne in disguise as something other than her "taxi-girl" role. Vincendeau is right in saying that in terms of the inter-relationship between *mise-en-scène* and performance, both songs are, in fact, very similar. Both showcase the same gestural charm and mobility of the performer. Both use the diegetic audience not only to position the body of the star as the central component of the screen's frame, but also as participants in the energy and communality of the moment. Chevalier gets the nightclub guests to sing-a-long in a cued refrain, for example, whilst at the *bal*, the song is a cue for everyone to start dancing. The point of this similarity is to emphasise the predictable nature of the Fleury persona as a somewhat hollow and unreliable man of spectacle, but Vincendeau then goes on to underline this fixity with recourse to two other fundamental tropes of Parisian representation – the *tradition comique-grivoise* and the depiction of the male poetic-realist hero. The song that Chevalier sings at the *bal* about a man who cannot stop weeping, even during sexual climax, belongs to the live tradition of Parisian ribald humour. This places the question of sexuality literally onto the field of the body itself where it then becomes an object – the externalised focus of derisive pleasure. When Chevalier is seen performing in disguise as a member of the working class, as well as simultaneously performing as a man who cannot stop crying before an audience, he is merely reaffirming the superficial, surface nature of his particular male identity. As a result of this emphasis on performance, Fleury (Chevalier) is denied the interiorised version of male subjectivity that is carried, for example, by the tragic Parisian proletarian hero embodied by Gabin in a poetic realist drama like LE JOUR SE LÈVE. Vincendeau argues that the Gabin persona in these types of films was allowed to be both the agent *and* the object of romantic sexual desire. In PIÈGES, on the other hand, Chevalier remains truly divided, caught "halfway between the comics of the *café-concert* and the tragic image of a Gabin" (97). The identity of "the man of spectacle" becomes, according to these terms, a meeting point – *the* site where division occurs and rests.

Thus it appears that even though PIÈGES was a film made by an émigré director, it had a steady hold on a range of meanings concerning Parisian popular culture. But it was also *because* of its émigré status that it presented a particular conception of the Chevalier Parisian persona. We can see this in the way in which the *mise-en-scène* elaborates on the theme of division that we have thus far outlined, and how the figure of Chevalier as Fleury specifically works in relation to the separation between the city of darkness and the city of light. In her article on PIÈGES, Vincendeau suggests that the characters of Fleury and

Brémontière are a kind of couple in the film to the extent that they are doubles of one another. An example of this is the way that Brémontière is seen as the serial killer, "the man of shadow", whilst Fleury is seen as the serial seducer, "the man of spectacle". This is certainly true in relation to the way the film contrasts the conventionally bright jocular banter of Fleury in his natural milieu and the noirish psychology of the office scene when Brémontière is finally unmasked. The distinction is also a matter of the difference between the performances of the two actors. The solidity and gravity of Pierre Renoir serves as a counter-weight to the extreme mobility and lightness of Chevalier's body language. However, the figure of Chevalier is further divided in the sense that the film also "performs darkness" on him whilst accommodating his "natural" milieu of performance and light spectacle. If we contrast the way, for example, Fleury is portrayed in his nightclub and the way he is portrayed when he is taken away to the police, we see more than a commentary on the inherent hollowness of his persona, we also discover a particular mode of choreography and artifice which chines with the works of other émigrés who worked in French cinema.

Fleury's nightclub is associated with space, light, whiteness and depth, with an emphasis on round forms, which is exemplified by the way that the milieu is established. Siodmak opens the sequence with a high-angle shot with a considerable depth of field. We see an extravagant decor of spiralling columns, a central oval stage and, in the foreground, a set of tables and spectators, which encircle the stage area. A flamenco dancer begins to move rightwards across the stage. This motif is continued in the subsequent medium long-shot in which we see Adrienne descending one of the stairways in the same direction. The camera commences with a slow rightwards, circular tracking movement at the moment when a waiter greets Adrienne and takes her to Fleury's table. During this, the luxurious, brightly lit features of the nightclub are deliberately highlighted. The importance of the setting supersedes that of the club's owner. In this sense, the *mise-en-scène* exemplifies what might be termed an émigré "double focus of attention" between "narrative intrigue" and the "playing for effect of set pieces" (Elsaesser 1984, 279). However, this disparity is subsequently abandoned during Chevalier's performance of *Mon amour*. Through its inherent energy and fusion of melody and physical display, Chevalier's performance draws fellow guests *together* to form part of a whole. The star moves his body and eyes to catch the gaze of the diegetic spectators. Even his hands re-iterate the circularity of the aforementioned decor in an inclusive fashion. The lighting is also softer in the sense that there are no harsh edges and the performer's features are well highlighted.

But during Fleury's interrogation at the police station, all of this is reversed. The emphasis here is on fragmentation and dislocation to the point where even Chevalier's trademark evening wear disintegrates; his shirt is unbut-

toned, his hair is ruffled, and his bow tie dangles loosely around his neck. It is
as if the Paris with which the performer has become identified has been over-
taken by a different, darker urban identity – an identity which anticipates the
noirish investigations of Siodmak's subsequent film career in Hollywood.
Again, we return to Elsaesser's remarks on the "use of cinematic *mise en scène*
as an instrument of abstraction" and the "ability to treat lighting or editing effects (...) as cinematic signifiers in their own right" (1984, 281). The space in the
room is compressed and shallow; there is no sense of integration based on the
inter-relationship of decor, light and actor. Instead, the lighting works independently and non-naturalistically in the form of a heightened commentary
on the proceedings. The police inspector is shot in medium close-up and is surrounded by pools of darkness. The overall lighting is dim but we see the dramatic use of a hard side light that accents the expressive contours of the man's
face in relief. When we cut to Fleury, he almost appears to be pinned down. His
body language is inert. As the discussion proceeds, the lighting takes on a life
of its own. Siodmak frequently cuts back to a slightly downwards-tilted medium close-up of Fleury in which Chevalier's former highlighted facial features are now flatly lit as if they are being viewed through a greyish gauze. A
black shadow is cast onto the upper part of his brow. As the interrogation
reaches its denouement and it appears that, according to the circumstantial evidence, Fleury is guilty after all, this shadow moves across the rest of Chevalier's face. His eyes, now blank and still, register disbelief. Whilst this disbelief
undoubtedly is supposed to be shared with the audience, the overall purpose
of this sequence is to unsettle the fixity of the "light" Paris embodied by Chevalier as "man of spectacle".

If PIÈGES is mostly concerned with the figure of the wealthy male Parisian
seducer, LILIOM is concerned with the world of another familiar trope of Parisian masculinity, the impoverished *mauvais garçon*. What is more, if Siodmak's
film works with the notion of a "light Paris" being troubled by criminality and
darkness, Lang's drama examines the disruption of the conventions of the
"city of darkness" by the metaphysics or mysticism of light and redemption.
More or less a synonym for the figure of the *apache*, the *mauvais garçon* was another incarnation of the criminal Parisian tough found in the popular films and
literature of the period. The term was such a clear signifier of a certain Parisian
culture that it even became celebrated in the light social comedy of disguise,
UN MAUVAIS GARÇON (Jean Boyer, 1936), which featured Henri Garat singing
the title song. Charles Boyer was cast against type in LILIOM although he had
already played a denizen of Berlin's underworld in the French-language version of Siodmak's TUMULTES. In Lang's film he plays a boyish, exuberant
ex-small criminal closely associated with the city milieux of the fairground life
and the rough terrain and small wooden houses of the *zone*. As with Chevalier

in PIÈGES, Boyer's physical performance is intimately linked with the social setting he occupies – in this case, the familiar milieu of dark Paris where popular urban entertainment and criminality meet.

The film begins with a medium long-shot of Madame Moscat at her booth. Moscat is lit distinctively by a strong, non-naturalistic light source from below which highlights her features against the shuffling shadows of local punters in the foreground. We first *hear* Liliom off-screen; he makes his living as a hawker with his distinctive voice. Guided by Moscat's gaze as it turns rightward, we cut to a long-shot of Liliom next to the merry-go-round, calling out to his audience. He is clearly the centre of attention. This is underlined in a subsequent shot taken from the window of the nearby hotel when we see Liliom framed in the rear of the image, surrounded by the local community, whilst in the foreground, the more or less soundless strongman stands there being ignored. The reason for the hawker's success is not just the attraction of his voice, although his ability to break out into raucous song is certainly part of it. As Lang's fluid camerawork demonstrates, it rests in the lithe inter-relationship between Liliom's "natural environment" and Boyer's charismatic gestural physicality. In this sense, Boyer's performance definitely "fits" in with the general requirements for the role. A good example of this is in the single shot in which Liliom lifts up a drunkard who has been stumbling around the outdoor tables of the cafe nearby. The drunkard's ineptitude is indicated by his diminutive frame and the comic effect of his pom-pom hat. In contrast, Liliom's virility is underlined by the way his close-fitting striped jersey seems designed to display his musculature. As Liliom tugs at the man and moves him forward onto the merry-go-round, the camera simultaneously pulls back to give a sensation of Boyer's mastery of the space around him. Everyone is watching him perform and the chaos of balloons and streamers just adds to the heightened atmosphere. The camera halts momentarily as the man stumbles into a woman seated on a nearby horse. Liliom and the woman help him into a chair. Liliom then turns around and the camera tracks his movement into the area at the back of the merry-go-round whilst maintaining Boyer's position in the centre of the frame. His body continues to turn, with his arms swinging or energetically gesturing toward the laughing crowd. Liliom continues to collect his money and moves to the left of the merry-go-round so that he is positioned midway between the horses and the locals gathered around him. He raises his arms and puts his hands to his ears as he suddenly notices something at a diagonal to him off-screen right. When he points and moves in the direction of his line of view, the camera this time does not move forward with Liliom. The effect of this is to heighten the intensity of Liliom's desire and to complete the single shot with an intensely focussed close-up of Boyer gazing at the object of his attention. In the subsequent shot this is revealed to be Julie and her female companion.

The problem with Boyer's performance in LILIOM is that it remains at the level of gesturality and mannerism. It forsakes depth, the seal of "authenticity" that would allow the film's depiction of the popular milieux of Paris to move closer to the currents of poetic realism. The matter is complicated by the inter-relationship between the various performance registers and the contributions of Lang and Rudolph Maté to the film's visual style. LILIOM feels divided between a conventionally dark realist representation of the city and a more moralistic and mystical sensibility, which combines moments of calculated theatrical abstraction. The difference between Madeleine Ozeray's interiority and Boyer's exteriority, for example, is evident in a key moment near the beginning of the film after the two have left the fairground and moved to a deserted park bench. By examining the sequence more closely, we can see how the émigré filmmakers' interest in the processes of visual narration counteracts, rather than complements, some aspects of Boyer's persona. A police raid has just interrupted Liliom and Julie and they are now alone standing in front of the bench under a lamppost. The police have warned Julie that Liliom is only after her money. The setting is an area of rough ground on the edge of the city. We can see the painted silhouettes of apartment blocks and factories in the background but the action takes place on a very shallow spatial plane, which allows Maté to distinctively manipulate the levels of light falling on their faces. At first, the camera maintains the same distance from the couple that it did when the police officers filled the frame. This effect of empty space reinforces the theatricality of the moment by creating a sense of a proscenium stage set. Throughout the sequence, the camera maintains it frontal position. A chance to mark space in a more fluid, cinematic way is avoided. Whilst Julie stands inertly and silently gazing at Liliom, Boyer turns around on his heels and walks toward her deliberately. He shrugs his shoulders dramatically and self-consciously turns to sit down. As Julie also sits down, Lang cuts closer, eliminating the foreground so that the couple fill the frame. The majority of their bodies are well lit in the chiaroscuro manner that is typical of Maté's cinematography; the edges of their features are juxtaposed sharply with the flattened black shadow behind them. Julie tells Liliom that if she had any money she would gladly give it to him. Startled by this, Liliom turns to her and the camera starts to track in. Whilst Ozeray is relatively quiet and her eyes move slowly and certainly, Boyer raises his arms and shakes his partner in disbelief. Suddenly, the lighting's pitch diminishes and the couple are now bathed in a more prominent shadow. We cut to a long shot of a man responsible for dousing the gaslights. Liliom points to the lamp next to him and asks if t is going to be extinguished. The man replies that it is only every other streetlight that is doused. This disruption of the narrative by the deliberate emphasis on the processes of the manipulation of light works in a twofold manner. Both circumvent the centrality of Boyer in the shot. Firstly, the foregrounding of light and darkness works in a textual fashion. Our attention is drawn to the shots' visual style rather than the characters and their words. Secondly, it prefigures the metaphysical motif which divides the film into two visual themes – that of the darkness of Paris and the light of the afterlife and heaven from which the earthly world can be reviewed and reassessed. As Liliom continues his seduction of Julie, the camera slowly tracks in to a remarkable full close-up of the couple's faces. There is more light on the face of Ozeray, as Boyer is remains in profile. Her eyes are turned towards the night sky as she declares that she doesn't have any fears, not even of death. The screen goes suddenly black, as a foreboding of what is to come. What could have been an intensely modulated exchange that rendered the ordinary city at night a place of poeticised desire – as in Marcel Carné's Hôtel du Nord, for example – becomes, instead, something more deliberate and abstract.

Journeys Across the Divided City

In Pièges and Liliom, the two main protagonists, Adrienne and Liliom, undertake significant journeys in relation to the city of Paris. Adrienne, by turning from a "taxi-girl" to police informer, is given a form of mobility which allows her to escape the world of the urban prostitute. Working undercover, she encounters a dark side to the surface of the Paris of luxury, wealth and glamour before finally joining that milieu when she ultimately marries the man hitherto suspected of the murders which she has been hired to investigate. Liliom, on the other hand, is denied his escape from the Parisian *faubourg* to the United States of his dreams. His death, however, takes him literally high above the city and into a fantastic other world where he is given a second chance to rediscover the values of mundane domesticity which he had previously ignored in favour of street crime and the dark world of the city's night life.

How do the two films stage these movements in relation to the issue of their status as émigré-related productions? And how does this shed light on certain prevalent mythologies of the city concerning gender and place?

The sensibility of Pièges is evident from the opening shots which, in the manner of numerous 1940s' Hollywood film noirs to come, present the city at night as an abstract site of dangerous motifs highlighted by a stylised conjugation of light and shadow. There are, at first, no discernible symbols or mentions of Paris to help orientate the audience. Instead, we begin with footsteps in the dark and a torch casting its beam on a discarded newspaper before shining its light on a nearby brick wall on which are illuminated the names of the film's cast. Following the credits, a Parisian newspaper headline fills the screen announcing the mysterious disappearance of a number of young girls. The newspaper is a key feature in the film. It has two aspects, which Siodmak used elsewhere in his French émigré productions. Firstly, it works as a cinematic emblem of the modern city: its speed and modernity in conveying urban information is matched by the nature of the film medium. Secondly, it is also, somehow, the voice of the city – the means by which the film suggests that the fabric of Paris is involved in the drama as an audience and as a commenting voice. In PIÈGES, a third dimension is introduced; the newspaper becomes the means by which the killer and other men lure young women to fulfill their desires.

Next, we see the shadow of a male figure passing in front of the doorways and walls of a darkened street. This is followed by a dramatically lit close-up of a gloved hand putting a letter addressed to the Paris police in a post box. The chain of the detective enquiry in the film is therefore established. The rest of the film will be concerned with the task of uncovering the identity of the stranger. At the police station, the film dissolves from a close-up of the letter's final line "You will leave for your last dance" to a flashing neon sign advertising "Taxi-girls. Dancing. La Danse. 2f". This form of urban display suggests more than the seedy marginality found in the "city of darkness". The notion of the "taxi-girl" is a curious extension of the film's themes since this euphemism for a prostitute can also be read as an evocation of the sense of journeying across the city which the film's narrative is mainly concerned with. The key to this journeying is the consistently uneven and dangerous power relationships between Adrienne and the men that she meets in the city. In the dance hall, for example, Adrienne's job is to sell a "ride" across the dance floor to an unknown male customer. In front of this dance space we see an extensive mural depicting the splendours of the Place de la Concorde. When Adrienne's real life journey across the city begins, the mural's suggestion of Parisian luxury, fashion and glamour actually comes to life as she meets Fleury and the other men. Her position in terms of power remains the same throughout, however. She is always being led by some male stranger around the sights of the French capital.

Adrienne makes two Paris car journeys in the film, which relate to the theme of division the film has established between the city of darkness and the city of light. In the first, Adrienne crosses the Seine over a bridge where she has just had her first mysterious encounter with Pears. Earlier she had met another stranger at a jazz club. The scene with Von Stroheim is shot as a Gothic melodrama, entirely at odds with the night-time modernity of the jazz venue. The lighting is low-key and Pears' intentions are vague as he makes an appointment with Adrienne for a rendezvous the following afternoon. The conclusion of their conversation is marked by a cut-away shot to the stranger at the jazz club waiting next to a car. After walking away from the bridge, Adrienne enters the frame of the shot of the waiting man. Her features emerge from the shadows. She accepts his offer to get into the vehicle and the shot fades out to black before swiftly fading into a two shot of the couple driving through the city. This dynamic of a pick-up on the street between a male and a female stranger, and the sense of motion through an unmarked urban environment at night, seems a strikingly modern anticipation of the iconography of the American film noir. Quite incidentally, this aspect of cultural translation is foretold by Adrienne's real occupation as a German, French and English translator, which serves rather nicely as an exact mirror of Siodmak's own professional career.[18] As other cars flash by, the occupants of the vehicle are momentarily illuminated, but the male's features remain barely visible. The frame of the windscreen, like that of the railway carriage in LA CRISE EST FINIE, is used as a secondary frame within the overall frame of the moving image. Adrienne tries to escape but she can't.

The scene cuts to another noir motif – the apartment staircase on which the troubled relationship between protagonists is underscored by disturbing sets of angles and the use of shadow. The journey to the top of the staircase takes even longer than the one in the car. This emphasises the way that the city of darkness, as fashioned by the contribution of the émigrés, can work as a signifying element in its own right, rather than as a simple backdrop to the processes of character interaction. In the first shot, for example, the pair enter the left hand frame at a diagonal. As they turn rightwards to climb the stairs, their enlarged shadows follow them on the wall in the background. As they pause, Adrienne turns around to look down at the man following her. Her face is completely blackened as she asks the stranger why he lied to her. "Don't play the innocent", he replies, "you were a taxi-dancer". As they continue up the stairs, the light begins to dim to create the effect that the characters are now an element in a highly choreographed interplay of shapes and abstract formal compositions. At another key instant, the shadow of one of the banisters falls across Adrienne's face as she speaks. This reproduces a sensation of division and disguise which the narrative has already established. The stranger then literally pulls her into the shadows when he tells he that he knows she is working for the police. It is only when Adrienne is pushed inside the apartment that we learn that the stranger is actually Inspector Batol who has been assigned as Adrienne's bodyguard. The effect of this sequence is multi-faceted. Firstly, it establishes the motif of disparity in relation to Adrienne's place in Paris. Her ability to read the desires of Parisian men that she learned while "picking up male passengers" at the dance hall is thwarted. Instead, she gets taken for a ride, both literally and metaphorically. Paris now becomes a site of vulnerability for her as she becomes the potential next victim of the killer. Secondly, the idea of hidden surfaces is also developed with the police and their agent working in disguise both against and with each other. Finally, in another aspect of the complex patterning of the narrative, just as Brémontière doubles Fleury, so Batol is set up here as competitor to Ténier.

Adrienne's mobility in the city is exemplified in the montage sequence involving "light Paris" that follows her decision to marry Fleury after it appears the murder case has been solved. The couple take a tour around the capital and go on a shopping spree in a convertible. Adrienne, to comic effect in the nightclub sequence, has always known the correct champagne to drink, and suddenly she is now able to purchase the city lifestyle she has always aspired to. What distinguishes the rapidly edited sequence of familiar Parisian tourist attractions and luxury establishments is the ironic ease with which Siodmak undermines the Chevalier persona. He is seen diegetically as a Parisian performer relaying his act as a seducer-dandy to the characters, whilst at the same time he breaks the boundaries of convention by involving the screen audience by winking at the end of the sequence. The lightness of the tone, the fluency of the montage, the witty interaction between image and score and the sense of space and movement all contrast with the darkness and menace of the previous intrigues. But it is this very ironic tone, along with a subtle commentary on the mechanics of visual display that marks the sequence's distinctiveness. It is as if Siodmak is also gently sending up the entire artifice of commonly held notions about Paris. The sequence is clearly dealing in surfaces. The imagery of the Arc de Triomphe, the Opéra and the rue de Rivoli flashing by, as well as the use of the chauffeur-driven convertible, all connote a touristic postcard image of the city. The dynamic inclusion of these differentiated aspects of the daylight city works in strong contrast to the way the city at night was excluded and rendered abstract in the film's previous noirish car journey. There is also a preponderance of mirrors in the *mise-en-scène* as well as obvious cinematic devices such as wipe cuts and various dissolves. In the fur salon, because of the large mirror on the wall in the background we see how the parade of models is linked to form a blur of reflection and reality. Each woman in this montage displays an item of clothing subsequently taken by Adrienne. At the same time, it is clear that these women have also been seduced by Fleury, thus establishing a chain of serial consumption that is simultaneously sexual and material.

Liliom's "journey" away from Paris begins with his suicide. The railway bridge and the *zone's* wasteland milieu, combined with the criminal act, make it similar to the opening scenes of Litvak's COEUR DE LILAS. Lang, however, is more interested in the spiritual, metaphysical bond between the dying man and his wife than the tragi-heroic fate of the poetic-realist male. He cuts immediately to a shot of Julie sewing at home. She clutches her chest in pain as if she is sympathetically feeling Liliom's suffering. From this moment on, the film's depiction of the city becomes more stylised with Maté's cinematography increasingly working against the currents of dark realism in favour of a more heightened display of technique. The contrasting worlds of Julie and Moscat, the two women in Liliom's life, are now marked with more exaggerated relief. At the fairground, for example, where Alfred goes to tell Moscat about what has happened, the shadows of the rotating poles of the merry-go-round on which Liliom used to work swirl disturbingly across the harshly lit features of the attraction's owner. As Elsaesser has noticed elsewhere, in relation to other French émigré films, space and light are used here to define time "as emotional intensity, as the passage from innocence to knowledge and regret" (1984, 282). Outside the worker's cottage where she lived with Liliom, Julie is framed in a pool of shadow. Her muteness and the stillness of her body work in direct contrast to the shrill banter and emotional arm waving of Florelle's Moscat. In a sense, these two women embody the two versions of the city that the film captures. In a not untypical association between femininity and Paris, Lang's film thus seems not only divided in terms of its metaphysics – between heaven and earth – but also in terms of its burdensome morality which contrasts the danger and pleasures of the fairground with the safety and order of the home. It is not surprising then, that it is at this point that popular Paris "dies", along with Liliom, whilst the spirituality and enduring values of Julie's domestic world endure.

The "death" of popular Paris in Lang's film is managed in a remarkable and heavily stylised sequence, which reveals the apparent umbilical relationship between Liliom and the city. As Julie holds Liliom's arm on the ground outside their home, the sounds of the fairground gradually fade into the soundtrack. We cut to a shot of a pensive Moscat who is approached screen right by the shadow of a police officer. The rotating shadows of Liliom's merry-go-round continue to flicker across her features. As she hears the news of Liliom's death, Moscat nearly collapses but she still manages to descend the stairs to tell the rest of the fair's members the news. The urban entertainment world, to which Liliom once belonged, comes to a halt in a succession of tableau shots. These images range from an abstract interest in decor and fairground machinery to a semi-documentary style depiction of the sorrow of the ordinary Parisian community. The shots almost suggest a formal division between the "Germanic" and "French" modes of filming the details of urban life.

We first see a carefully composed close-up of three of the merry-go-round's mechanical musical figures as they come to a halt. Lang then cuts to a complex shot depicting the slowing down of the merry-go-round's shadow on the walls of a nearby hotel. There is a couple in the upper right-hand corner watching

10. Liliom (Charles Boyer) leaves Paris in LILIOM (BFI)

and listening to the stop in the flow of music and energy. The shot of the re-
volving figures on the wall suggests a ghostly transference of the real bodies of
the local city dwellers onto the actual body surface of the city itself. Next we
see a man stop a fortune wheel's spin. Lang cuts to the somewhat abstract image of a gramophone horn before shifting to a shot of one of the fairground
workers announcing Liliom's death. A succession of images then re-enacts
Liliom's passing away through the depiction of various clockwork toy devices
that grind spontaneously to a silent standstill. The fairground seems to have a
life of its own. This sense of the uncanny sits uneasily with the following near
still-life shots of local faces caught in the process of private mourning. One
particular image, that of a group of figures in a local city bar, looks as if it has
been taken from a contemporary illustrated magazine rather than the
worked-over formal vision of a Fritz Lang drama.

This specific disjunction in the portrayal of Paris may account for the relative failure of the film at the box office. Lang and his fellow émigrés, as many
critics noted, simply got the tone wrong. The film was, in this sense, *too* heterogeneous. Jean Fayard, for example, suggested that "the old commonplaces of
populist cinema [were] badly situated".[19] Jean Laury, as noted earlier, argued
that LILIOM was in fact a German film that was "at once realist and mystical".[20]

The key to this conflation of the "realist" and the "mystical" rests in the way that LILIOM's narrative is divided between the city of Paris and "the city of God". The manner in which Lang blends the urban ordinary and the extraordinary in the scenes of Liliom's ascension to heaven recalls the director's use of the uncanny in his preceding film, DAS TESTAMENT DER DOCTOR MABUSE. There is, however, a significant difference here due to the important inclusion of the French capital as a site of meaning. MABUSE represented an unsettling of the general artefacts of urban modernity such as railway lines, gasworks, and chemical factories. LILIOM works, instead, with the specificities of a *Parisian* male *mauvais garçon* who is trapped in the film between an abstract form of moral redemption and the particularly French fatalism of the poetic realist hero.

This conjugation of the bizarre with the everyday is most apparent when the celestial white-faced messengers, dressed in black with white gloves, arrive to take the film's eponymous hero away. Their visit is accompanied by an unreal, mechanised humming sound. One of the figures raises a hand and in the next shot Liliom rises from the ground. As the camera pulls away, the back lighting fades so that by the time Liliom is upright, the background is completely dark. The messengers then lift Liliom up and are shown ascending with him, leaving the empty shell of Liliom's body behind. As the trio soars higher and higher, the diminishing figure of Liliom remains centre-frame until the image fades into a mottled blur. The point which he occupied in the frame is replaced by the outlines of a building. The camera begins to move across an aerial view of the city at night. Street lamps shine through the nocturnal gloom, though Paris below remains indistinct – there is no formal point of reference. Suddenly, we are high enough to be able to make out the familiar grid of the French capital with the River Seine and its islands. For a moment Paris returns to us but we are, by now, far away from the *quartier populaire*. This is the iconic city one would see as a visitor. This is the Paris, indeed, one would see on a journey – the city of someone who now, like Fritz Lang himself, was indeed on a journey to another destination.

6 Conclusion

The French film journalist Henri Calef, in a 1933 interview with the émigré director Kurt Bernhardt, observed that "the cinema is an excellent vehicle for the intensification of relations between two nations – it permits not only a richer mutual knowledge but also a greater mutual understanding".[1] Calef's utopian ideals were apparently akin to those of the future director of CARREFOUR who, in another meeting with the Parisian press, argued that the presence of foreign filmmakers in France "was the only means by which to achieve an international cinema".[2] This book has examined what happened to these aspirations in relation to a number of different émigré filmmakers' encounters with the French capital in the 1930s. Some, like Fritz Lang and Billy Wilder, stayed but briefly, their eyes firmly fixed on the next stage of their journey: the United States. Others stayed longer. Bernhardt himself turned down an offer by Hollywood's Columbia Studios in 1936, preferring to remain, for the time being, in Europe. Filmmakers like Robert Siodmak and Victor Trivas worked in France for the rest of the decade with varying degrees of professional and financial success. Whilst Siodmak eventually directed a number of features, Trivas made but one film and spent the rest of the 1930s fitfully engaged in various scriptwriting opportunities before narrowly evading arrest by moving to the South of France.

The arrival in Paris of various film personnel from the studios of Berlin must be seen within the context of a complex history of travel and exchange between France and Germany. This history was framed by a pattern of ambivalence which in turn informed the way that the two countries' respective film industries tilted between mutual rivalry and mutual concern as they both responded to the increasingly hegemonic position of the United States in the world film market. The city was an important location from which to understand this process; not least because of the significant fact that each country's capital had long been central to dominant definitions of national cinema in terms of production, exhibition and representation. As Siegfried Kracauer observed, contemporary cinema in the post-First World War period had a particular affinity for the contingent aspects of urban life. This was "strikingly demonstrated by its unwavering susceptibility to the 'street' – a term designed to cover not only the street, particularly the city street in the literal sense, but also its various extensions, such as railway stations, dance and assembly halls, bars, hotel lobbies [and] airports" (in Gleber 1999, 145). The urban-based films which had emanated from the Berlin studios in the 1920s were admired by the French for their technical sophistication and complex handling of visual style; but they were also seen, simultaneously, as harbingers of a particular response to modernity which French film culture seemed unwilling to make. The arrival of émigré filmmakers on French soil was therefore also viewed ambiguously. On the one hand, the travellers were welcomed for the degree of proficiency that they would bring to an under-resourced native industry; but on the other hand, they were regarded with suspicion – because they were perceived as a threat to an already precarious employment situation, and because of their potential to disrupt governing notions of what constituted French cultural identity.

The journeying foregrounded by the real experience of the filmmakers was paralleled by wider notions of transition that were illustrated in a number of their films. The recurring narrative thread of a journey to or across the capital suggested a sense of the city as a destination to be viewed as a bright spectacle. Other journeys of exploration to the city at night relayed a sense of social concern and investigative curiosity. In this sense, many émigré films made specific use of pre-existing Parisian mythologies dating back to nineteenth century practices of portraying the city. The films went on to extend this analogous relationship to pre-cinematic forms of urban representation by largely insisting on a seamless continuum of remembering and nostalgia in order to evoke a familiar and pleasurable sense of a past urban community. In fact, far from helping to create a completely new practice of international co-production – one which foregrounded the very cosmopolitan modernity their own identities signified – the émigrés, to a great extent, colluded with existing French modes of cultural representation. Instead of turning to the immediacies of modern city life, as might be expected, they largely helped to consolidate the previous discourses of light and darkness in Parisian live entertainment and contemporary literature and photography.

This phenomenon must be seen as part of the inevitable transformative process of cultural assimilation and adaptation that all immigrants undergo upon arriving in a new host culture. As Hamid Naficy notes, this process relates to the ways all kinds of émigrés "transcend and transform themselves to produce hybridised, syncretic, performed or virtual identities" (2001, 13). Having said this however, the émigré filmmakers described in this book clearly contravene the model of film practice Naficy uses to describe present-day exilic cinema. Naficy suggests that because exilic films are deterritorialised, they "are deeply concerned with territory and territoriality" (5). This is certainly true in the case of the German émigrés, but only in the reverse, rather melancholic, sense. The émigrés were, of course, deracinated, but their fleeting fascination with French film culture was truly bittersweet. To survive professionally, they had to portray a new homeland rather than engage with a direct screen memory of their previous domicile. Furthermore, they then had to depict this alien city in more or less nostalgic terms. The émigrés were thus excluded twice over: first, because they would never truly belong to present-day Paris, and second, because the urban world they were working so hard at to represent was one that they had never known or could ever imagine belonging to in the first place.

To a certain extent then, the distinguishing features of the film émigrés' settlement within the host culture of Paris remain hard to place. This is also partly because the émigrés were already part of a functioning European trade network, and partly because, upon their arrival, many of the filmmakers were subjected to the fitful and often precarious commercial nature of the French film industry in the 1930s. Having said this however, many of the émigrés *did* noticeably mediate traditional Parisian representational tropes with an incoming awareness of the expressive possibilities of film form. In some cases, this meant new attention paid to the processes of cinematic narration; in other instances, it meant a sophisticated and revelatory handling of light. In his interview with *Paris Midi*, Kurt Bernhardt suggested that one of the major faults of the German cinema had been to place too much visible attention on technique. "A good film", he declared, "should make the audience forget the presence of the camera".[3] Previous scholarship on the émigrés in Paris has largely concurred with this assessment, arguing that the French films of the German émigrés suffered from an over-determined sense of form in which objects and visual effect may have mattered more than actorly performance.

It is certainly true that one way of understanding the specificity of many of the émigrés' Paris productions is to see them as hybrid or multiple on the basis of their singular contribution to visual style. Unlike other figures in the broader history of 1930s German emigration, the émigrés did not need to rely so heavily on the professional significance of the written word. Indeed, as mostly newcomers to France and to French cinema, they were naturally inclined to favour visual language over an indigenous interest in the cultural specificities of written dialogue. Naficy has even argued that an aesthetic of self-referentiality may be an indicative trait of exilic filmmaking (2001, 271). But in some cases, the émigrés' heightened attention to the processes of visual storytelling specifically served the needs of cultural adaptation. This was especially true in the case of the dark city film which privileged a sense of visual uncovering and looking, and a particularly concentrated and intense awareness of the interplay between light and shadow in relation to the urban decor. Here it was largely thanks to their specific technical prowess that the émigrés were allowed to fit in while simultaneously remaining different. By being adept at both meeting and contravening expectations of what a "French film" about Paris should look like, they sidelined Bernhardt's broader aspirations of becoming a truly international counter-ballast to American hegemony, and instead contributed more directly to the specific viability of the French film industry.

Thanks to sustained investment and their training in the Berlin studios, cinematographers like Kurt Courant and Eugen Schüfftan attained a level of tech-

nical expertise that was unrivalled in all of Europe. They were able to experiment effectively with faster film stocks and new lighting technology. The
results of this sophisticated expertise was revealed not only in the films they
made, but also in their beneficial role as educators to native French professionals. The importance of the attention the émigrés paid to the expressive visual
possibilities of the medium therefore clearly went beyond the hollow mechanics of any formalistic argument. Their contribution rests on the fact that their
presence often went to the heart of an ongoing debate over the direction that a
competitive French cinema should take regarding the relative significance of
the image and the spoken word in relation to the new sound technologies.
They made lasting contributions to the development of what Anatole Litvak
termed "real cinema" especially in the field of lighting and cinematography.
This type of filmmaking went on to achieve numerous critical and commercial
successes towards the end of the decade, especially in the genre of poetic realism. It remains an interesting irony that French efforts to create a meaningful
and internationally successful cinema were so explicitly aided by their leading
industrial rivals.

This technical and expressive awareness had also been shaped during the
Berlin studios' heyday when a predilection for a more unsettling and modern-day style of cinematic urban darkness resulted in a number of successfully
exported films in the 1920s and early 1930s. A further irony can be found in the
fact that it was partly the very success of these earlier films that lent weight to
the outbreak of xenophobic French voices protesting the arrival of the
post-1933 wave of émigrés. By conflating German Jewishness with urban disorder and "morbidity", the French right-wing turned what might have been
merely an economic argument into a critical and political dispute over the direction of how one should understand the city. A study of the work of the German émigrés in Paris therefore raises fascinating historical questions about
both the nature of European film culture and the wider terrain of national political life. Paris may have been a natural destination for fellow European filmmakers to take advantage of a pre-existing web of contacts, but it was also, for
many, a place of refuge for those with vulnerable ethnic identities.

Most of the journeys made to the French capital after 1933 were made for
political reasons by Jewish personnel. Their arrival thus helped to raise important questions about assimilation and cultural difference. These issues went
beyond the immediacies of the French film industry. France's right-wing generally portrayed Jews as symbolising the perils of mass industrialisation and
modernity. They served as the locus for resentments concerning the heterogeneous nature of urban culture which were fed, in turn, into the general fears of
instability engendered by economic recession. Thus, the relationship between
the émigrés and Parisian representation matters in more ways than one. The ti-

tle of this book may foreground the era's recuperative and essentially nostalgic cultural conventions surrounding Parisian representation, but it also has a set of other, more immediately relevant, historical resonances.

The arrival of so many émigré filmmakers on French soil in the 1930s clearly forces us to revise our untroubled assumptions about what constituted a French national cinema of that particular period. The French capital was a site of wide-ranging cultural, social and political significance for both the migrant and the native. Finally, if a sense of divided perception remains in the way the spaces of the city were variously portrayed, perhaps this can be only expected. As refugees on a journey from an oppressive political regime and faced with a far from embracing welcome from a fractured French film industry, many of the émigré filmmakers were literally divided within themselves.

Notes

Notes to Chapter One

1   For further discussion of this important analogy see, amongst others, Wolfgang Natter (1994) "The City as Cinematic Space: Modernism and Place" in Aitken and Zonn (eds.) (1994); Guiliana Bruno (1993) *Streetwalking on a Hidden Map*; and Anne Friedburg (1994) *Window Shopping*.

2   See, for example, Jacques Belmans (1977) *La Ville dans le cinéma de Fritz Lang à Alain Resnais*; Catherine Boulègne et al (eds.) (1987) *Cités-Cinés*; Hillairet, Prosper et al (eds.) (1985) *Paris vu par le cinéma de l'avant garde 1923-1983*; François Niney, (ed.) (1994) *Visions Urbaines* and Michael Sheringham (ed.) (1996) *Parisian Fields*.

3   Many émigré films, of course, were not even set in Paris and thus fall out with the immediate concerns of this book. These titles include, for example, most of the body of work that Max Ophüls produced whilst in the French capital – ON A VOLÉ UN HOMME (1933); LA TENDRE ENNEMIE (1936); YOSHIWARA (1937); LE ROMAN DE WERTHER and SANS LENDEMAIN (1940). Similarly I have not discussed the French émigré projects of G.W. Pabst such as MADEMOISELLE DOCTEUR (1936) and LE DRAME DE SHANGHAI (1938).

4   Books which discuss the Hollywood work of the German émigrés include: John Baxter (1976) *The Hollywood Exiles*; Anthony Heilbut (1997) *Exiled in Paradise*; Graham Petrie (1985) *Hollywood Destinies. European Directors in America, 1922-1931*; Gene D. Phillips (1998) *Exiles in Hollywood: Major European Film Directors in America*; and John Russell Taylor (1983) *Strangers in Paradise: The Hollywood Emigrés 1933-1950*.

Notes to Chapter Two

1   Pierre Mac Orlan (1882-1970) was a novelist, screenwriter (*L'Inhumaine* [Marcel L'Herbier, 1924]), poet and journalist whose written work was widely circulated in the periodicals and literary texts of the period. Two of his novels (both Prix Goncourt winners) were adapted for the screen: LA BANDERA by Julien Duvivier in 1935 and QUAI DES BRUMES by Marcel Carné in 1937. The latter relied on émigré cinematographer Eugen Schüfftan for many of its atmospheric effects. Mac Orlan had a keen interest in Parisian visual culture. For Rifkin (1995), his way of seeing the urban decor in his writings on photography "resembles the metonymizing viewpoint of the detective, from the startling initiatives of Poe and Gaboriau to the popular currency of Mac Orlan's own time – the atmosphere-swilling figure of Inspector Maigret" (99). Grosz illustrated Mac Orlan's stories *Port d'Eaux-Mortes* (1926).

2   *Cinématographie Française* 19 January 1929, p. 12.

3   As Abel (1988, 12) points out, Bernard's film, like so many others of the time, di-
      vided Parisian critics along political fault lines. For Paul Reboux (in Abel, 94), the
      film didn't go far enough in condemning the "monstrous absurdities" of war. It
      only served "to confirm world opinion as it currently exists on the subject of
      France: an isolated country (...) imposing harsh economic measures and regula-
      tions on its neighbours". On the other hand, for the right-wing journalist Lucien
      Rebatet (in Abel, 95), the film demonstrated "the vitality of the masculine virtues
      of our race".

4   See also Georg Simmel's earlier influential comments on the inter-relationship be-
      tween nervous stimulation and the regulation and exchange of money in contem-
      porary city life in his 1903 essay "The Metropolis and Mental Life" (in Frisby and
      Featherstone (eds.) 1997, 174-185).

5   There is now a significant body of literature drawing upon the correlations be-
      tween urban Weimar society and the cinema culture of the period. See, in particu-
      lar, Sabine Hake (1993) *The Cinema's Third Machine*; Patrice Petro (1989) *Joyless
      Streets*; Bruce Murray (1990) *Film and the German Left in the Weimar Republic*; and the
      various articles collected in *New German Critique* 40 (Winter 1987). The following is
      a selection of the vast number of texts which treat the Weimar republic more
      broadly: Keith Bullivant (1977) *Culture and Society in the Weimar Republic*; Peter Gay
      (1974) *Weimar Culture: The Outsider as Insider*; John Willet (1978) *The New Sobriety:
      Art and Politics in the Weimar Period*; and Edward Dimendberg et al. (eds.) (1994)
      The Weimar Republic Sourcebook. For a cultural study of Berlin see Haxthausen and
      Heidrun (eds.) (1991) *Berlin: Culture and Metropolis*.

6   The *Straßenfilm*, according to Elsaesser (in Vincendeau [ed.] 1995), was a "German
      film genre (...) describing a particular German urban melodrama made between
      1923 and 1930, in which a middle class (generally male) protagonist strays onto
      'the street' seeking relief from the *ennui* and the moral confinement of bourgeois
      existence, while a lower class (generally female) protagonist tries to escape the un-
      derworld milieu. Typically, the protagonists are chastised or destroyed by the ex-
      perience of the city's darker or licentious side (personified in the figure of the
      prostitute). While testifying to the iniquities of modern urban life (...) [they]
      tended to end up deterministically reaffirming existing class divisions and the pri-
      macy of middle class values" (409). See also Anton Kaes (1996) "Sites of Desire:
      The Weimar Street Film" in Neumann (ed.) (1996).

7   The *Kammerspielfilm*, again according to Elsaesser (in Vincendeau [ed.] 1995), was
      "a German genre designating films produced during the early 1920's which drew
      on the conventions of contemporary German theatre. The scriptwriter Carl Mayer
      created the genre's narrative model in his screenplays for *Scherben / Shattered*
      (1921), *Hintertreppe* (1921), *Sylvester – Tragödie einer Nacht* (1923) and *Der letze Mann
      / The Last Laugh* (1924). Characteristically, the plot is a realist drama portraying ser-
      vants or members of the lower middle class who meet with a tragic end through
      murder or suicide. Most *Kammerspiele* films were set indoors and drew on innova-
      tive cinematic techniques (...) exemplified in (...) minimal use of titles and expres-
      sive camera movements" (235).

8   Other important work on the inter-relationship between femininity, modernity
      and the city includes: Andreas Huyssen (1986) "Mass Culture as Woman. Modern-
      ism's Other" in Modleski (1986); Janet Woolf (1990) *Feminine Sentences: Essays on*

Women and Culture; Elizabeth Wilson (1991) *The Sphinx in the City: Urban Life and the Control and Disorder of Women*; Anne Friedburg (1992) *Window Shopping* and Elizabeth Wilson (1992) "The Invisible Flaneur", *New Left Review* no. 191 (January/February 1992).

9   For a further discussion of this relationship between mass entertainment, modernity and "Americanisation" see Peter Wollen (1991) "Cinema / Americanism / the Robot" in Naremore and Brantlinger (1991).

10   For Benjamin on Paris and Berlin, see in particular: "On Some Motifs in Baudelaire" in *Illuminations* (1992) and "A Berlin Chronicle" in *One-Way Street* (1997).

11   Paul Morand (1888-1976) was a novelist who also specialized in travel and short story writing. He prospered as an international diplomat under the patronage of the cultural annex of the French Foreign Ministry which was established in the immediate post-World War One period. His novel *L'Europe galante* (1925) surveyed the corrupt nature of European high society whilst the impressionistic stories published in *Ouvert la nuit* centred on a series of short-lived entanglements between the narrator and a succession of foreigners. Morand tried his hand at scriptwriting for the equally international Paramount outlet in France but only his script based on the afore-mentioned short-story collection was accepted and made into a film. He became increasingly outspoken against the influx of foreigners entering France after 1933, and after his duties as Vichy ambassador to Rumania and Switzerland during World War Two, his reputation became permanently compromised.

12   Tobis-Klangfilm came into being on 13 August 1929 as the result of an accord between the two most significant German sound patent holders: Tonbild-Syndicat A.G. (Tobis) who held the Tri-Ergon patent and Klangfilm G.m.b.H. The bulk of the finance for the Klangfilm organisation came from the German electrical concerns Siemens and A.G.E. See Icart (1974) "L'Avenement du film parlant" in *Les Cahiers de la cinémathèque* no. 13-15.

13   *Cinématographie Française* 23 February 1929, p. 11.

14   See Kristin Thompson (1999) "The Rise and Fall of Film Europe" in Higson and Maltby (1999) (eds.).

15   Feyder was also one of a number of French directors and performers employed by Hollywood in the early sound period to make French language version films actually in the United States. These included M.G.M.'s popular successes *Le Spectre vert* (Jacques Feyder, 1929) with André Luguet and *Big House* (Paul Féjos, 1930) with Charles Boyer.

16   Film production figures from *Cinématographie Française* 4th January 1930. Film export figures from *Cinématographie Française* 2 May 1931, p. 15. It should be noted, however, that the relative weakness of the French export position to Germany was not solely the fault of the French film industry. Throughout the early sound era, French film exports were placed in a disadvantageous position vis-à-vis the Germans because of a strictly enforced system of export license payments. French exporters continued, despite vigourous negotiations between the two countries, to pay between 200, 000 and 300, 000 French francs per film to the German authorities (source: *Cinématographie Française* 2 May 1931. p. 15). C.F. Tavano wrote in the same issue of Cinématographie Française that "reciprocation between France and Germany has only been a *trompe l'oeil*, almost a bluff. The colonisation of our screens (...) is a danger as serious as that of a war" (11). From the point of view of

the Germans, however, they were put in this invidious position by the significant downturn in receipts and the collapse of many small businesses and corporations following the onslaught of the Depression.

17 German and American representatives met in Paris in June 1930 to agree on terms upon which to divide up the world market according to their mutual interests. France was the most significant European market left to the forces of open competition. The "Paris Agreement" was never formally ratified and despite the efforts of a second conference held in 1932, it was not until 1935 that the matter was formally resolved. See Crisp (1993), 99.

18 *Cinématographie Française* 23 February 1929, p. 14.

19 *Cinématographie Française* 23 March 1929, p. 35.

20 The actor, playwright and film director Sacha Guitry was still making the same point in his 1932 article "Pour le théâtre et contre le cinéma". In it he declared that he did not like current French films "because they [were] not deservedly French. When they make a film in France, they do everything to make it international. (...) If the French cinema is to exist one day, it must stand clear of the American formulas; it must absolutely be itself" (in Abel 1988, 101).

21 *Cinématographie Française* 22 June 1929, p. 22.

22 The film, based on material developed by G.W. Pabst and starring Louise Brooks, was eventually released directed by Augusto Genina.

23 This an interesting reversal of the Franco-German reception of *Das Cabinett des Dr Caligari* (Robert Wiene, 1920) when the film was first lauded by the French before subsequent success in Germany. See Kristin Thompson (1990) "Dr Caligari at the Folies-Bergère, or, The Success of an Early Avant-Garde Film" in Budd (1990).

24 *Cinématographie Française* 30 August 1930, p. 36. For further commentary on this crucial question of the specific potential of early 1930s' French-language sound cinema, see also Abel (1988) *French Film Theory and Criticism 1907-1939: A History/Anthology 1907-1939 Vol. II*; Ginette Vincendeau (1990) "In the name of the father: Marcel Pagnol's 'trilogy' *Marius* (1931), *Fanny* (1932), *César* (1936)" in Hayward and Vincendeau (eds.) (1990), and Christopher Faulkner (1994a) "René Clair, Marcel Pagnol and the Social Dimension of Speech", *Screen* vol. 35 no. 2 (Summer 1994).

25 The first actual German-French sound production had been *La Nuit est à nous/Die Nacht gehört uns* (1929) which was directed respectively by Henry Roussell and Carl Froelich in Berlin for U.F.A. Marie Bell, Henry Roussell and Jean Murat starred in the French-language version, whilst Hans Albers and Charlotte Ander starred in the German version. The sound for the film was recorded on both disc and film.

26 *Cinématographie Française* 14 March 1930, p. 7. Carl Froelich in Berlin for U.F.A. Marie Bell, Henry Roussell and Jean Murat starred in the French-language version, whilst Hans Albers and Charlotte Ander starred in the German version. The sound for the film was recorded on both disc and film.

27 *Cinématographie Française* 8 February 1930, p. 15.

28 *Pour Vous* 31 July 1930, p. 14.

29 *Cinématographie Française* 4 July 1931.

30 *Le Courier cinématographique* no. 18 (4 May 1929), (in Courtade 1978, 65).

31 Raoul Ploquin (1900-unknown) worked as a journalist and publicist in Paris before he was engaged by Films Albatros in 1924. He wrote a number of film scripts

in the early 1930s and was then employed as a production supervisor for A.C.E. in Berlin on films such as L'ETRANGE MONSIEUR VICTOR (Jean Grémillon, 1938) and ADRIENNE LECOUVREUR (Marcel L'Herbier, 1938). Between 1940 and 1942 he was the director of the Comité de l'organisation de l'industrie cinématographique (C.O.I.C.) which managed French film production during the Occupation of France. In 1943, he founded his own production company, Les Films Raoul Ploquin, which went on to make Robert Bresson's LES DAMES DU BOIS DE BOULOGNE (1945). "I make two sorts of films," he said. "First those of which I'm certain, that's to say films with Brigitte Bardot for which I select subjects which allow her to be seen in an appropriate light. Then, films which shouldn't be made, but which it would be a shame not to make; those also which, thanks to the tact and talent of the director, incorporate some degree of experimentation" (in Crisp, 282-83).

32 *Cinématographie Française* 30 November 1929, p. 14.
33 *Pour Vous* 26th July 1932, p. 11.
34 *Le Radical* 11 February 1932.
35 *L'Intransigeant* 24 April 1932.
36 *Pour Vous* 15 January, 1931, p.3.
37 in *Cinématographie Française*, 13 September 1930, p. 24.
38 Ibid.
39 *Pour Vous* 23 October 1930, p.6.
40 *Le Radical* 11 February 1932.
41 The story of the Russians in France is told, in much greater detail, in the following: François Albera (1995) *Albatros: Des Russes à Paris 1919-1929*; Lenny Borger (1989) "From Moscow to Montreuil: the Russian Émigrés in Paris 1920-1929" in *Griffithiana* no. 35-36 (October 1989), and Kristin Thompson (1989) "The Ermolieff Group in Paris: Exile, Impressionism, Internationalism" in *Griffithiana* no. 35-36 (October 1989).
42 *Cinématographie Française* 8 February 1930, p. 16.
43 in *Cinématographie Française* 17 October 1931, p. 11.
44 *Cinématographie Française* 31 October 1931, p. 15.
45 *Cinématographie Française* 19 December 1931, p. 115.
46 *Cinématographie Française* 10 October 1931, p. 11. The following year, in an article in the *Cinématographie Française* (25 June 1932, p. 47), Lucie Derain suggested that "films shot with more than 20 per cent foreign personnel (...) shouldn't be called 'French' but 'Franco-German', 'Franco-Russian', 'Franco-American' etc.".
47 *France-Soir* 17 December 1974.
48 *Pour Vous* 22 June 1933, p. 11.
49 *Le Jour se lève* had been previously photographed by Kurt Courant, Litvak's cinematographer on *Coeur de lilas* and *Cette Vieille canaille*. (Interestingly, the title of the remade film, *The Long Night* (1947), puts the emphasis on darkness rather than light). Litvak also directed his own American remake of *L'Équipage*, *The Woman I Love*, in 1937.
50 *Cinémonde* 31 December 1931.
51 *Cinématographie Française* 30 November 1929, p. 14.
52 For an interesting reversal of the commonly perceived distinctions between Clair and Pagnol in relation to the depiction of social reality see Faulkner (1994a). Ac-

cording to Faulkner's argument, it was Pagnol's manipulation of the expressive potential of the French language that accorded his sound films a greater degree of authenticity. Unlike Clair who constructed "an ideal, universal, and trans-historical spectator", Pagnol assumed a spectator who had "a local, particular and material existence" (164).

53 *Cinématographie Française* 25 November 1933, p. 39.
54 Francis Carco (1886-1958), was the writer of many books about "dark Paris" which included such emblematic titles as *La Lumière noire, La Rue*, and *L'Ombre*. He had sung in *café-concerts* as "Le Petit Mayol" and by the 1930s, particularly because of the novel, *Jésus la caille*, he was a celebrated literary figure. Carco featured in Parisian magazine photo-spreads and even cropped up in the film PRISONS DE FEMMES (Roger Richebé, 1938) as himself. He wrote the sub-titles for the French release of DEAD END (William Wyler, 1937) known as *Rue sans issue*. As Andrew (1995, 158) points out, the film that he scripted such as PARIS-BÉGUIN (Augusto Genina, 1931) and PARIS LA NUIT both involved "wealthy women seduced by swarthy criminals or lured to the climate of the criminal *quartiers*" (158). In his obituary published in *Aurore* (27th May 1958) it was claimed "nobody knew like him the appeal of pavements wet with rain, the mist of mornings in Montmartre and the equivocal atmosphere of cafés populated with girls and ruffians."
55 *Cinémonde* 11 December 1930.
56 *Cinémonde* 31 December 1931.
57 *Cinématographie Française* 3 June 1933, p. 15.
58 *Cinématographie Française* 24 January 1931, p. 24.
59 *Le Temps* 14 January 1939.
60 Ibid. The critic Georges Altman makes the same point in his review of Courant's subsequent work on *Le Jour se lève* which he calls a "pure *film noir*" (in Abel 1988, 266).
61 In *Cinématographie Française* 16 January 1932, p. 22.
62 The words of P.A. Harlé in *Cinématographie Française* 11 March 1933, p. 7.
63 *Cinémonde* 6 April 1933.
64 Ibid.
65 *Cinématographie Française* 1 April 1933, p. 10.
66 *La Guerre des valses* (Ludwig Berger, 1933) and *Tout pour l'amour* (Joe May, 1933).
67 *Cinématographie Française* 22 July 1933, p. 20.
68 Lucien Rebatet (1903-1972) wrote under the pseudonym of François Vinneuil. He was the film critic for *Action Française* between 1932 and 1939. From 1938 and during the Occupation he was an editor and film reviewer at *Je suis partout*. Rebatet was openly fascist in his sentiments – his essays in *Les Tribus du cinéma et du théâtre* (1941) are shockingly pernicious. He was found guilty of treason after the Liberation and sentenced to ten years imprisonment.
69 The breakdown of this figure is as follows: artists (425); liberal professions (424); intellectuals (904); businessmen (1,189); employees (980); labourers (117); general (1,085) and unemployed (1,830).
70 Several of these personnel, as already mentioned, were not of German origin but arrived, instead, from Berlin after working in the studios there. Litvak, Trivas, Granowsky and Ozep were Russian and Richard Pottier (né Ernst Deutsch) was Hungarian, for example. Some of these names never left France. Granowsky and

Wiene died before the end of the decade and Pottier was successful in obtaining full French citizenship.

71   Among the figures who stayed there at this time were Rudolph Joseph (G.W. Pabst's assistant); Billy Wilder, Hanns G. Lustig; Peter Lorre; Friedrich Hollaender and Franz Waxman. See Kevin Macdonald (1996) *Emeric Pressburger. The Life and Death of a* Screenwriter, 103.

72   On 9 January 1934 Alexandre Stavisky, a petty Parisian criminal with high society connections, was found dead – either a suicide or a murder – by the police. Stavisky, a Jew, had been suspected of financial fraud by selling bonds which later proved to be worthless. His case revealed a murky series of jurisdicially and politically corrupt entanglements. Stavisky's trial had been postponed 19 times by the Paris procurator, the brother-in-law of the Prime Minister Camille Chautemps and Chautemps' Minister for the Colonies, Albert Dalimier, had advocated the bonds. The resulting lack of accountability lead to street protests which culminated in the eventual resignation of the leading political protagonists.

73   Eugène Dabit (1898-1936) also edited E.E. Noth's émigré novel *L'Enfant écartelé* for the journal *Europe* and participated in the activities of the Associations des écrivains révolutionnaires. He was an important spokesman for the League Against Anti-Semitism. *Hôtel du nord* had won the first French Prix populiste for a literary work of populist fiction. Dabit produced other works of fiction, memoirs, and criticism before his premature death while visiting the U.S.S.R. with André Gide.

74   *Pour Vous* 26 January 1933, p. 3.

75   *Pour Vous* 18 May 1933, p. 2.

76   *Cinémonde* 25 May 1933.

77   *La Cinématographie française* 30 June 1933, p. 45.

78   This debate was not restricted to the film industry. An argument also raged about how truly French those Germans were who had been naturalised as French citizens. In a culturally symbolic moment in 1935, the newly elected Miss France, a naturalised German named Mlle. Pitz, was forced to resign and was replaced by the more appropriate Mlle. Giselle Préville. A newspaper declared that this time "Miss France will be French!" in Weber (1995) 92 .

79   Pathé's subsidiary was Literaria, Gaumont's was Deutsche Gaumont-Gesellschaft and Eclair's was Deutsche Eclair Film.

80   See Hardt (1996) *From Caligari to California: Erich Pommer's Life in the International Film War* s, 87-93 for more on the intricacies of the so-called Parafumet agreements.

81   It was later suggested by Ophüls in his memoirs that it would have been better if he and Lang had reversed their assignments. "Had we exchanged the films, Lang most likely would have made an extraordinary mystery and I a very good romantic comedy" he said (in Hardt 1996, 142).

82   *Pour Vous* 31 August 1933, p. 14.

83   Ibid.

84   The film, *Music in the Air* was to be Pommer's first Hollywood feature after leaving France. It was produced almost entirely by fellow émigrés with Joe May as director, Billy Wilder as co-scriptwriter and Franz Waxman as musical director.

85   *Cinématographie Française* 28 October 1933, p. 30.

86   *Action Française* 28 April 1934.

87   In 1934, Goebbels ordered the integration of the company into the Tobis trust un-
     der the name of Rota-Film AG.
88   *Paris-Midi* 21 May 1933.
89   Siodmak in *Cinémonde* 8 June 1933.
90   *Je Suis Partout* 2 September 1933.
91   See *Cinématographie Française* 30 June 1934.

Notes to Chapter Three

1   *Cinémonde* 8 June 1933.
2   For a further example of this mythologising, listen to Josephine Baker's famous
     song *J'ai deux amours*.
3   The actual premiere of the operetta was 31 October 1866 at the Palais Royal.
4   This association between light and spectacle was literally embodied in the alterna-
     tive project considered to mark the 1889 Exposition – Jules Bourdais's Tour Soleil.
     The Tour Soleil was planned to be equipped with enough arc-lighting to illumi-
     nate the entire capital. Other international public events designed to link Paris
     with light included the 1881 Paris Electricity Exhibition and the Palace of Electric-
     ity exhibit at the 1900 Exposition Universelle. Paris was, in fact, the centre of many
     of the 19th-century's technological light-related innovations including incandes-
     cent street lighting in 1886. See Wolfgang Schivelbusch (1988) *Disenchanted Night:
     The Industrialisation of Light in the Nineteenth Century.*
5   Jacques Offenbach was born the son of Jewish parents in Cologne in 1819. He came
     to Paris in 1833 to train at the Conservatoire.
6   "We are coming / Arriving / From all the countries of the world / By land or even
     by sea / Italians / Brazilians / Dutch / Spanish / Gypsies / Egyptians / Peruvi-
     ans / We are coming / Arriving! / The steam leads us / We are going to invade /
     The sovereign city / The place of pleasure / We rush, gather pace / To get to know
     Paris / To get to know drunkenness / And your days and your nights. / All de-
     lighted foreigners / Are rapidly moving to Paris! / We are going to sing / We are
     going to shout / We are going to dine / We are going to love / Oh my God, we're
     all going / To be crazy and have fun".
7   See Wolfgang Schivelbusch (1986), *The Railway Journey: Trains and Travel in the
     Nineteenth Century* on how the development of the railway removed "spatially in-
     dividual or autonomous" (197) localities and produced a new inter-relationship
     between the consumer commodity and the subject's sense of place.
8   "No town is as romantic as Paris / Montmartre and Montparnasse are paradise".
9   "The young live there on love and fresh water and one says to oneself / You only
     see that in Paris".
10   "Every day 100,000 taxis go around making noise / In the evening 100,000 lights
     make you forget the night / And 100,000 pretty girls have sweet dreams / You
     only see that in Paris".
11   "The hoodlums are polite, their gestures are exact / After having taken every-
     thing, they say thank you / No town is as romantic as Paris / Montmartre and

Montparnasse are paradise / One says it to oneself seeing all these chants and shouts / You only see that in Paris".

12 See M. Boyer (1994) *The City of Collective Memory* for a further discussion on the shifting relationship between urban space and theatrical space. Taking as her starting point that "the Greek word 'theatron'" means literally "place for seeing" (74) she argues that "both the theater and urban space are places of representation, assemblage and exchange between actors and spectators, between the drama and the stage set" (74).

13 Ginette Vincendeau (1985a) develops this point by claiming that "the histories of theatre (and music hall) and cinema [are] (...) intimately linked in France in the 1930s, on the level of production, finance, and personnel" (113). She argues that cinema and live entertainment, by co-existing through an inter-textual relationship, shared genres, extra-textual practices such as printed publicity and song recordings, modes of performance and even audience loyalties. Vincendeau sees "the privileging of the actor's performance [in so many French films of the 1930s] as the crucial link with the audience" (137). She goes on to claim that, very often, "performance in these films is not what the actor does in addition to his or her function in the plot, but it *is* that very function" (141). Dudley Andrew (1995a) also notes that "within most of the hundreds of films built around or including formalised songs, dances, recitations, and the like, simple reverse shots display an original audience whose admiration or disapproval of the performance serves as a model for our own reaction. (...) It could be said with only slight exaggeration that the French cinema of the 1930s (...) is a cinema of reaction" (97).

14 Caradec and Weill (1980) mention that the "Paris Guide", produced by Lacroix for as far back as the *Exposition* of 1867, signalled to visitors that the *Café de Géant*, *l'Eldorado*, and *l'Alcazar* were worthy of exploration (7). By the time of the 1900 *Exposition*, according to the *Guide des plaisirs* specially produced for the occasion, Paris was "a city of extraordinary pleasures, the pleasure capital of the whole world" (145).

15 Bach and Milton, two of the most popular comic male entertainers in the 1930s' film industry, both came from *café-concert* backgrounds.

16 Mainly the 9th and 10th *arrondisements* or what Maurice Chevalier called "the quadrilateral of song" to describe the world of theatres, agents, publishers, and *costumiers* based in this area. See Jando (1979) *Histoire mondiale du music-hall* (25).

17 Sung by the *chanteuse réaliste* Lys Gauty in the famous recorded version.

18 Images of street children playing and visual accounts of the urban working classes integrating leisure and national pride can also be found in the myriad of photo-journalistic publications of the era.

19 See also Kelley Conway (2001) "Diva in the Spotlight: Music Hall to Cinema" in Alex Hughes and James S. Williams (eds.) (2001). In this interesting article she explores gender issues in relation to the performances of a number of music hall divas in four French films of the 1930s.

20 Date of first publication: 1880.

21 This attitude was the norm for wealthy male visitors in Paris at the time. Take, for example, this prescient quote (in terms of the narrative of LA VIE PARISIENNE) taken from an article written by Léon Gozlan in 1852 on "What It Is That Makes a Parisienne" in Goulemot and Oster (1989) *La Vie Parisienne. Anthologie des Moeurs*

du XIX siècle. According to the opinion of foreigners "she is a composite of spirit, grace and sensibility; an inexhaustible source of seduction, the resounding justification for the superiority of France above other nations; the woman one dreams of at sixteen and the one, one remembers at sixty" (249).

22   Liane de Pougy actually starred in the Offenbach Revue at the Moulin Rouge in 1904.

23   There is a very similar sequence, two years later, in LE CRIME DE M. LANGE (Jean Renoir, 1936).

24   Kracauer (1937) has even gone so far as to suggest that "the operetta would never have been born had the society of the time not itself been operetta-like; had it not been living in a dream world, obstinately refusing to wake up and face reality. Only in Paris were there present all the elements, material and verbal, that made the operetta possible" (174).

25   Charles Lecocq, in an article in 7 Jours, March 1905, also made the point that the cost of putting on "true" operetta had become almost prohibitive.

26   Soir, 19 August 1925.

27   9 November 1925.

28   Ami du peuple, 5 January 1930.

29   See Roger Icart (1974, 169-175) for further discussion of the early German sound musicals.

30   Shot in a contemporaneous German-language version called MAMSELL NITOUCHE by Carl Lamac. The original operetta with librettos by Meilhac and Millaud and music by Hervé was a huge national success in the early years of the Third Republic.

31   This "magical" shift in space and time across the city might be a distinctive feature of the émigré portrayal of the capital. In LA CRISE EST FINIE, after a shot of Marcel pointing off stage, Marcel and Nicole suddenly find themselves gazing into a shop window. Barry Salt (1992, 217) argues that jump-cuts were frequently used by Ophüls in the mid-1930s.

32   Excelsior, 18 May 1934.

33   Date unknown.

34   Perhaps the idea of having the theatre in the film represented as one of a number of venues which have fallen into disuse is a slightly disingenuous one. It might make sense in terms of the film's "impossible" project of reconciling live performance and the cinema, but as Vincendeau (1985a) argues "statistically, after an initial drop between 1926 and 1933, Parisian music halls, concert halls, theatres, and other live entertainments maintained a fairly constant level of box-office receipts" (119).

35   MAUVAISE GRAINE was remade in England by Gainsborough as FIRST OFFENCE (Mason, 1936).

36   Waxman also shares a music credit on LA CRISE EST FINIE.

37   Source and date unknown. This is rather ironic because one of the proudest boasts of the tie-thief Jean-la Cravatte (Raymond Galle) is that one of his ties was stolen from Marcel Pagnol. The actor Maupi, who plays another gang member, was also a regular in Pagnol's troupe.

Notes to Chapter Four

1 See, for example, the following illustrated articles published in *Pour Vous*: "Le Drame de la foule et son decor" (23 November 1933), "Vues de Paris" (11 November 1937), "Paris Romanesque populiste" (9 November 1938) and "Paris, Studio de cinéma" (6 September 1939).

2 *Paris Midi* 16 November 1933.

3 Ibid.

4 *Cinéopse* March 1934.

5 Andréjew also worked with the other émigré directors discussed in this chapter: with Anatole Litvak in CETTE VIEILLE CANAILLE (1933) and MAYERLING (1935); Kurt Bernhardt in L'OR DANS LA RUE (1934); and LE VAGABOND BIEN-AIMÉ/THE BELOVED VAGABOND (1936). He travelled between France and Britain throughout the 1930s. For further information on Andréjew, see my chapter "A Cosmopolitan Film Culture: Exile and Emigration in Classical French Cinema" in Temple and Witt (eds.) *The French Cinema Book* (London: British Film Institute, 2004). For an informative discussion of Eisler's subsequent work in the United States, see Claudia Gorbman (1991) "Hanns Eisler in Hollywood", *Screen*, vol. 32 no. 3 (Autumn 1991).

6 See Abel (1988), 34.

7 For further discussion of literary adaptations in the French cinema of the 1930s, see Andrew (1990) "The Impact of the Novel on French Cinema of the 1930s", *L'Esprit Créateur* vol. XXX no. 2 (Summer 1990).

8 The "Zille film" was a more politically self-conscious off-shoot of the German *Straßenfilme* which took its name from the work of the influential Berlin city artist Heinrich Zille. As Bruce Murray (1990) observes in his analysis of DIE VERRUFENEN (Gerhard Lamprecht, 1925), while "the street films warned middle class and lower middle class spectators about the possibility of downward social mobility and advised them to avoid social interaction with the lower classes, the Zille films offered hope to those who began to question the myth of upward social mobility" (84). See Petro (1989, 90-94) for more on the inter-relationship between the development of German photojournalism and late-silent cinema.

9 *La Cinématographie française* 8 April 1933.

10 See Vincendeau (1998) *Pépé le moko*, 31.

11 Known in France as SUR LE PAVÉ DE BERLIN.

12 *Pour Vous* 14 January 1932.

13 *L'Intransigeant* 20 February 1932.

14 Dédé seems to be a popular name for a male street criminal. The name appears in numerous other dark city films of the period. See, for example: PARIS BÉGUIN (Alberto Genina, 1931), PRISONS DE FEMMES (Roger Richebé, 1938) and FAUBOURG MONTMARTRE (Raymond Bernard, 1931).

15 Related to this point of documenting Paris, one should also note the work of Marcel Poëte who was instrumental in setting up the Écoles des Hautes Études Urbaines in 1919. See Norma Evenson *Paris: A Century of Change* (1979), 266.

16 For an interesting discussion of the 1930s' feature films of Pierre Chenal, see Andrew (1995a) *Mists of Regret*, 160-66.

17 *Pour Vous* 9 June 1932.

18 *Cinémonde* no. 277 (8 February 1934), previously cited by Andrew (1995a, 371). This translation is mine.

19 *Petit Bleu* 4 February 1934.

20 *Candide* 8 February 1934.

21 *Gringoire* 2 March 1934.

22 *Pour Vous* 15 September 1932, p. 9.

23 According to Jack Edmund Nolan (1967) and Kelley Conway (1995, 166), the film is set in the Porte des Lilas district of Paris. The area was celebrated in popular Parisian culture for the profusion of flowering lilacs in small local gardens.

24 The term *apache* relates to a bourgeois conception of proletarian Paris as a savage wilderness both in terms of the quality of its living conditions and the perceived correlation between the working class and criminality. It goes back to the nineteenth century, and might well have been formulated in connection with the popularity of the American "wilderness" novels of James Fennimore Cooper. By the early years of the twentieth century, *apaches* increasingly became the focus of sensational press coverage. They had "dens" in areas like the Bastille and even became, bizarrely enough, the focus of tourist interest. According to a book quoted by Joachim Schlör (1998, 138), one could actually go on a "Paris By Night" tour and drink a glass of wine with a local character. For other details on the figure of the *apache* see also Vincendeau (1998, 39-41).

25 *L'Intransigeant* 20 February 1932.

26 *L'Avenir* 12 February 1932.

27 *Gringoire* 11 March 1932.

28 *Ciné-Miroir Almanach* (1933). The quotation should also be placed in the context of the career of Luguet who had worked previously in Hollywood on French-language version and English-language version films. COEUR DE LILAS makes use of its star's linguistic talents in a scene, set in the police station, when he is able to serve as interpreter on behalf of a detained American sailor.

29 *Cinémonde* 24 September 1931.

30 See Adrian Rifkin (1993) *Street Noises* (120-27) and David H. Walker (1991) "Cultivating the *Faits Divers: Détective*" *Nottingham French Studies* vol. 32 no. 1 (Spring 1993), for more on *Détective*'s seminal coverage of "notable crimes and trials ... features on clandestine immigrants, international drug trafficking, the white slave trade, the criminally insane, *les bagnards*, *la pègre*, *les irregulières*, *les moeurs des quartiers réservés*, and so on" (Walker, 75).

31 In his memoirs (1989, 105), René Lucot argues the opposite and actually suggests that the atmospheric world of the street outside the Pathé studios at rue Francoeur blended neatly with the set inside. He claims that the street in the film is modelled on nearby rue Cyrano-de-Bergerac in Montmartre.

32 *Le Courrier* 26 September 1931.

33 *Dès qu'on a vu se barrer l'soleil / Tous les jours, c'est pareil / Sans hâte, on descend sur le trottoir / Pour chercher les coins noir / Fuyant le regard du flic / On a des espoirs de fric.*
As soon as you see the sun setting / Everyday it's the same / You go down to the pavement unhurriedly / In search of darkened corners / Keeping out of the copper's sight / You hope to make a bit of cash.
(The song is performed again in Litvak's subsequent French émigré film, CETTE VIEILLE CANAILLE, in a scene set in a women's prison).

34 *Cinéopse* March 1934, p. 225.

35 See Lotte Eisner (1973) *The Haunted Screen* (119-127) for a discussion on the German cinema of the 1920s and its use of stairways and corridors.

36 See also Kelley Conway (1995). Other appearances by Fréhel in "dark" Paris films of the 1930s include LA RUE SANS NOM (Pierre Chenal, 1933), LE PURITAIN (Jeff Musso, 1937), LA RUE SANS JOIE (André Hugon, 1938) and L'ENTRAÎNEUSE (Albert Valentin, 1938).

37 Chenoune (1993) explains how the fashions for the Parisian *apache* during the inter-war period were fundamentally a revolt against bourgeois taste. Every sartorial detail was heightened so that "stripes were wider than normal ... ties more colourful, shoulders more pronounced, waists more tailored, hips more marked [and] trouser bottoms floppier". The felt hat, of the kind worn by Martousse, often had a wide ribbon whose colour changed according to the season. All these details "far from operating as camouflage, ultimately functioned like warrior dress" (196).

38 *Cinémagazine* January 1933.

39 *Pour Vous* 21 April 1932, p. 4.

40 The figure of the Parisian industrialist who encounters a world of criminal intrigue was a common trope in French "dark city" film dramas. Other examples include Novian who is murdered in COEUR DE LILAS and the sober, unwitting husband in PRISONS DE FEMMES (Roger Richébé, 1937) who discovers the secret past criminal milieu of his wife.

41 See, for example, *Pour Vous* 26 November 1936, p. 6.

42 *Le Matin* 29 October 1938.

43 *Cinémonde* 29June 1933.

44 Another example of how the space of the nightclub could be both French and international is shown in different scenes in L'ENTRAÎNEUSE. At the beginning of the film, Fréhel is the house *chanteuse* at *La Dame de Coeur* whilst later on in the narrative the club is pulsating with hot jazz music. There is also a black barbershop quintet that plays at *Chez Jenny* in JENNY.

45 *Cinémonde* 29 June 1933.

46 Les Halles, because of its historical proximity to many of the city's leisure and prostitution *quartiers*, was also a meeting point of the city's various social classes.

47 *Cinémonde* 27 October 1938.

Notes to Chapter Five

1 *Gringoire* 21 December 1940.

2 *Action Française*, 28 April 1934.

3 PIÈGES was re-made in the United States by another German émigré, Douglas Sirk, as LURED (1947).

4 *Le Figaro* 29 April 1934.

5 Lang later had his own temporary lodgings at 11, rue Labie.

6 It is somewhat appropriate, therefore, that the Fox Europa offices were in the *New York Herald Tribune* building.

7   Undated documents concerning the French stage production of LILIOM from the
     Bibliothèque de l'Arsenal, Paris.
8   *Pour Vous*, 31 August 1933.
9   *Paris-Midi* 20 January 1934.
10   9 December 1933.
11   Billy Wilder was working as a taxi-dancer in Berlin in the 1920s at the time he met
     Robert Siodmak.
12   *Le Jour*, 18 January 1939.
13   For more on Boyer's early sound career in Hollywood see Phillips (2002)
     "Changing Bodies/Changing Voices: Success and Failure in Hollywood in the
     Early Sound Era" *Screen* vol. 43 no. 2 (Summer 2002).
14   The French-language version of this film was actually shot in Joinville, France.
15   February 1932.
16   *Pour Vous*, 7 June 1939. The continuing "loyalty" of Chevalier to his home country
     needed some promotion however. For the French-language version of INNOCENTS
     OF PARIS (Richard Wallace, 1929), LA CHANSON DE PARIS (Richard Wallace, 1929),
     for example, Paramount added a special prologue by Chevalier to reassure the
     French public that he was still a *gars de faubourg* (lad of the *faubourg*). See Rearick
     (1997, 120).
17   *Mon Film*, May 1937.
18   For further speculation on this trajectory between Berlin, Paris, and Hollywood,
     especially in relation to the vexing question of the determinants of film noir, see
     Vincendeau (1992b) "Noir is also a French Word: The French Antecedents of Film
     Noir" in Cameron (1992); Andrew (1996) "Film Noir: Death and Double Cross
     Over the Atlantic", *Iris* no. 21 (Spring 1996); Janice Morgan (1996) "Scarlet Streets:
     Noir Realism from Berlin to Paris to Hollywood", *Iris* no. 21 (Spring 1996), and
     Elsaesser (1996a) "A German Ancestry to Film Noir? – Film History and its Imagi-
     nary", *Iris* no. 21 (Spring 1996).
19   *Candide* 10 March 1934.
20   *Le Figaro* 29 April 1934.

Notes to Chapter Six

1   *Paris Midi* 19 June 1933.
2   *Cinémonde* 29 June 1933.
3   *Paris Midi* 19 June 1933.

Appendices

Appendix One: Tobis in Paris Filmography 1929-1939

(glv: German-language version; flv: French-language version)

1929   Le Requin (Henri Chomette)

1930   Sous les toits de Paris (René Clair)

1931   Allô Berlin, ici Paris (Julien Duvivier)
À Nous la liberté (René Clair)
Le Million (René Clair)

1932   La Femme en homme (Augusto Genina)
Quartorze juillet (René Clair)

1933   L'Ange gardien (Jean Choux)
Du haut en bas (Georg-Wilhelm Pabst)
Primerose (René Guissart)
Toi que j'adore (Geza von Balvary and Albert Valentin);
   glv Ich Kenn' Dich nicht und liebe Dich (Geza von Balvary)

1934   La Banque Nemo (Marguerite Viel)
Pension Mimosas (Jacques Feyder)

1935   La Kermesse héroïque (Jacques Feyder);
   glv Die klugen Frauen (Jacques Feyder)
Stradivarius (Geza von Balvary and Albert Valentin),
   glv Stradivari (Geza von Balvary)

1937   Les Gens du voyage (Jacques Feyder);
   glv Fahrendes Volk (Jacques Feyder)
Le Tigre du Bengale (Richard Eichberg); glv Der Tiger von
Eschnapur (Richard Eichberg)

1938   Le Joueur (Gerhard Lamprecht and Louis Daquin);
   glv Der Spieler or Roman eines Spielers (Gerhard Lamprecht)

Appendix Two: Osso Filmography 1930-1939

1930   ARTHUR (Léonce Perret)
MÉPHISTO (Henri Debain)
MYSTÈRE DE LA CHAMBRE JAUNE (Marcel l'Herbier)
PARFUM DE LA DAME EN NOIR (Marcel l'Herbier)

1931   L'AIGLON (Victor Tourjansky);
glv DER HERZOG VON REICHSTAG (Victor Tourjansky)
LE CHANT DU MARIN (Carmine Gallone)
CIRCULEZ! (Jean de Limur)
LE COSTAUD DES P.T.T. (Jean Bertin, Rudolph Maté)
LA FEMME DE MES RÊVES (Jean Bertin);
glv EINE NACHT IM GRANDHOTEL (Max Neufeld)
JE SERAI SEULE APRÈS MINUIT (Jacques de Baroncelli)
MA COUSINE DE VARSOVIE (Carmine Gallone);
glv MEINE COUSINE AUS WARSCHAU (Carl Boese)
PARIS-BÉGUIN (Augusto Genina)
UN SOIR AU FRONT (Alexandre Ryder)
UN SOIR DE RAFLE (Carmine Gallone)
TOUT S'ARRANGE (Henri Diamant-Berger)

1932   LE DERNIER CHOC (Jacques de Baroncelli)
FAUT-IL LES MARIER? (Carl Lamac);
glv DIE GRAUSAME FREUNDIN (Carl Lamac)
UN FILS D'AMERIQUE (Carmine Gallone)
L'HOMME QUI NE SAIT PAS DIRE SON NOM (Heinz Hilpert);
glv ICH WILL DICH LIEBE LEHREN (Heinz Hilpert)*
UNE JEUNE FILLE ET UN MILLION (Max Neufeld and Fred Ellis);
glv SEHNSUCHT 202 (Max Neufeld)
MARIE, LÉGENDE HONGROISE (Paul Féjos);
glv MARIE (Paul Féjos)**
LE ROI DES PALACES (Carmine Gallone)***
ROULETABILLE AVIATEUR (Istvan Szekely)****

1937   L'AMOUR VEILLE (Henri Roussel)

*   French version never released in France because the German actress wanted to play both versions and her French accent was too lamentable
**   Also shot in Hungarian, Rumanian and English versions
***   Also shot in English version
****   Also shot in Hungarian version

Appendix Three: Anatole Litvak Filmography 1930-1936

1930   DOLLY MACHT KARRIERE

1931
Berlin   CALAIS DOUVRES; glv NIE WIEDER LIEBE

Paris   COEUR DE LILAS

1932
Vienna   CHANSON D'UNE NUIT; glv DAS LIED EINER NACHT*

1933
Paris   CETTE VIEILLE CANAILLE

1935   L'EQUIPAGE **

1936   MAYERLING

---

*   Also shot in English-language version. The film was remade in the United States as BE MINE TONIGHT (Anatole Litvak).
**   Remake of L'EQUIPAGE (Maurice Tourneur, 1927). The film was remade in the United States as THE WOMAN I LOVE (Anatole Litvak).

Appendix Four: Kurt Courant Filmography 1929-1939

1929
Berlin DAS BRENNENDE HERZ (Ludwig Berger)
DIE FRAU IM MOND (Fritz Lang)

1930
Paris LE ROI DE PARIS (Leo Mittler); glv DER KÖNIG VON PARIS
(Leo Mittler)

Berlin L'HOMME QUI ASSASSINA (Kurt Bernhardt and Jean Tarride);
glv DER MANN, DER DEN MORD BEGING (Kurt Bernhardt)
DIE SINGENDE STADT (Carmine Gallone)
DER WEISSE TEUFAL (Alexandre Volkoff)
DER HAMPELMANN (E.W. Emo)

1931
Paris SON ALTESSE D'AMOUR (Erich Schmidt and Robert Péguy);
glv IHRE MAJESTÄT DIE LIEBE (Joe May, 1930) (Berlin)
LE CHANTEUR INCONNU (Victor Tourjansky) (decor Serge Pimenoff)
COEUR DE LILAS (Anatole Litvak) (decor Serge Pimenoff)

Berlin MA COUSINE DE VARSOVIE (Carmine Gallone);
glv MEINE COUSINE AUS WARSCHAU (Carl Boese)
WER NIMMT DIE LIEBE ERNST? (Erich Engel)

1932
Berlin L'HOMME QUI NE SAIT PAS DIRE NON (Heinz Hilpert); glv ICH WILL
DICH LIEBE IEHREN (Heinz Hilpert) (French version unreleased)
SCAMPOLO EIN KIND DER STRASSE (Hans Steinhoff)*
GITTA ENTDECKT IHR HERZ (Carl Froelich)
DIE—ODER KEINE (Carl Froelich)
RASPUTIN (DER DÄMON DER FRAUEN) (Adolf Trotz)

Budapest
UN FILS D'AMÉRIQUE (Carmine Gallone) (decor Serge Pimenoff)

1933
Paris CES MESSIEURS DE LA SANTÉ (Pierre Colombier)
(flv of SCAMPOLO EIN KIND DER STRASSE)

CETTE VIEILLE CANAILLE (Anatole Litvak) (decor Serge Pimenoff)
CIBOULETTE (Claude Autant Lara)
UN PEU D'AMOUR (Hans Steinhoff)
LE VOLEUR (Maurice Tourneur)

Britain   THE PERFECT UNDERSTANDING (Gardner)

1934
Paris   AMOK (Fédor Ozep)

Britain   THE MAN WHO KNEW TOO MUCH (Alfred Hitchcock)
THE IRON DUKE (Victor Saville)

1935
Britain   THE PASSING OF THE THIRD FLOOR (Bernard Viertel)

1936
Britain   BROKEN BLOSSOMS (Septan)
SPY OF NAPOLEON (Knowles)
THE MAN IN THE MIRROR (Maurice Elvey)

1937
Paris   LE MENSONGE DE NINA PETROVNA (Victor Tourjansky)
(decor Serge Pimenoff)
LE PURITAIN (Jeff Musso, 1937)

1938   LA BÊTE HUMAINE (Jean Renoir)
LE DRAME DE SHANGHAI (G.W. Pabst)
LUMIÈRES DE PARIS (Richard Pottier)
LA MAISON DE MALTAIS (Pierre Chenal)
TARAKANOWA (Fédor Ozep)

1939   LE JOUR SE LÈVE (Marcel Carné)
LOUISE (Abel Gance)
MONSIEUR BRETONNEAU (Alexandre Esway)

*   Also shot in Austrian German-language film version.

Appendix Five:
Erich Pommer French-Language Filmography 1930-1934

1930

Berlin   LE CHEMIN DU PARADIS (Wilhelm Thiele); glv DIE DREI VON DER
            TANKSTELLE (Wilhelm Thiele)
            FLAGRANT DÉLIT (Hanns Schwartz); glv EINBRECHER

1931   AUTOUR D'UNE ENQUÊTE (Robert Siodmak);
                glv VORENTERSUCHUNG (Robert Siodmak)
            LE CONGRÈS S'AMUSE (Eric Charell);
                glv DER KONGRESS TANZT (Eric Charell)
            LA FILLE ET LE GARÇON (Wilhelm Thiele);
                glv ZWEI HERZEN UND EIN SCHLAG (Wilhelm Thiele)
            TUMULTES (Robert Siodmak); glv STÜRME DER LEIDENSCHAFT

1932   À MOI LE JOUR, À TOI LA NUIT (Ludwig Berger and Claude
                Heymann); glv ICH BIN TAG UND DU BEI NACHT (Ludwig Berger)
            I.F.I. NE RÉPOND PAS (Karl Hartl);
                glv F.P.I. ANTWORTET NICHT (Karl Hartl)
            MOI ET L'IMPÉRATRICE (Friedrich Hollaender);
                glv ICH UND DIE KAISERIN (Friedrich Hollaender)
            QUICK (Robert Siodmak); glv QUICK (Robert Siodmak)
            UN RÊVE BLOND (Paul Martin);
                glv EIN BLONDER TRAUM (Paul Martin)
            LE VAINQUEUR (Hans Hinrich); glv DER SIEGER (Hans Hinrich)

1933

Paris   ON A VOLÉ UN HOMME (Max Ophüls)

1934   LILIOM (Fritz Lang)

Appendix Six:
Robert Siodmak French-Language Filmography 1931-1939

1931 AUTOUR D'UNE ENQUÊTE; glv VORUNTERSUCHUNG

1932 TUMULTES; glv STÜRME DER LEIDENSCHAFT
QUICK; glv QUICK, KÖNIG DER CLOWNS

1933 LE SEXE FAIBLE

1934 LA CRISE EST FINIE
LE ROI DES CHAMPS-ELYSÉES (uncredited)

1935 LA VIE PARISIENNE

1936 LE GRAND REFRAIN
MISTER FLOW
LE CHEMIN DE RIO

1937 MOLLENARD

1938 ULTIMATUM
LES FRÈRES CORSES (uncredited)

1939 PIÈGES

Appendix Seven: Nero Films Filmography 1930-1939

1930   LES SALTIMBANQUES (Jacquelux and Robert Land)

1931   LA TRAGÉDIE DE LA MINE (G.W. Pabst)

1932   L'ATLANTIDE (G.W. Pabst)

1933   LE SEXE FAIBLE (Robert Siodmak)
            LE TESTAMENT DU DR. MABUSE (Fritz Lang)

1934   LA CRISE EST FINIE (Robert Siodmak)
            LE ROI DES CHAMPS-ELYSÉES (Max Nosseck and Robert Siodmak)

1935   LA VIE PARISIENNE (Robert Siodmak)

1936   MAYERLING (Anatole Litvak)
            LE CHEMIN DE RIO (Robert Siodmak)

1938   LE ROMAN DE WERTHER (Max Ophuls)
            TAKARANOWA (Fédor Ozep)

1939   LES OTAGES (Raymond Bernard)

Appendix Eight: La Crise est finie

Nero Films, 1934
Distributed by S.A.F. Paramount
74 mins.

Director	Robert Siodmak
Producer	Seymour Nebenzahl
Script	Jacques Constant (after the novel by Frédéric Kohner and Kurt Siodmak)
Cinematography	Eugen Schüfftan
Decor	Renoux
Music	Jean Lenoir and Franz Waxman
Costume	Elkins and Mme. Laget
Sound	Wilmarth
Cast	Danielle Darrieux (Nicole)
	Albert Préjean (Marcel)
	Suzanne Dehelly (Mme. Olga)
	René Lestelly (René)
	Jeanne Loury (Mme. Bernouillin)
	Marcel Carpentier (Emile Bernouillin)
	Milly Mathis (la concièrge)
	Pitoutot (Hercule)
	Paul Velsa (le machiniste)
	Paul Escoffier (le manager)
	The girls: Donell, Barcella, Belly, De Silva, Sherry, Ossipova, Trinkel, Wendler

Plot synopsis

A troupe of theatrical performers, led by Parisian old hands, Olga and Marcel, decide to seek their fortunes in the capital following the collapse of their show in the provinces. They arrive to find no work available. Down on their luck, the troupe make their shelter in a disued theatre. Nicole, a young novice, and Marcel try to trick M. Bernouillon, a lecherous piano seller, into lending them a piano to put on a show. Eventually Olga uses her savings to purchase the piano but meanwhile Bernouillon buys up the theatre with the aim of turning it into a cinema. Desperate measures are called for to ensure that the first night can live up to its promise and the crisis is really over. The troupe traps Bernouillon under the theatre's stage and enlists the city's working classes to be their make-shift audience. The film ends with the performance of the show "La Crise est finie".

Review

"After Le Chemin du paradis, le Congrès s'amuse, Symphonie inachevie, le 42e rue, it was difficult to avoid repetition, to invent a new tone for a musical comedy. Siodmak has succeeded with ease. Three rousing and heady songs promise success and are intimately linked to the action. All of this is managed with a fast pace and a clownish sense of fantasy which mixes strong jokes and a slightly crazy sense of humour".

Pour Vous (date unknown)

Appendix Nine: LA VIE PARISIENNE

Nero Films, 1935
95 mins.

Director	Robert Siodmak
Producer	Seymour Nebenzahl
Script	Emmerich Pressburger, Marcel Carré, Bruno Vigny (based on operetta by Meilhac and Halévy)
Cinematography	Armand Thirard, Jean Ismard
Decor	Jacques Colombier
Music	Jacques Offenbach (adaptation and original music: Maurice Jaubert)
Costume	Jean Patou, Marcel Roches, Elkins
Choreography	Ernst Mattray
Cast	Max Dearly (Don Ramiro de Mendoza)
	Conchita Montenegro (Helenita)
	Georges Rigaud (Jacques Mendea)
	Marcelle Praince (Liane d'Ysigny)
	Germaine Aussey (Simone)
	Jean Périer, Roger Dann, Jacques Henley, Jane Lamy, Austin Trevor, Claude Roussel, Enrico Glori

Plot synopsis

Paris 1900. At the "La Vie Parisienne" revue Don Ramiro makes his farewells to Paris and to his mistress Liane. Paris 1935. Don Ramiro returns to the capital with his innocent grand-daughter Helenita and installs himself at the "Hôtel-Mondial". The current management of the "La Vie Parisienne" hopes that Don Ramiro will help sort out their financial affairs. Jacques, an impecunious aristocrat, makes himself known to the couple. Much to the disapproval of Helenita's actual father, who also arrives in the city, Jacques and Helenita fall in love. Don Ramiro, by chance, meets Liane again at the theatre. The two set about hatching a plan to thwart the father's resistance to the romance, which ultimately involves the ordinary people of Paris. In the end, all is resolved: Jacques and Helenita stay together and Don Ramiro decides never to leave Paris again.

Review

"You could certainly shoot LA VIE PARISIENNE in the way that Offenbach, Meilhac and Halévy are famous for by trying to recreate the atmosphere of 1867 which was Paris's merriest and finest year. But, in the film of LA VIE PARISIENNE, wasn't it a more interesting idea to compare the former LA VIE PARISIENNE with the current one, to use the brio, the spirit, and situations of the operetta but transpose them into a modern setting? ... What makes the film especially unlike any old drama is the fact that it freely adapts a previous success by exploiting the title. Maurice Jaubert has taken up the famous manner of the operetta to accompany, underline and comment on the action with exactly the same mocking verve as that of Offenbach".

Le Figaro, 19 August 1935

Appendix Ten: MAUVAISE GRAINE

Compagnie Nouvelle Cinématographique, 1933
Distributed by C.N.C.
80 mins.

Director	Billy Wilder and Alexandre Esway
Producer	M. Corniglion-Molinier
Script	Alexander Esway and H.G. Lustig
Cinematography	Paul Coteret, Maurice Delattre
Production Design	Jacqueline Gys
Music	Walter Gray and Franz Waxman
Cast	Danielle Darrieux (Jeannette)
	Pierre Mingand (Pasquier)
	Raymond Galle (Jean)
	Jean Wall ("The Zebra")
	Michel Duran ("The Chief")
	Paul Escoffier (Dr. Pasquier)
	Maupi (Man in Panama hat)

Plot synopsis

Pasquier, the spoilt son of a prominent *haute-bourgeois* doctor, is forced by his father to relinquish his cherished automobile. He later sees a car of the same model on the street and decides to steal it. However, he is observed by a gang of car thieves who had their eyes on the vehicle as well. A spectacular chase ensues through the city streets. After the chase, the thieves decide to offer Pasquier a job and he begins working for them. Pasquier befriends Jean, one of the younger members of the gang, and eventually falls in love with Jean's sister, Jeannette. When Pasquier criticises the behaviour of the gang's boss, he and Jeannette are sent on a mission to Marseilles. They make it, despite the fact that their car that has been tampered with, and they decide to flee by setting sail overseas. Meanwhile, the gang's headquarters is raided and Jean dies in a shootout.

Reviews

"René Clair has already struck a youthful note in his stories of smart and resourceful types which suits the tag of 'made in France' ... With MAUVAISE GRAINE, which will next be shown at the Paramount Theatre, the public will be exposed to a style of direction which represents a true renewal, a reaction against the 'Pagnolisation' of cinema".

Source unknown

"With the combination of the charming music of Alan Gray and Franz Wachsmann, which we have already tasted in EMIL ET LES DÉTECTIVES, a completely innovative use of sound, which promises us passionately created rhythms, and the work of these young actors and technicians we'll see new kinds of images unfurl in a sharp and vivacious style".

La Comédia, 8 October 1934

Appendix Eleven: COEUR DE LILAS

Fifra Film, 1931
Distributed by United Artists
Date of First Screening: 3 March 1932 (Paris)
90 mins.

Director	Anatole Litvak
Assistant Directors	Dimitri Dragomir and H. Blanchon
Producer	Dorothy Farnum and Maurice Barber
Script	Dorothy Farnum, Anatole Litvak and Serge Veber, based on a play by Charles-Henry Hirsch and Tristan Bernard
Cinematography	Kurt Courant
Assistant Camera	Louis Née
Decor	Serge Pimenoff
Music	Maurice Yvain
Sound	Loirel
Cast	Marcelle Romée (Coeur de lilas)
	André Luguet (André Lucot)
	Jean Gabin (Martousse)
	Madelaine Guitty (Mme. Charignoul)
	Carlotta Conti (Mme. Novion)
	Marcel Delaître (Darny)
	Georges Paulais (le juge d'instruction)
	Fréhel (la Douleur)
	Lydie Villars (La Crevette)
	Fordyce (Mme. Darny)
	Paul Amiot (Merlu)
	Fernandel (le garçon d'honneur)
	Pierre Labry (Charignoul)
	Georges Pally, René Maupré, Edouard Rousseau

Plot synopsis

Novion, a Parisian industrialist, is found murdered in "*la zone*". Darny, one of his employees is arrested but Inspector André Lucot doesn't share the opinion of the examining judge and decides to do his own personal investigation. A glove belonging to Coeur de lilas, a well-known girl at the *bals musettes*, is found near the corpse. Using the identity of an unemployed mechanic, Lucot rents a room at the local Charignoul lodgings in order to meet her. He fights over Lilas with Martousse, a local *apache* and former lover of the girl. Martousse is arrested in the course of a police raid. Lucot takes Lilas to a hotel on the banks of the Marne. Martousse escapes from prison, finds them and tells Lilas that her new lover is a police officer interested in arresting her. Struck sideways by the revelation she makes off but eventually turns herself in to be charged with the offence.

Review

"It is at once a detective story, a sentimental comedy, and a picturesque portrait of the criminal underworld with heroes and heroines which will please both the adolescent and the rather more mature bourgeois. Honest people will be able to almost smell the romance of the slums as well as the odour of crimes they have not committed and risks they have not run because of family obligations and educational goals. It is also a slice-of-life story by Charles-Henry Hirsch, which is further seasoned with some underground irony by Tristan Bernard, as a Cornellian tragedy, a debate between passion and duty in the soul of a police officer ... All of this is pictorially facilitated with great ease. There is a wealth of just and piquant images integrated with fertile invention and a precise sense of cinema by the director Anatole Litvak. ... Jean Gabin, the *apache*, has created an admirable character. It would be impossible to come up with a personality who carried more truth and conviction. The felt hat balanced on the head in the best style, the fixed cigarette butt, the fold of the scarf, the shrug of the shoulders, the clean-shaven face, the forelock, the slow accent, the voice with a delayed sense of cocky cheek, the loose abandon of the body leaning on the counter of the bar; a certain sympathy but, at the same time, a sense of squalour, all lead to the idea that we have formed of the criminal type which converges in this flawless silhouette. I have met many rogues in the course of my life but none of them could have taught Jean Gabin a thing."

Alexandre Arnoux in *L'Intransigeant*, 20 February 1932)

Appendix Twelve: DANS LES RUES

Société Internationale Cinématographique, 1933
Filmed at Studios Films Sonores Tobis Paris, Epinay-sur-Seine
90 mins.
Date of First Screening: 26 July 1933 (Paris)

Director	Victor Trivas
Producer	Pierre O'Connell
Script	Victor Trivas, Alexandre Arnoux, Henri Duvernois
	after a novel by Joseph-Henry Rosny aîné
Cinematography	Rudolph Maté
Assistant Camera	Louis Née
Decor	Andrej Andréjew
Music	Hanns Eisler
Sound	Hermann Storr, Georges Leblond
Cast	Wladimir Sokoloff (père Schlamp)
	Madeleine Ozeray (Rosalie)
	Marcelle-Jean Worms (Mme Lérande)
	Jean-Pierre Aumont (Jacques)
	Lucien Paris (Maurice)
	Paulette Dubost (Pauline)
	Charlotte Dauvia (Jeanne)
	Germaine Michel (concièrge)
	Patachou (Moustique)
	Humbert (Cigare)
	Roger Legris (Moutarde)
	Emile Rosen (Gobiche)
	François Llénas (Main Droite)
	René Prat (Main Gauche)
	Pierre Lugan (Rosengart)
	Rose Mai (child)
	Jean Marais (child)

Plot synopsis

Maurice and Jacques, two sons of a war widow, live in the tenements of a Paris *quartier*. Maurice, a worker, is resigned to his lot but his younger brother, Jacques, is dissatisfied with the terms of his life. Jacques is involved with a band of petty criminals who regularly fall foul of the law. The object of his affections is Rosalie – the daughter of Father Schlamp, a second-hand goods dealer. The gang steals a car and pass a day in the country. Cigare, a rival gang leader, is snubbed by Rosalie. A party at Father Schlamp's storeroom is raided by Cigare's gang and a heated scuffle ensues. Jacques decides to burgle the property of a wealthy local widow. He enters the property by seducing the maid at a *bal*. Startled by the intruders, the widow dies and Jacques is forced to take to the streets on the run from the law. The young man is released from prison because of his mother's pleas for clemency which cite his tormented upbringing.

Reviews

"A film by Victor Trivas is always an event. The creator of No Man's Land has proven himself such a master that we know full well that a production bearing his imprint will contain certain qualities. ... The script of Dans les rues has a theme of incontestable value. It was inspired by the novel by J.-H. Rosny the elder of the Academie Goncourt. ... In the novel, Rosny the elder knows how to express with feeling and humanity the kind of vague melancholy which, in the adolescent of the *faubourg*, is freely translated into a hesitation regarding which path to take. ... Trivas knows admirably well exactly how to get our attention. At the screening at the Marignan cinema, a difficult public was united and captivated from the opening images. ... His masterly technique is in evidence throughout the film and it never weakens or strikes a false note. This is particularly true concerning the atmosphere. ... At the very least, a popular milieu has been skillfully created. It is somewhat disturbing, a bit too low in social standing, even lower than Quatorze juillet, but it makes good use of its elements: the images of a fairground, the astonishing shambles of père Schlamp, a second-hand goods dealer and especially the interiors of the houses with their principle component, the soul of these humble areas, the staircase".

Le Cinéopse, March 1934

"The atmosphere here is so heavy, so dark, the scenes are so poorly aerated that one is frustrated. I believe that the principle fault of the film ... is that there are a succession of too rigourously compartmentalised scenes, heaped up one after the other and separated by an overly rigourous visual punctuation. The staging, similarly fragmented, reminds one strongly of a certain Russian-German theatricality which one finds in Grand Hotel and Crime and Punishment. ... In any case this film is a masterpiece of photographic interpretation. ... Certain exteriors such as the grey dawn over the Seine with Notre Dame in the distance are especially miraculous. ... Dans les rues is a succession of passably banal anecdotes, swiftly treated and crowned by a pompous, pseudo-social and falsely humanist ending served up with fake pity and sugary tears".

Mon Ciné, 7 December 1933

Appendix Thirteen: CARREFOUR

British Unity Pictures Française, 1938
84 mins.

Director	Curtis Bernhardt
Producer	Eugène Tuscherer
Script	M. Kafka, André-Paul Antoine
Cinematography	Léonce-Henry Burel, Henri Tiquet, Georges Régnier
Decor	Jean d'Eaubonne, Raymond Gabutti
Music	Michel Emer
Sound	Marcel Courmes
Editor	Lantz
Cast	Suzy Prim (Michèle Allain)
	Tania Fédor (Mme de Vétheuil)
	Marcelle Géniat (Mme Pelletier)
	Charles Vanel (Roger de Vétheuil)
	Jules Berry (Lucien Sarrou)
	Jean Claudio (le petit Paul)
	Christian Argentin (l'avocat)
	Pierre Palau (le duc)
	Robert Rollys (un elève)
	Marcel Duhamel (le domestique)
	Liliane Lesaffre
	Otto Wallburg
	Auguste Boverio
	Jean Tissier
	Jenny Hecquet
	Paul Amiot
	Edy Debray
	Marcel Pérès
	Jacques Cléry
	Pierre de Ramey

Plot synopsis

Roger de Vetheuil, a prominent Parisian industrialist, is accused by a newspaper of actually being Jean Pelletier, a one-time criminal. At an ensuing trial, a mysterious stranger named Lucien provides evidence to clear Vetheuil. Shortly thereafter, Lucien attempts to blackmail Vetheuil by saying that he had lied on his behalf. Vetheuil, who is suffering from amnesia caused by a war injury, visits a Montmartre nightclub and meets its hostess, Michèle, who recognises him. Michèle is currently Lucien's mistress and accomplice but was once Pelettier's lover. Realising the truth, Vetheuil-Pelletier is caught in a quandary. Eventually, he is saved from his plight by Michèle who shoots Lucien after an argument. She allows him to return to his new post-war identity.

Review

"It has been said and written that CARREFOUR is a good and fine piece of work. Far be it for me to contradict such affirmation which with deserved credit must go to the director Kurt Bernhardt. I would, however, like to rectify the word 'work' which may have a perjorative sense when applied to a cinematic production. I would like to draw out its real meaning, which I am sure colleagues would have liked to have used. No confusion must be produced when one finds oneself in the presence of a film which is as coherent and as finely and scrupulously observed as CARREFOUR. ... [Kurt Bernhardt and A.P. Antoine] have conserved on film, through the immense possibilities of cinema, a unity of danger and menace that presents itself as a moving, poignant, human drama. Each of the characters from the victim of the atrocious amnesia to the unscrupulous blackmailer combine to create an atmosphere admirably maintained by the succession of images."

Jean Néry, publication unknown, 16 November 1938

Appendix Fourteen: Pièges

Speva Films, 1939
99 mins.

Director	Robert Siodmak
Producer	Michel Safra
Script	Jacques Companeez, Ernest Neuville, Simon Gantillon
Cinematography	Michel Kelber, Jacques Mercanton, Marcel Fredetal
Decor	Georges Wakhévitch
Music	Michel Michelet
Sound	Pierre Calvet
Editor	Yvonne Martin
Cast	Marie Déa (Adrienne Charpentier)
	Maurice Chevalier (Robert Fleury)
	Pierre Renoir (Brémontière)
	André Brunot (le commissaire Ténier)
	Jean Temerson (Batol)
	Erich von Stroheim (Pears)
	Jacques Varennes (Maxime)
	Mady Berry (Sidonie)
	Milly Mathis (Rose)
	Madelaine Geoffrey (Valérie)
	Catherine Farel (Lucie Barral)
	Yvonne Yma (Mme. Batol)
	Henri Bry (Oglou Vacapoulos)
	Robert Seller (Carioni)
	Raymond Rognoni, André Nicolle (les inspecteurs)
	Pierre Magnier (l'homme d'affaires)
	André Numès fils (le spectateur barbu)
	Jean Brochard (le speaker)
	Pierre Labry (le danseur)
	André Carnège (le juge d'instruction)
	Nicolas Rimsky (Rouski)
	Philippe Richard (l'avocat)
	Léon Arvel (le greffier)
	Albert Malbert (le chauffeur)
	Anthony Gildès (le jardinier)
	Jacques Beauvais (le chef-cuisinier)
	Julienne Paroli

Liliane Lesaffre
Robert Berri
Eugène Stuber
Charles Vissières

Plot synopsis

A serial killer is loose in Paris and is sending mysterious notes to the police. Commissioner Ténier and his assistant Batol recruit a young girl, Adrienne, to help them in their efforts to track down the criminal. Adrienne answers a series of anonymous announcements in the papers and comes across a number of individuals including Pears, a former fashion designer and Maxime, the head butler of a large household. She also meets Robert Fleury, a nightclub owner and his assistant, Brémontière. Fleury pursues Adrienne and they decide to marry after Maxime's arrest for his involvement in a sex slave ring and the disappearance of a number of young girls. However, the killer continues to strike, and with Adrienne's help, Fleury becomes the prime suspect. Fleury is arrested but Ténier remains unconvinced and eventually Brémontière is unmasked as the real killer. Adrienne and Fleury are reunited.

Reviews

"The grumpy ones will perhaps say that there are some implausibilities in the script by Jacques Companez and Ernest Neuville. This isn't untrue, but it nonetheless remains true to say that PIÈGES is an excellent film, well constructed, never boring, and perfectly played by Maurice Chevalier, Pierre Renoir, André Brunot, Temerson, Jacques Varenne, Erich von Stroheim and a newcomer, Marie Déa who is fresh, ravishing, adroit, and wears her clothes beautifully".
Pour Vous, 27 December 1939

"PIÈGES by Robert Siodmak isn't a great film but it is a very good production that merits attention for its well-constructed script and the mystery and intrigue which are not uncovered until the final images. ... Marie Déa who plays the principal role is a revelation. She has a simple, nuanced, and meticulous manner of acting and a clarity in her gestures and language that confirm her as a real gift for the screen".
Candide, 20 December 1939

"You could say that it is a matter of a police film ... but Pièges has neither the cut nor the rhythm of a police film. What it seems to be is a succession of sketches destined to bring its comical or bizarre characters to life in front of us. The slowness and, it must be said, the talent with which the director Robert Siodmak describes the social milieu of each of his characters scarcely contributes to strengthening the film's illusion".

Georges Champeux, *Gringoire*, 21 December 1939

"Here is one of the greatest French films released since the war. ... Its intrigue is well constructed, composed as a rising movement of mystery and violence which is nuanced, however, by charm and humour. ... Throughout there is a dramatic atmosphere which is admirably composed as much by Wakhévitch's well-researched décor as the knowing shadows of Michel Kelber's beautiful cinematography".

La Cinématographie Française, 23 December 1939

Appendix Fifteen: LILIOM

Fox Europa, 1934
120 mins.
Date of First Screening: 27 April 1934

Director	Fritz Lang
Assistant Director	Jean-Pierre Feydeau
Producer	Erich Pommer
Script	Fritz Lang, Robert Liebmann, Bernard Zimmer after the play by Ferenc Molnar
Cinematography	Rudi (Rudolph) Maté, Louis Née
Decor	Paul Colin, René Renoux, Ferdinand Earle
Music	Jean Lenoir, Franz Waxman
Costume	René Hubert
Sound	E. Zylberberg
Cast	Charles Boyer (Liliom)
	Madeleine Ozeray (Julie)
	Florelle (Mme Moscat)
	Pierre Alcover (Alfred)
	Vivianne Romance (la marchande de cigarettes)
	Maximilienne (Mme Menoux)
	Roland Toutain (le marin)
	Mimi Funès (Marie)
	Alexandre Rignault (Hollinger)
	Mila Parély (le dactylo)
	Robert Arnoux (le tourneur)
	Henry Richard (le commissaire)
	Raoul Marco (l'inspecteur)
	Barencey (le policier)
	Antonin Artaud (le rémouleur)
	René Stern (le caissier)
	Léon Arvel (l'employé)
	Josiane Lisbey
	Blanche Estival

Plot synopsis

Liliom is a hawker for a merry-go-round at a fairground in the Parisian *zone*.
His boss, Mme Moscat, has strong feelings for him but he falls in love with the

demure and innocent Julie. The couple establish a home and a photography business with Julie's aunt, Mme Menoux, who harbours strongly voiced doubts about Liliom's character. Liliom frequently loses his temper with his partner. Julie becomes pregnant and because they are short of money, Liliom plans a robbery with his criminal cohort Alfred. The scheme goes awry and Liliom kills himself. He goes to heaven where he is reprimanded for his actions. Many years later, Liliom is allowed to return to Earth where he meets his daughter. Back in heaven again, because of his tears, Liliom is absolved.

Reviews

"The screen is currently taking up an interest in LILIOM and the version that Fritz Lang has given us is both loose with and faithful to the original. It has a flavour of humanity which the cinema is unused to. Situated within the particular order that realism has so often painted with its minutiae and taste for telling detail, LILIOM escapes from the simplistic art which attempts to just photograph life. Molnar is a poet and it is from the basis of the poetry that his fantasy evolves".
   Comedia, 28 April 1934

"The Parisian public is not going to unanimously welcome the first French work by Fritz Lang... the Judeo-Hungarian collaboration between Lang and Molnar doesn't treat the metaphysical jokes with enough lightness. ... The first part of the film offers nothing original and there is an accumulation of the old commonplaces of populist cinema: the fair, the merry-go-rounds, the *bistro*, the *zone* and so on. The greatest fault of all of this is that it is false, stiff, and badly situated. The action, we are told, unfolds in Paris but all the characters have a profoundly forlorn and pessimistic German disposition to the point of obsession".
   Jean Fayard, *Candide*, 10 March 1934

"The first scenes make you think immediately of Francis Carco ... the lighting is in this dark manner of the German studios which worsens still further the overly considered style of the visuals. The effect is to sacrifice the whole for a number of less important effects".
   Le Journal, 4 May 1934

"The concern of the director was, it appears, to make a French film where in fact LILIOM is a German film par excellence, at once realist and mystical. The first part unwinds in the '*zone internationale*' with the banal decor of the fair and the *fortifs*. The second, takes place at the gateway to heaven and is inspired by that marvellous form of fantasy whose typical form of expression is the Germanic Christmas tree".

Jean Laury, *Le Figaro*, 29 April 1934

"Because of the 'cleaning' performed by the German studios, the Jew Erich Pommer has settled in our country. ... These crude details of *faubourg* life: the turned up nose of Florelle, the *gavroche*-like air of Roland Toutain are lost under the weight of the lighting of the Berlin studios so that the result is nothing but a heterogeneous spectacle. ... this French-Jewish-Hungarian collaboration doesn't create a breathable atmosphere. We return to that bizarre and boring cinematic country produced by UFA's French-German dramas, a 'no man's land' a lot closer to the Sprée than to the Seine, a Babel emptied of all character".

François Vinneuil, *Action Française*, 28 April 1934

"Those who will be taken in by LILIOM will go up in the skies with him. They will see the angels and the heavens. They will hear the song of the stars. The others will remain on earth. They will only see in the film the rather banal story of a carefree and lazy fairground hawker who has a bad head but a good heart and doesn't know very well how to manage his life. ... A pace that's rather too slow spoils the movement of the film. Each image is on the screen for too long. It is too insistent on details. In particular, there is too much dialogue when the lighting and sound effects would suffice to create the atmosphere. Bernard Zimmer's dialogue is too literary ... what a relief the images are! Fritz Lang and his cinematographer Maté have understood how to express the tragedy of the *faubourgs* with an ambiguous and painfully emotional *clair-obscur* light".

Jean Vidal, *Pour Vous*, 3 May 1934

Filmography

ÄLLO BERLIN, ICI PARIS (Julien Duvivier, 1931)
ASPHALT (Joe May, 1928)
ATALANTE, L' (Jean Vigo, 1934)
AVEC LE SOURIRE (Maurice Tourneur, 1936)
BAS FONDS, LES (Jean Renoir, 1936)
BERLIN-ALEXANDERPLATZ (Piel Jützi, 1931)
BERLIN SYMPHONIE DES EINER GROSSE STADT (Walter Ruttman, 1927)
BÊTE HUMAINE, LA (Jean Renoir, 1938)
DIE BLAUE ANGE (Josef Sternberg, 1930)
BOUDU SAUVÉ DES EAUX (Jean Renoir, 1932)
BÜCHSE DER PANDORA, DIE (G.W. Pabst, 1928)
CARREFOUR (Kurt Bernhardt, 1938)
CETTE VIEILLE CANAILLE (Anatole Litvak, 1933)
CHACUN SA CHANCE (Hans Steinhoff, 1930)
CHIENNE, LA (Jean Renoir, 1931)
COEUR DE LILAS (Anatole Litvak, 1931)
CRIME DE M. LANGE, LE (Jean Renoir, 1936)
CRIME ET CHÂTIMENT (Pierre Chenal,)
CRISE EST FINIE, LA (Robert Siodmak, 1934)
DANS LES RUES (Victor Trivas, 1933)
DREIGROSCHENOPER, DIE / THE THREEPENNY OPERA (G.W. Pabst, 1931)
DU HAUT EN BAS (G.W. Pabst, 1934)
ENTRAÎNEUSE, L' (Albert Valentin, 1938)
FANTÔMAS (Paul Fejos, 1932)
FAUBOURG-MONTMARTRE (Raymond Bernard, 1931)
GARDEZ LE SOURRIRE (Paul Fejos, 1933)
GOUALEUSE, LA (Fernand Rivers, 1938)
GUELE D'AMOUR (Jean Grémillon, 1937)
HÔTEL DU NORD (Marcel Carné, 1938)
JENNY (Marcel Carné, 1936)
JOUR SE LEVE, LE (Marcel Carné, 1939)
LILIOM (Fritz Lang, 1933)
LUMIÈRES DE PARIS (Richard Pottier, 1938)
M (Fritz Lang, 1931)
MAM'ZELLE NITOUCHE (Carl Lamac, 1931)
MATERNELLE, LA (Jean Benoit-Levy and Marie Epstein, 1933)
MAUVAISE GRAINE (Billy Wilder, 1933)
METROPOLIS (Fritz Lang, 1926)

MÜTTER KRAUSENS FAHRT INS GLÜCK (Piel Jützi, 1929)
PARIS (Jean Choux, 1936)
PARIS-BÉGUIN (Alberto Genina, 1931)
PARIS, MÉDITERRANÉE (Joe May, 1931)
PARIS LA NUIT (Henri Diamont-Berger, 1930)
PETITE LISE, LA (Jean Grémillon, 1931)
PÉPÉ LE MOKO (Julien Duvivier, 1937)
PIÈGES (Robert Siodmak, 1939)
PRISONS DE FEMMES (Roger Richebé, 1938)
PRIX DE BEAUTÉ (Augusto Genina, 1931)
PURITAIN, LE (Jeff Musso, 1937)
QUARTORZE JUILLET (René Clair, 1932)
RUE SANS JOIE (André Hugon, 1938)
SEXE FAIBLE, LA (Robert Siodmak, 1933)
SOUS LES TOITS DE PARIS (René Clair, 1930)
TAGEBUCH EINER VERLOREN, DAS (G.W. Pabst, 1929)
TESTAMENT DES DR. MABUSE, DAS / LE TESTAMENT DU DOCTEUR MABUSE
    (Fritz Lang, 1933)
TÊTE D'UN HOMME, LA (Julien Duvivier, 1932)
TUMULTES / STÜRME DER LEIDENSCHAFT (Robert Siodmak, 1931)
TUNNEL, LE (Kurt Bernhardt, 1933)
VIE PARISIENNE, LA (Robert Siodmak, 1935)
ZOU-ZOU (Marc Allégret, 1934)

Bibliography

Abel, Richard (1984) *French Cinema: The First Wave 1915-1929*, Princeton, NJ: Princeton University Press.

Abel, Richard (ed.) (1988) *French Film Theory and Criticism 1907-1939: A History/Anthology 1907-1939* 2 vols., Princeton: Princeton University Press.

Ades, Dawn (1996) *Photomontage*, London: Thames and Hudson.

Adorno, Theodor W. and Eisler Hanns (1972) *Musique de cinéma*, Paris: L'Arche.

Agulhon, Maurice (1996) "Paris: A Traversal from East to West" in Kritzman (1996), 523-554.

Aitkin, Stuart C. and Zonn, Leo E. (1994) (eds.) *Place, Power, Situation and Spectacle: A Geography of Film*, Lanham: Rowman and Littlefield.

Albera, François (1995) *Albatros. Des Russes à Paris 1919-1929*, Paris: Mazzotta / La Cinémathèque Française.

Albrecht, Donald (1986) *Designing Dreams: Modern Architecture in the Movies*, New York: Harper & Row.

Alékan, Henri (1987) "Le Bon vieux cinéma" in Boulègne (1987), 190-198.

Alékan, Henri (1991) *Des Lumières et des ombres*, Paris: La Librairie du collectionneur.

Allen, Robert C. and Gomery, Douglas (eds.) (1985) *Film History, Theory and Practice*, New York: Knopf.

Anderson, Benedict (1996) *Imagined Communities*, London: Verso.

Andrew, Dudley (1983a) "Sound in France: The Origins of a Native School" in Bandy, 57-65.

Andrew, Dudley (1983b) "Poetic Realism" in Bandy (1983), 115-120.

Andrew, Dudley (1990) "The Impact of the Novel on French Cinema of the 1930s", *L'Esprit Créateur* vol. XXX no. 2 (Summer 1990), 3-13.

Andrew, Dudley (1992) "Family Diversions: French Popular Cinema and the Music-Hall" in Dyer and Vincendeau (1992), 15-30.

Andrew, Dudley (1995a) *Mists of Regret*, Princeton, NJ: Princeton University Press.

Andrew, Dudley (1995b) "Appraising French Images", *Wide Angle* vol. 16, no. 3 (February 1995), 53-65.

Andrew, Dudley (1996) "Film Noir: Death and Double Cross Over the Atlantic", *Iris* no. 21 (Spring 1996), 21-30.

Ankum, Katharina von (1997) *Women in the Metropolis*, Berkeley: University of California Press.

Armes, Roy (1985) *French Cinema*, London: Secker and Warburg.

Ashby, Justine and Higson, Andrew (eds.) (2000) *British Cinema Past and Present*, London: Routledge.

Atwell, Lee (1977) *G.W. Pabst*, Boston: Twayne.

Augé, Marc (1996a) "Paris and the Ethnography of the Contemporary World" in Sheringham (1996), 175-179.

Augé, Marc (1996b) *Paris Années 30*, Paris: Hazan.

Aumont, Jean-Pierre (1957) *Souvenirs provisoires*, Paris: René Jüillard.

Aumont, Jacques and Païni, Dominique (eds.) (1992) *Les Cinéastes en exil*, Paris: La Cinémathèque Française.

Aurich, Rolf, Jacobsen, Wolfgang and Schnauber, Cornelius (eds.) (2001) *Fritz Lang: His Life and Work*, Berlin: Filmmuseum Berlin-Deutsche Kinemathek and Jovis Verlang GmbH.

Badia, Gilbert (ed.) (1979) *Les barbelés de l'exil*, Paris: Presses Universitaires de Grenoble.

Badia, Gilbert (1979) "L'émigration en France: ses conditions et ses problèmes" in Badia (ed.) (1979), 11-96.

Badia, Gilbert (ed.) (1982) *Exilés en France. Souvenirs d'antifascistes allemands émigrés 1933-1945*, Paris: François Maspero.

Badia, Gilbert et al (eds.) (1984a) *Les Bannis de Hitler. Accueil et lutte des exilés allemands en France 1933-1939*, Paris: Études et Documentation Internationales, Presses Universitaires de Vincennes.

Badia, Gilbert (1984b) "Défense de la culture allemande" in Badia et al. (eds.) (1984), 365-378.

Balzac, Honore (1987) (date of first publication 1837-43) *Lost Illusions*, Harmondsworth: Penguin.

Balzac, Honore (1991) (date of first publication 1834-35) *Old Goriot*, Harmondsworth: Penguin.

Bandy, Mary Lea (1983) *Rediscovering French Film*, New York: Museum of Modern Art.

Bardèche, Maurice, and Brassilach, Robert (trans. and ed. Iris Barry) (1938) *History of the Film*, London: George Allen and Unwin Ltd.

Barron, Stephanie (ed.) (1997) *Exiles and Emigrés: The Flight of European Artists From Hitler*, New York: Harry Abrams, Inc.

Barrot, Olivier, and Jeancolas, Jean-Pierre (1973) *Les Français et leur cinéma, 1930-1939*, Créteil: Maison de la Culture, Losfield.

Barsacq, Leon (1976) *Caligari's Cabinet and other Illusions*, Boston: New York Graphic Society.

Barthes, Roland (1993) "The Eiffel Tower", in Sontag (1993), 236-250.

Bates, Robin (1997) "Audiences on the Verge of a Fascist Breakdown: Male Anxieties and Late 1930s French Film", *Cinema Journal* vol. 36 no. 3 (Spring 1997), 25-55.

Bauche, Freddy (1965) *G.W. Pabst*, Paris: Premier plan.

Baudelaire, Charles (1995) *The Painter of Modern Life and Other Essays*, London: Phaidon.

Bazin, André (1974) *Jean Renoir*, London: W.H. Allen.

Belmans, Jacques (1977) *La Ville dans le cinéma de Fritz Lang à Alain Resnais*, Brussels: Editions A. de Boeck.

Benjamin, Walter (1997) *One Way Street*, London: Verso.

Benjamin, Walter (1992) *Illuminations*, London: Fontana.

Bergfelder, Tim (1996) "The Production Designer and the *Gesamtkunstwerk*: German Film Technicians in the British Film Industry of the 1930's" in Higson (1996), 20-37.

Bergfelder, Tim (2000) "The Nation Vanishes: European Co-Productions and Popular Genre Formulae in the 1950s and 1960s" in Hjort and Mackenzie (2000), 139-152.

Berghaus, Günter (ed.) (1981) *Theater and Film in Exile: German Artists in Britain, 1933-1945*, Oxford: Berg.

Bergut, Bob (1960) *Eric von Stroheim*, Paris: Roger Dupuis.

Berman, Marshall (1983) *All That is Solid Melts Into Air*, London: Verso.

Bernhardt, Curtis (date unknown) *Curtis Bernhardt*, Metuchen, NJ: The Directors Guild of America / The Scarecrow Press.

Berthomé, Jean Pierre (1981) "Entretien avec Max Douy", *Positif* no. 246-247 (July/August 1981, September 1981), 2-12, 22-33.

Besnard, Annick and d'Hoop Jean-Marie (1980) *La France et l'allemagne 1932-1936*, Paris: Éditions du Centre National de la Récherche Scientifique.

Besnard-Bernadac, Marie-Laure and Metken, Günter (eds.) (1992) *Paris-Berlin. Rapports et contrastes france-allegmagne 1900-1933*, Paris: Éditions du Centre Georges Pompidou / Éditions Gallimard.

Bessy, Maurice and Chirat, Raymond (1988) *Histoire du cinéma Français. Encyclopedie des films 1929-1934*, Paris: Pygmalian / Gérard Watelet.

Bessy, Maurice and Chirat, Raymond (1988) *Histoire du cinéma Français. Encyclopedie des films 1935-1939*, Paris: Pygmalian / Gérard Watelet.

Billard, Pierre (1995) *L'Age classique du cinéma français. Du cinéma parlant à la Nouvelle Vague*, Paris: Flammarion.

Billia, Laurent and Le Roy, Eric (1995) *Eclair: Un siècle de cinéma à Epinay-sur-Seine*, Paris: Calman-Levy.

Bleys, Jean-Pierre (1988) "Les Chefs opérateurs étrangers dans le cinéma français des années trente", *Positif* no. 323 (January 1988), 51-53.

Bock, Hans-Michael and Jacobson, Wolfgang (eds.) (1996) *Victor Trivas*, Hamburg; Berlin: Cinegraph.

Bocock, Robert and Thompson, Kenneth (eds.) (1992) *Social and Cultural Forms of Modernity*, Oxford/Cambridge: Polity / O.U. / Blackwell.

Bodeen, Dewitt and Ringgold, Gene (1973) *Chevalier: The Films and Career of Maurice Chevalier*, Secaucus, New Jersey: The Citadel Press.

Borde, Raymond (1975) *La France des années trente vue par son cinéma*. Toulouse: La Cinémathèque de Toulouse, la Bibliothèque Municipale de Toulouse et le Musée des Augustins.

Borde, Raymond (1976) "La France des années 30", *L'Avant-scène du cinéma*, no. 173 (October 1976), 23-28.

Borger, Lenny (1983) "*Les Croix de bois* de Raymond Bernard", *Cinématographe* no. 91 (July-August 1983), 31-35.

Borger, Lenny (1989) "From Moscow to Montreuil: the Russian Émigrés in Paris 1920-1929" *Griffithiana* no. 35-36 (October 1989), pp. 28-39.

Boston, Richard (1994) *Boudu Saved From Drowning*, London: British Film Institute.

Boulègne, Catherine et al (eds.) (1987) *Cités-Cinés*, Paris: Éditions Ramsay et la Grande Halle / La Villette.

Bouqueret, Christian (1998) *Les Femmes photographes de la nouvelle vision en France 1920-1940*, Paris: Marval.

Bourget, Jean-Loup (1992) "L' 'Hybridation' des genres Hollywoodiens par les metteurs en scènes Européens" in Aumont and Païni (1992), 39-51.

Bousinnot, Roger (ed.) (1995) *Encyclopedie du cinéma*, Paris: les Savoirs Bordas.

Boyer, M. (1996) *The City of Collective Memory*, Cambridge, Mass.: M.I.T. Press.

Brasillach, Robert (1941) *Notre avantguerre*, Paris: Librairie Plan.

Brasillach, Robert (1968) *Une Génération dans l'orage*, Paris: Plon.

Brassaï (1997) *Letters to My Parents*, Chicago: The University of Chicago Press.

Bresler, Henri (1996) "Le Pittoresque investit la ville" in Lucan (1996), 149-159.

Brieu, Christian et al. (eds.) (1985) *Joinville, le cinéma: le temps des studios*, Paris: Ramsay.

Briginshaw, Valerie A. (1997) "'Keep Your Great City!' – The Lament of the Empress and other Women" in Thomas (1997), 35-49.

Brunelin, André (1987) *Gabin*, Paris: Éditions Robert Laffont.

Bruno, Guiliana (1993) *Streetwalking on a Ruined Map*, Princeton: Princeton University Press.

Brunsdon, Charlotte (1989) "Little Shop Girls (And Other Women) Go to the Movies", *Screen* vol. 30, no. 4 (Summer 1989), 69-73.

Budd, Mike (ed.) (1990) *The Cabinet of Dr Caligari: Texts, Contexts, Histories*, New Brunswick: Rutgers University Press.

Bullivant, Keith (1977) *Culture and Society in the Weimar Republic*, Manchester: Manchester University Press.

Burch, Noël and Sellier, Geniève (1996) *La Drôle de guerre des sexes du cinéma français 1930-1956*, Paris: Nathan.

Burns, Rob (1995) *German Cultural Studies*, Oxford: Oxford University Press.

Caillois, Roger (1937) "Paris, mythe moderne", *Nouvelle revue Française*, vol. XXV no. 284 (May 1937), 682-699.

Calvino, Italo (1974) *Invisible Cities*, London: Martin Secker and Warburg.

Cameron, Ian (ed.) (1992) *The Movie Book of Film Noir*, London: Studio Vista.

Caradec, François and Weill, Alain (1980) *Le Café-concert*, Paris: Atelier Hachette / Massin.

Carbaud, Michel (1982) *Paris et les Parisiens sous le Second Empire*, Paris: Pierre Belfond.

Carcasonne, Philippe (1978) Interview with Louis Daquin, *Cinématographe*, no. 38 (May 1978), 27-30.

Carcasonne, Philippe and Cuel, François (1982) Interview With Alexandre Trauner, *Cinématographe*, no. 76 (March 1982), 12-17.

Carcasonne, Philippe and Cuel, François (1982) Interview With Lucien Aguettand, *Cinématographe*, no. 76 (March 1982), 18-22.

Carné, Marcel (1933) "When Will the Cinema Go Down the Street?" in Abel (1988), 127-129.

Cartier, Jacqueline (1989) *Monsieur Vanel*, Paris: Robert Laffont.

Caws, Mary Ann (ed.) (1991) *City Images: Perspectives From Literature, Philosophy and Film*, New York: Gordon and Breach.

Charney, Leo and Schwartz, Vanessa R. (eds.) (1996) *Cinema and the Invention of Modern Life*, Berkeley: University of California Press.

Chauveau, Philippe and Sallée, Andrée (1985) *Music-hall et café-concert*, Paris: Bordas.

Chenal, Pierre (1985) *Souvenirs du cinéaste*, Paris: Éditions Dujarric.

Chenoune, Farid (1993) *A History of Men's Fashion*, Paris / New York: Flammarion.

Chevalier, Louis (1980) *Montmartre du plaisir et du crime*, Paris: Robert Laffont.

Chevalier, Maurice (1946) *Ma Route et mes chansons*, Paris: René Julliard.

Chirat, Raymond (1983) *Le cinéma français des années trentes*, Paris: Hatier.

Chirat, Raymond (1987) *Atmosphères: sourires, soupirs et délires du cinéma Français des années 30*, Paris: Hatier.

Ciment, Michel (1975) "Entretien avec Jean Renoir", *Positif* no. 173, 15-21.

Cinématographie Française 1929-1939.

Cinémonde 1931-1933.

Clair, René (1946) "Du Théatre au cinéma" in Lapierre (1946), 264-270.

Clark, Tim (1996) *The Painting of Modern Life: Paris in the Art of Manet and his Followers*, London: Thames and Hudson.

Clarke, David B. (ed.) (1997) *The Cinematic City*, London: Routledge.

Clifford, James (1992) "Traveling Cultures" in Grossberg et al (1992), 96-112.

Cobb, Richard (1983) *French and Germans, Germans and French*, Hanover, New Hampshire: University Press of New England.

Cobb, Richard (1998) *Paris and Elsewhere*, London: John Murray.

Colpart, Gilles *Billy Wilder*, Paris: Edilig.

Colette (1960) *The Vagabond*, Harmondsworth: Penguin.

Comes, Philippe de and Marmin, Michel (eds.) (1984) *Le cinéma français 1930-1960*, Paris: Éditions Atlas.

Conley, Tom (1996) "*Le cinéaste de la vie moderne*: Paris as Map in Film, 1924-34" in Sherringham (1996), 71-84.

Conway, Kelley (1995), "Les goualeuses de l'écran" in Toulet (ed.) (1995), 162-171.

Conway, Kelley (2001) "Diva in the Spotlight: Music Hall to Cinema" in Hughes and Williams (eds.) (2001), Oxford: Berg.

Cook, Pam (ed.) (1994) *The Cinema Book*, London: British Film Institute.

Copjec, Joan (ed.) (1993) *Shades of Noir*, London: Verso.

Corbin, Alain (1996) "Paris-Province" in Kritzman (1996), 426-464.

Courant, Curtis (1956) "Cameraman in the Golden Age of Cinema", *Film Culture* vol. 2 no. 3, 17-19.

Courtade, Francis (1963) *Fritz Lang*, Paris: Le Terrain vague.

Courtarde, Francis (1978) *Les Malédictions du cinéma Français*, Paris: Alain Moreau.

Courtade, Francis (1991) "Les coproductions franco-allemandes et versions multiples des années 30" in Gassen and Hurst (1991), 173-184.

Cozarinsky, Edgardo (1983) "Foreign Filmmakers in France" in Bandy (1983), 136-140.

Cozarinsky, Edgardo (1992) "Cinéma de France, cinéastes d'ailleurs" in Aumont and Païni (1992), 1-14.

Crisp, Colin (1993) *The Classic French Cinema 1930-1960*, Bloomington and Indianapolis: Indiana University Press.

Cronin, Vincent (1994) *Paris: City of Light 1919-1939*, London: Harper Collins.

Crowe, Cameron, (1999) *Conversations With Billy Wilder*, London: Faber.

Czaplicka, John (1990) "Pictures of a City at Work. Berlin, Circa 1890-1930: Visual Reflections on Social Structures and Technology in the Modern Urban Construct" in Haxthausen and Heidrun (1990), 3-36.

Dabit, Eugène (1990a) *Faubourgs de Paris*, Paris: Éditions Gallimard.

Dabit, Eugène (1990b) *Ville lumière*, Paris: le Dilettante.

Dale, R.C. (1986) *The Films of René Clair*, Metuchen, NJ: Scarecrow Press.

Damare, Jacques (1960) *les Folies du music-hall*, Paris: Éditions Spectacles.

Dany, Serge (1987) "Ville-Ciné et Télé-Banlieue" in Boulègne (1987), 121-127.

Darrieux, Danielle (1995) *Filmographie commentée par elle-même*, Paris: Ramsey.

Dethier, Jean and Guiheux, Alain (eds.) (1994) *La Ville, art et architecture en Europe, 1870-1993*, Paris: Éditions du Centre Pompidou.

Diamant-Berger, Henri (1977) *Il Était une fois le cinéma*, Paris: Éditions Simoën.

Dimendberg, Edward; Jay, Martin and Kaes, Anton (eds.) (1994) *The Weimar Republic Sourcebook*, Berkeley: University of California Press.

Doane, Mary Ann (1991) *Femmes Fatales: Feminism, Film Theory, Psychoanalysis*, London: Routledge.

Donald, James (1989) *Fantasy and the Cinema*, London: British Film Institute.

Donald, James (1992) "Metropolis: The City as Text" in Bocock and Thompson (1992), 418-461.

Donald, James (1995) "The City, The Cinema: Modern Spaces" in Jenks (1995).

Douchet, Jean (1987) "La Ville tentaculaire" in Boulègne (1987), 61-71.

Douchet, Jean and Nadeau, Gilles (1987) *Paris-une ville vue par le cinéma, de 1895 à nos jours*. Paris: Éditions du May.

Douy, Max and Jacques (1993) *Décors de cinéma. Les Studios français de Meliès à nos jours*, Paris: Éditions du Collectioneur.

Dubois, Jacques (1952) "Entretien avec Francis Carco", *Les Lettres Françaises* 6th-13th November 1952, 3-7.

Dumont, Hervé (1991) *Robert Siodmak. le Maître du film noir*, Lausanne: L'Age d'homme.

Eisner, Lotte (1976) *Fritz Lang*, London: Secker and Warburg.

Eisner, Lotte (1983) *The Haunted Screen*, London: Secker and Warburg.

Elert, Nicolet et al (eds.) (1997) *International Dictionary of Films and Filmmakers*, Detroit: St. James Press.

Elsaesser, Thomas and Vincendeau Ginette (1983) *Les Cinéastes allemands en France. Les Années trente*, Paris: Goethe Institute.

Elsaesser, Thomas (1983a) "Introduction" in Elsaesser and Vincendeau (1983), 1-3.

Elsaesser, Thomas (1983b) "Une mise-en-scène des objets" in Elsaesser and Vincendeau (1983), 7-11.

Elsaesser, Thomas (1983c) "Lulu and the Meter Man. Louise Brooks, Pabst and Pandora's Box", *Screen* vol. 24, no. 4-5 (July-October 1983), 4-36.

Elsaesser, Thomas (1984a) "The German Émigrés in Paris During the 1930s. Pathos and Leavetaking", *Sight and Sound*, vol. 53 no. 4 (Autumn 1984), 278-283.

Elsaesser, Thomas (1984b) "Film History and Visual Pleasure: Weimar History", in Mellencamp and Rosen (1984), 54-81.

Elsaesser, Thomas (1985) *German Cinema: Seven Decades, Seven Films*, London: Goethe Institut.

Elsaesser, Thomas (1989) "Social Mobility and the Fantastic: German Silent Cinema", in Donald (ed.) (1989), 23-38.

Elsaesser, Thomas (1996a) "A German Ancestry to Film Noir? Film History and its Imaginary", *Iris* no.21 (Spring 1996), 129-144.

Elsaesser, Thomas (1996b) ""Chacun au monde a deux patries". Robert Siodmak und das Paris der 30er Jahre" in Sturm and Wohlgemuth (eds.) (1996), 81-100.

Elsaesser, Thomas (1999) "Ethnicity, Authenticity, and Exile: A Counterfeit Trade? German Filmmakers and Hollywood" in Naficy (ed.) (1999), 97-124.

Elsaesser, Thomas (2000) *Weimar Cinema and After: Germany's Historical Imaginary*, London: Routledge.

Espaces et sociétés no. 86 (March 1996) "Ville et cinéma", Paris: L'Harmattan.

Evenson, Norma (1979) *Paris: A Century of Change*, New Haven: Yale University Press.

Ezra, Elizabeth (1996) "Silents are Golden: Staging Community in *Zouzou*", *French Cultural Studies* vol. 7 part 2 no. 2 (June 1996), 149-161.

Faulkner, Christopher (1985) *The Social Cinema of Jean Renoir*, Princeton: Princeton University Press.

Faulkner, Christopher (1992) "Theory and Practice of Film Reviewing in France in the 1930s: Eyes Right (Lucien Rebat and the *Action Française*, 1936-1939)", *French Cultural Studies* vol. 3 no. 8 (June 1992), 133-155.

Faulkner, Christopher (1994a) "René Clair, Marcel Pagnol and the Social Dimension of Speech", *Screen* vol. 35 no. 2 (Summer 1994), 157-170.

Faulkner, Christopher (1994b) "Affective Identities: French National Cinema and the 1930s", *Canadian Journal of Film Studies* vol. 3 no. 2 (Fall 1994), 3-23.

Featherstone, Mike and Frisby, David (eds.) (1997) *Simmel on Culture*, London: Sage.

Feuer, Jane (1995) "The Self-Reflexive Musical and the Myth of Entertainment" in Grant (1995), 441-455.

Flanner, Janet (1988) *Paris Was Yesterday: 1925-1939*, New York: Harcourt Brace Jovanovich.

Flitterman Lewis, Sandy (1996) *To Desire Differently: Feminism and the French Cinema*, New York: Columbia University Press.

Forbes, Jill (1996) *Les Enfants du Paradis*, London: British Film Institute.

Ford, Charles and Jeanne René (1969) *Paris vu par le cinéma*, Paris: Hachette.

Ford, Charles and Jeanne René (1958) *Histoire encyclopédique du cinéma vol. IV Le cinéma parlant (1929-1945)*, Paris: S.E.D.E.

Fornairon, E. (1932) "La Renaissance de l'opérette", *Lectures Pour Tous* (October 1932).

Frank, Nino (1950) *Petit cinéma sentimental*, Paris: La Nouvelle Édition.

Friedberg, Anne (1994) *Window Shopping*, Berkeley: University of California Press.

Frieden, S., McCormick, R.W., Peterson, V.R., Vogelsang, L., (eds.) (1993) *Gender and German Cinema*, Oxford: Berg.

Frisby, David (2001) *Cityscapes of Modernity*, Cambridge: Polity Press.

Garb, Tamar and Nöchlin, Linda (1995)*The Jew in the Text: Modernity and the Construction of Identity*, London: Thames and Hudson.

Gardies, André (1993) *L'Espace au cinéma*, Paris: Meridiens Klincksieck.

Gassen, Heiner and Hurst, Heike (eds.) (1991) *Tendres ennemis: France-Allemagne*, Paris: L'Harmattan.

Gauteur, Claude and Vincendeau, Ginette (1993) *Jean Gabin: Anatomie d'un mythe*, Paris: Natan.

Gay, Peter (1974) *Weimar Culture: The Outsider as Insider*, Harmondsworth: Penguin.

Gilloch, Graeme (1996) *Myth and Metropolis*, Oxford / Cambridge: Blackwell / Polity.

Gleber, Anke (1999) *The Art of Taking a Walk: Flanerie, Literature, and Film in Weimar-Culture*, Princeton: Princeton University Press.

Golan, Romy (1995a) *Modernity and Nostalgia: Art and Politics Between the Wars*, New Haven and London: Yale University Press.

Golan, Romy (1995b) "From Fin de Siècle to Vichy. The Cultural Hygienics of Camille (Faust) Mauclair" in Garb and Nöchlin (eds.) (1995), 156-173.

Gomery, Douglas and Staiger, Janet (1979) "The History of World Cinema: Models for Economic Analysis" in *Film Reader* 4 (1979), 35-44.

Gorbman, Claudia (1991) "Hanns Eisler in Hollywood", *Screen*, vol. 32 no.3 (Autumn 1991), 272-285.

Gough-Yates, Kevin (1989) "The British Feature Film as an European Concern: Britain and the Émigré Film Maker 1933-1945" in Berghaus (1989), 135-166.

Goulemot, Jean and Oster, Daniel (1989) *La Vie Parisienne. Anthologie des Moeurs du XIX siècle*, Paris: Sand/Conti.

Grant, Barry Keith (ed.) (1995) *Film Genre: Reader II*, Austin: University of Texas Press.

Green, Mary Jean (1987) *Fiction in the Historical Present: French Writers and the Thirties*, Hanover, New Hampshire: University Press of New England.

Green, Mary Jean (1989) "Fascists on Film: the Brasillach and Bardèche Histoire du cinéma", *South Central Review* vol. 6 no. 2 (Summer 1989), 32-47.

Green, Nancy L. (1989) "Les Juifs Étrangers à Paris" in Kaspi and Marès (eds.) (1989), 105-118.

Greenburg, Joel and Higham, Charles (1969) *The Celluloid Muse*, Chicago: Henry Regnery.

Grossberg, Lawrence et al (eds.) (1992) *Cultural Studies*, London: Routledge.

Gunning, Tom (2000) *Fritz Lang: Allegories of Vision and Modernity*, London: British Film Institute.

Hake, Sabine (1993) *The Cinema's Third Machine: Writing on Film in Germany 1907-1933*, Lincoln: University of Nebraska Press.
Hake, Sabine (1996) "Legacies: Mabuse, Lang and the Sound of Noir", *Iris* no. 21 (Spring 1996), 54-73.
Hall, Stuart (ed.) (1997) *Representation*, London: Sage and Open University Press.
Hamblett, Charles (1963) *Anatole Litvak*, (publisher unknown).
Hamilton, Peter (1995) *Willy Ronis. Photographs. 1926-1995*, Oxford: M.O.M.A.
Hamilton, Peter (1997) "Representing the Social: France and Frenchness in Post-war Humanist Photography" in Hall (1997), 75-150.
Hansen, Miriam Bratu (1995) "America, Paris and the Alps: Kracauer (and Benjamin) on Cinema and Modernity" in Charney and Schwartz (eds.) (1995), 362-402.
Hardt, Ursula (1996) *From Caligari to California: Erich Pommer's Life in the International Film Wars*, Providence: Berghahn Books.
Haxthausen, Charles W. and Heidrun, Suhr (eds.) (1990) *Berlin: Culture and Metropolis*, Minneapolis: University of Minnesota Press.
Hayward, Susan and Vincendeau, Ginette (eds.) (1990) *French Film: Texts and Contexts*, London: Routledge.
Hayward, Susan (1993) *French National Cinema*, London: Routledge.
Heilbut, Anthony (1997) *Exiled in Paradise: German Refugee Artists and Intellectuals in America From the 1930s to the Present*, Berkeley: University of California Press.
Hewitt, Nicholas and Rigby Brian (1991) *France and the Mass Media*, Basingstoke: Macmillan.
Hewitt, Nicholas (1996) "Shifting Cultural Centres in Twentieth Century Paris" in Sheringham (1996), 30-45.
Higson, Andrew (ed.) (1996) *Dissolving Views: Key Writings on British Cinema*, London: Cassell.
Higson, Andrew and Maltby, Richard (eds.) (1999) *"Film Europe" and "Film America". Cinema, Commerce and Cultural Exchange 1920-1939*, Exeter: Exeter University Press.
Higson, Andrew and Maltby, Richard (1999) "'Film Europe' and 'Film America': An Introduction" in Higson and Maltby (eds.), 1-31.
Higson, Andrew (1999) "Cultural Policy and Industrial Practice: Film Europe and the International Film Congresses of the 1920s" in Higson and Maltby (eds.), 117-131.

Higson, Andrew (2000a) "The Limiting Imagination of National Cinema" in Hjort and Mackenzie (2000), 63-74.

Higson, Andrew (2000b) "The Instability of the National" in Ashby and Higson (2000), 35-47.

Hillairet, Prosper et al (eds.) (1985) *Paris vu par le cinéma de l'avant garde 1923-1983*, Paris: Paris Experimental.

Hjort, Mette and Mackenzie, Scott (eds.) (2000) *Cinema and Nation*, London: Routledge.

Horak, Jan-Christopher (1996) "German Exile Cinema, 1933-1950", *Film History* vol. 8 (1996), 373-389.

Hughes, Alex and Williams, James S. (2001) *Gender and French Cinema*, Oxford: Berg.

Huyssen, Andreas (1986) "Mass Culture as Woman: Modernism's Other" in Modleski (1986), 188-207.

Hyman, Paula (1986) *From Dreyfus to Vichy: The Remaking of French Jewry 1906-1939*, New York: Columbia University Press.

Icart, Roger (1974) "L'Avenement du film parlant" in *Les Cahiers de la cinémathèque* no. 13-15, 25-219.

Jacobs, Jerome *Billy Wilder*, Paris: Rivages.

Jacobsen, Wolfgang and Prinzler, Hans Helmut (1998) *Siodmak Bros. Berlin-Paris-London-Hollywood*, Berlin: Stiftung Deutsche Kinemathek and Argon Verlag GmbH.

Jando, Dominique (1979) *Histoire mondiale du music-hall*, Paris: Jean-Pierre Delarges.

Jeancolas, Jean Pierre (1983a) *15 ans d'années trente: le cinéma des français, 1929-1944*, Paris: Stock.

Jeancolas, Jean-Pierre (1983b) "Délicieuse ... Mauvaise Graine", *Positif* no. 271 (September 1983), 31.

Jeancolas, Jean Pierre (ed.) (1988) Dossier: Les immigrés du cinéma français, *Positif* no. 323 (January 1988), 36-53.

Jeffrey, Ian (1981) *Photography. A Concise History*, London: Thames and Hudson.

Jelavich, Peter (1990) "Modernity, Civic Identity, and Metropolitan Entertainment: Vaudeville, Cabaret, and Revue in Berlin, 1990-1933" in Haxthausen and Heidrun (1990), 95-110.

Jenks, Chris (1995) *Visual Culture*, London: Routledge.

Johnson, Douglas and Madelaine (1987) *Age of Illusion: Art and Politics in France 1919-1940*, London: Thames and Hudson.

Kaes, Anton (1996) "Sites of Desire: The Weimar Street Film" in Neumann (1996), 26-32.

Kaes, Anton (1998) "Leaving Home: Film, Migration, and the Urban Experience", *New German Critique* no. 74 (Spring/Summer 1998), 179-192.

Kaplan, Alice Yaeger (1986) *Reproductions of Banality. Fascism, Literature and French Intellectual Life*, Minneapolis: University of Minnesota Press.

Karasek, Helmut and Wilder, Billy (1973) *Et tout le reste est folie. Memoires*, Paris: Robert Laffont.

Kaspi, André and Marès, Antoine (eds.) (1989) *Le Paris des étrangers depuis une siècle* Paris: Imprimerie nationale.

Kear, Jon (1996) "*Vénus noire*: Josephine Baker and the Paris Music-Hall" in Sheringham (1996), 46-70.

Kelber, Michel (1981) "Interview", *Cinématographe* no. 68 (June 1981), 29-33.

Kelber, Michel (1984) "Interview", *Film Dope* no.30 (September 1984), 2-10.

Kelber, Michel (1996) "Interview", *Projections* no. 6, 229-254.

Kelley, David and Timms, Edward (eds.) (1985) *Unreal City: Urban Experience in European Literature and Art*, Manchester: Manchester University Press.

Kessler, Frank and Usai, Paolo Cherchi (eds.) (1991) *Cinéma et architecture*, Paris: Meridiens Klincksieck.

Kingston, Paul J. (1983) *The Genesis and Evolution of the Theme of Anti-Semitism in France 1933-1944*, Oxford: University of Oxford thesis.

Kirgener, Claudine (1988) *Itinérie d'un inconnu célèbre*, Paris: Vernal/Lebaud.

Koch, Gertrud (1990) "The Stairway to Exile" in Rentschler (1990), 103-115.

Koch, Gertrud (1991) "'Not Yet Accepted Anywhere' Exile, Memory, and Image in Kracauer's Conception of History" in *New German Cinema* no. 54 (Fall 1991), 95-110.

Koch, Gertrud (2000) *Siegfried Kracauer. An Introduction*, Princeton, NJ: Princeton University Press.

Kracauer, Siegfried (1937) *Offenbach and the Paris of his Time*, London: Constable.

Kracauer, Siegfried (1947) *From Caligari to Hitler: A Psychological History of the German Film*, Princeton: Dennis Dobson.

Kracauer, Siegfried (1995) *The Mass Ornament: Weimar Essays*, Cambridge, Mass.: Harvard University Press.

Kritzman, Lawrence D. (ed.) (under the direction of Pierre Nora) (1996) *Realms of Memory: Rethinking the French Past*, New York: Columbia University Press.

Kruse, Joseph A. and Werner, Michaël (eds.) (1991) *Heine à Paris*, Paris: Goethe Institut.

Lagny, Michèle; Ropars, Marie-Claire et Sorlin, Pierre (1986) *Genérique des années trentes*, Paris: Presses Universitaires de Vincennes.

Lally, Kevin (1996) *Wilder Times: The Life of Billy Wilder*, New York: Henry Holt.

Lapierre, Marcel (ed.) (1946) *Anthologie du cinéma*, Paris: La Nouvelle Édition.

Lazaroff Alpi, Deborah (1998) *Robert Siodmak: A Biography*, Jefferson North Carolina: Mc Farland and Company.

Léglise, Paul (1970) *Histoire de la politique du cinéma français vol. I*, Paris: R. Pichon et R. Durand-Auxias.

Lenauer, Jean (1930) "Dix jours à Berlin", *La revue du cinéma* no. 11 (June 1930), 46-51.

Leprohon, Pierre (1957) *Préscences contemporaines: Cinéma*, Paris: Nouvelles Editions Debresse.

Llopès, Marie-Claire et al (1992) *Paris-Paris 1937-1957* Paris: Éditions du Centre Georges Pompidou / Éditions Gallimard.

Lucan, Jacques (1986) *Paris des faubourgs. Formation. Transformation*, Paris: Éditions du Pavillon de l'Arsenal.

Lucot, René (1989) *Magic City*, Paris: Pierre Bordas.

Lynch, Kevin (1960) *The Image of the City*, Cambridge, Mass.: M.I.T. Press.

MacDonald, Kevin (1996) *Emeric Pressburger: The Life and Death of a Screenwriter*, London: Faber.

Malverti, Xavier and Picard, Aleth (1996) "La Voie publique annexe les faubourgs" in Lucan (1996), 135-144.

Mann, Carol (1996) *Paris: Artistic Life in the Twenties and Thirties*, London: Lawrence King.

Marchand, Bernard (1993) *Paris, histoire d'une ville*, Paris: Éditions du Seuil.

Marie, Michel (1990) "'Let's sing it one more time': René Clair's *Sous les toits de Paris* (1930)" in Hayward and Vincendeau (1990), 51-66.

Marion, Denis. (ed.) (1949) *Le Cinéma par ceux qui le font*, Paris: Arthème Fayard.

Martin, John W. (1983) *The Golden Age of French Cinema*, Boston: Twayne.

Masson, Alain (1982) "Des Genres creux, du clinquant, du simili", *Positif* no. 259 (September 1982), 32-37.

McCormick, Richard W. (1993) "From *Caligari* to Dietrich: Sexual, Social and Cinematic Discourses in Weimar Film", *Signs* 18:3, 640-668.

McGilligan, Patrick (1997) *Fritz Lang: The Nature of the Beast*, London: Faber.

Meilhac, Henry and Halévy, Ludovic (musique de Jacques Offenbach) (1889) *La Vie Parisienne*, Paris: Calmann Lévy.

Mellencamp, Patricia and Rosen, Phil (eds.) (1984) *Cinema Histories, Cinema Practices*, Los Angeles: A.F.I / University Publications of America, Inc.

Metken, Günter (1992) "Regards sur la France et l'Allemagne" in Besnard-Bernadac and Metken (1992), 26-39.

Meyer, Alain and Revie, Ian (1994) *Mythologies of Paris*, Stirling: University of Stirling.

Michelson, Annette (1985) "Dr. IXE et Mr. Clair" in Hillairet et al (1985), 19-29.

Minden, Michael (1985) "The City in Early Cinema. *Metropolis*, *Berlin* and *October*" in Kelley and Timms (1985), 193-213.

Missiaen, Jean Claude and Siclier, Jacques (1988) *Jean Gabin*, Paris.

Mitry, Jean (1980) *Histoire du cinéma vol. 4, 1930-40*, Paris: Jean Pierre Delarge.

Modleski, Tania (ed.) (1986) *Studies in Entertainment: Critical Approaches to Mass Culture*, Bloomington and Indianapolis: Indiana University Press.

Molnar, Ferenc (1944) *Liliom*, New York: Samuel French.

Monaco, Paul (1976) *Cinema and Society: France and Germany in the Twenties*, New York: Elsenier.

Morand, Paul (1934) *France la doulce*, Paris: Gallimard.

Morgan, Janice (1996) "Scarlet Streets: Noir Realism from Berlin to Paris to Hollywood", *Iris* no. 21 (Spring 1996), 31-53.

Moullet, Luc (1963) *Fritz Lang*, Paris: Seghers.

Müller, Lothar (1990) "The Beauty of the Metropolis: Towards an Aesthetic Urbanism in Turn-of-the-Century Berlin" in Haxthausen and Heidrun (1990), 37-57.

Munby, Jonathan (1996) "The "Un-American Film Art: Robert Siodmak and the Political Significance of Film Noir's German Connection", *Iris* no. 21 (Spring 1996), 74-88.

Murray, Bruce (1990) *Film and the German Left in the Weimar Republic*, Austin: University of Texas Press.

Murray, Bruce (1993) "The Role of the Vamp in Weimar Cinema: An Analysis of Karl Grune's *The Street (Die Straße)*" in Frieden et al (1993), 33-41.

Naficy, Hamid (ed.) (1999) *Home, Exile, Homeland: Film, Media and the Politics of Place*, New York: Routledge.

Naficy, Hamid (2001) *An Accented Cinema: Exile and Diasporic Filmmaking*, Princeton, NJ: Princeton University Press.

Naremore, James and Brantlinger, Patrick (1991) *Modernity and Mass Culture*, Bloomington and Indianapolis: Indiana University Press.

Natter, Wolfgang (1994) "The City as Cinematic Space: Modernism and Place in *Berlin, Symphony of a City*" in Aitken and Zonn (1994), 203-227.

Neumann, Dietrich (ed.) (1996) *Film Architecture: From Metropolis to Blade Runner*, Munich/New York: Prestel.

Niney, François (ed.) (1994) *Visions Urbaines*, Paris: Editions Centre Georges Pompidou.

Noiriel, Gérard (1996) "French and Foreigners" in Kritzman (1996), 145-180.

Nolan, Jack Edmund (1967) "Anatole Litvak", *Films in Review* vol. 28 no. 9 (November 1967), 548-565.

Nolan, Jack Edmund (1969) "Robert Siodmak Might Have Been As Popular As Hitchcock But For The Stockmarket", *Films in Review*, vol. 30 no. 4 (April 1969), 218-240.

Nora, Pierre (1989) "Between Memory and History: *Les Lieux de Mémoire*", *Representations* vol. 26 (Spring 1989), 7-25.

Nowell-Smith, Geoffrey (ed.) (1997) *The Oxford History of World Cinema*, Oxford: Oxford University Press.

O'Brien, Charles (1996) "Film Noir in France: Before the Liberation", *Iris* no. 21 (Spring 1996), 7-20.

Olsen, Daniel J. (1986) *The City as a Work of Art*, New Haven, Conn.: Yale University Press.

O'Shaughnessy, Martin (2001) "The Parisian Popular as Reactionary Modernisation", *Studies in French Cinema* vol. 1 no. 2, 80-88.

Ott, Frederick W. (1979) *The Films of Fritz Lang*, Secaucus, New Jersey: Citadel Press.

Païni, Dominique (1992) "le Passage en France: Lang, Siodmak, Trivas, Wilder" in Aumont and Païni (1992), 53-66.

Palmier, Jean-Michel (1984) "La décision d'émigrer" in Badia et al (eds.) (1984), 17-36.

Palmier, Jean-Michel (1988) *Weimar en exil. vol. I. Exil en Europe*, Paris: Payout.

Palmier, Jean-Michel (1991) "Quatre destins de cinéastes émigrés en France" in Gassen and Hurst (1991), 147-172.

Passek, Jean Loup (ed.) (1991) *Dictionnaire du cinéma*, Paris: Larousse.

Paul, Eliot (1947) *A Narrow Street*, Harmondsworth: Penguin.

Petrie, Graham (1985) *Hollywood Destinies: European Directors in America, 1922-1931*, London: Routledge & Kegan Paul.

Petro, Patrice (1989) *Joyless Streets*, Princeton, NJ: Princeton University Press.

Philippe, Claude-Jean (1987) "La Fascination de la ville" in Boulègne (1987), 128-137.

Phillips, Alastair (2004) "*Liliom*: A Fateful Divide" in Pye (ed.) (2004).

Phillips, Alastair (2004) "A Cosmopolitan Film Culture. Exile and Emigration in Classical French Cinema 1930-1960" in Temple and Witt (eds.).

Phillips, Alastair (2002) "Changing Bodies/Changing Voices: Success and Failure in Hollywood in the Early Sound Era" *Screen* vol. 43 no. 2 (Summer 2002), 187-200.

Phillips, Alastair (2000) "The Camera Goes Down the Streets. *Dans les rues* (Victor Trivas, 1933) and the Paris of the German *émigrés*" *Modern and Contemporary France* vol. 8 no. 2 (August 2000), 325-334.

Phillips, Alastair (1999) "Performing Paris. Myths of the City in Robert Siodmak's Émigré Musical *La Vie Parisienne*" *Screen* vol. 40 no. 3 (Autumn 1999), 257-276.

Phillips Gene D. (1998) *Exiles in Hollywood: Major European Film Directors in America*, Lehigh: Lehigh University Press.

Pollock, Griselda (1991) *Vision and Difference*, London: Routledge.

Pour Vous 1930-1939.

Prédal, Réné (1972) *La Société française 1914-1945 à travers le cinéma*, Paris: Armand Colin.

Préjean, Albert (1956) *The Sky and the Stars. The Memoirs of Albert* Préjean, London: Harvill.

Préjean, Patrick (1979) *Albert Préjean par Patrick Préjean*, Paris: Candeau.

Prendergast, Christopher (1995) *Paris and the Nineteenth Century*, Oxford: Blackwell.

Prouty, Richard (1996) "The Well Furnished Interior of the Masses: Kirsanoff's *Ménilmontant* and the Streets of Paris", *Cinema Journal* (Autumn 1996).

Puaux, Françoise (ed.) (1995) "Architecture, décor et cinéma", *Cinémaction* (1985).

Pye, Douglas (2004) *Fritz Lang*, Moffat: Cameron Books.

Rancière, Jacques (1989) *The Nights of Labour – The Worker's Dream in Nineteenth Century France*, Philadelphia: Temple University Press.

Rearick, Charles (1997) *The French in Love and War: Popular Culture in France 1914-1945*, New Haven, Conn.: Yale University Press.

Rebatet, Lucien (1941) *Les Tribus du cinéma et du théatre*, Paris: Nouvelles Éditions Françaises.

Reader, Keith and Vincendeau, Ginette (eds.) (1986) *La Vie est à nous*, London: British Film Institute.

Réda, Jacques (1996) *The Ruins of Paris*, London: Reaktion.

Remarque, Erich (1947) *Arch of Triumph*, London: Hutchinson.

Renoir, Jean (1974) *Ma Vie et mes films*, Paris: Flammarion.

Rentschler, Eric (ed.) (1990) *The Films of G.W. Pabst. An Extraterritorial Cinema*, New Brunswick: Rutgers University Press.

Reynolds, Siân (1993) "Camera Culture and Gender in Paris in the 1930's: Stills and Movies", *Nottingham French Studies* vol. 32 no. 1 (Spring 1993), 39-51.

Rice, Shelley (1997) *Parisian Views*, Cambridge, Mass.: M.I.T. Press.

Rifkin, Adrian (1987) "Musical Moments", *Yale French Studies* no. 73, 121-155.

Rifkin, Adrian (1991) "French Popular Song: Changing Myths of the People" in Hewitt and Rigby (1991), 200-219.

Rifkin, Adrian (1994) *Street Noises: Parisian Pleasures, 1900-1940*, Manchester: Manchester University Press.

Roger, Philippe (1991) "L' Obscure clarté – la lumière allemande du cinéma français" in Gassen and Hurst (1991), 111-138.

Rollet, Patrice (1985) "Passages des panoramas" in Hillairet et al (1985), 9-18.

Roud, Richard (ed.) (1980) *Cinema: A Critical Dictionary, The Major Filmmakers* (2 vols.), New York: Viking.

Rouleau, Bernard (1996) "Des contrastes nécessaires à la ville. La formation des faubourgs" in Lucan (1996), 14-19.

Sadoul, George (1979) *Chroniques du cinéma français 1939-1961, Écrits I*, Paris: UGE.

Sadoul, George (1953) *French Film*, London: Falcon.

Salachas, Gilbert (1994) *Le Paris d'Hollywood*, Paris: Caisse nationale des monuments historiques et des sites.

Salt, Barry (1979) "From Caligari to Who?", *Sight and Sound* vol. 48, no. 2 (Spring 1979), 119-123.

Salt, Barry (1992) *Film Style and Technology: History and Analysis*, London: Starword.

Schivelbusch, Wolfgang (1979) *The Railway Journey: Trains and Travel in the Nineteenth Century*, New York: Urizen Books.

Schivelbusch, Wolfgang (1988) *Disenchanted Night: The Industrialisation of Light in the Nineteenth Century*, Berkeley: University of California Press.

Schlör, Joachim (1998) *Nights in the Big City*, London: Reaktion.

Schor, Ralph (1989) "Le Paris des libertés" in Kaspi and Marès (1989), 13-33.

Schwartz, Vanessa (1998) *Spectacular Realities*, Berkeley: University of California Press.

Sellier, Geneviève (1981) "Les Singuliers héritiers du cinéma français des années 30", *Cinéma* no. 268 (April 1981), 4-26.

Sellier, Geneviève (1983) "Charles Vanel. Un nom-séducteur" du cinéma français", *Cinéma* no. 298 (October 1983), 63-66.

Sellier, Geneviève (1989) *Jean Grémillon le cinéma est à vous*, Paris: Méridiens Klincksieck.

Sesonske, Alexandre (1980) *Jean Renoir, the French Films, 1924-1939*, Cambridge, Mass.: Harvard University Press.

Sheringham, Michael (ed.) (1996) *Parisian Fields*, London: Reaktion.

Sheringham, Michael (1996) "City Space, Mental Space, Poetic Space: Paris in Breton, Benjamin and Réda", in Sheringham (1996), 85-114.

Silberman, Marc (1996) "What is German in the German Cinema?", *Film History* vol. 8 (1996), 297-315.

Simmel, George (1971) "The Metropolis and Mental Life" in Featherstone and Frisby (eds.) (1997), 174-185.

Siodmak, Robert (1980) *Zwischen Berlin und Hollywood*, Munich: Herbig.

Sontag, Susan (ed.) (1993) *A Roland Barthes Reader*, London: Vintage.

Sorlin, Pierre (1981) "Jewish Images in the French Cinema of the 1930s", *Historical Journal of Film, Radio and Television* vol. 1, no. 2, 139-149.

Soupault, Philippe (1979) *Écrits de cinéma 1918-1931*, Paris: Librairie Plon.

Strebel, Elizabeth Grottle (1980) *French Social Cinema of the 1930's. A Cinematographic Expression of Popular Front Consciousness*, New York: Arno.

Sturm, Sibylle and Wohlgemuth, Arthur (eds.) (1996) *Hallo? Berlin? Ici Paris!*, Munich: Cinegraph.

Sutcliffe, Anthony (1984) *Metropolis 1890-1940*, London: Mansell.

Swindell, Larry (1983) *Charles Boyer*, London: Weidenfield and Nicholson.

Taylor, John Russell (1983) *Strangers in Paradise: The Hollywood Emigrés 1933-1950*, London: Faber and Faber.

Technique cinématographique 1930-1939.

Temple, Michael and Witt, Michael (eds.) (2004) *The French Cinema Book*, London: British Film Institute.

Thalmann, Rita (1980) "L'immigration allemande et l'opinion publique en France de 1933 à 1936" in Besnard and d'Hoop (1980), 149-172.

Thalmann, Rita (1989) "Topographie de l'émigration du IIIe Reich à Paris" in Kaspi and Marès (eds.) (1989), 91-103.

Thiher, Allen (1979) *The Cinematic Muse: Critical Studies in the History of French Cinema*, Columbia and London: University of Missouri Press.

Thomas, Helen (ed.) (1997) *Dance in the City*, London: Macmillan.

Thompson, Kristin (1989) "The Ermolieff Group in Paris: Exile, Impressionism, Internationalism" in *Griffithiana* no. 35-36 (October 1989), pp. 50-57.

Thompson, Kristin (1990) "Dr Caligari at the Folies-Bergère, or, The Success of an Early Avant-Garde Film" in Budd (1990), 121-170.

Thompson, Kristin (1999) "The Rise and Fall of Film Europe" in Higson and Maltby (eds.) (1999), 56-81.

Toulet, Emmanuelle (ed.) (1995) *Le Cinéma au rendez-vous des arts*, Paris: Bibliothèque nationale de France.

Trauner, Alexandre (1988) *Décors de cinéma*, Paris: Jad-Flammarion.

Tudor, Andrew (1974) *Image and Influence. Studies in the Sociology of Film*, London: George Allen and Unwin.

Turim, Maureen (1990) "Poetic Realism as psychoanalytical and ideological operation: Marcel Carné's *Le jour se lève* (1939) in Hayward and Vincendeau (1990), 103-116.

Turk, Edward (1989) *Child of Paradise: Marcel Carné and the Golden Age of French Cinema*, Cambridge, Mass.: Harvard University Press.

Ungar, Steven (1997) "Atmosphère, atmosphère: On the Study of France Between the Wars", *Studies in 20th Century Literature*, vol. 21 no. 2 (Summer 1997), 381-397.

Van Damme, Charlie (1987) *Lumière actrice*, Paris: Fondations Européene des metiers de l'image et du son.

Verne, Maurice (1932) *Les Amuseurs de Paris*, Paris: Les Éditions de France.

Vernet, Marc (1993) "Film Noir on the Edge of Doom" in Copjec (1993), 1-32.

Vidler, Anthony (1996) "The Explosion of Space: Architecture and the Filmic Imaginary" in Neumann (1996), 13-25.

Vincendeau, Ginette (1983) "France, terre d'accueil?" in Elsaesser and Vincendeau (1983), 4-6.

Vincendeau, Ginette (1985a) *French Cinema in the 1930s* (unpublished Ph.D. thesis), University of East Anglia.

Vincendeau, Ginette (1985b) "Community, Nostalgia and the Spectacle of Masculinity", *Screen* vol. 26 no. 6, 18-39.

Vincendeau, Ginette (1987) "The Mise-en-Scène of Suffering. French Chanteuses Réalistes" *New Formations*, no. 3 (Winter 1987), 107-128.

Vincendeau, Ginette (1988a) "'Des portes ouvertes seulement à contrecoeur'. Les cinéastes allemands en France pendant les années trente", *Positif*, no. 323 (January 1988), 45-50.

Vincendeau, Ginette (1988b) "Daddy's Girls (Oedipal Narratives in 1930s French Films)", *Iris* no. 8 (1988), 70-81.

Vincendeau, Ginette (1988c) "Hollywood Babel", *Screen*, vol. 29 no. 2 (1988), 24-39.

Vincendeau, Ginette (1989) "Melodramatic Realism: On Some French Women's Films in the 1930s", *Screen*, vol. 30 no. 3 (Summer 1989), 51-65.

Vincendeau, Ginette (1990) "In the name of the father: Marcel Pagnol's 'trilogy' *Marius* (1931), *Fanny* (1932), *César* (1936)" in Hayward and Vincendeau (eds.) (1990), 67-82.

Vincendeau, Ginette (1992a) "From the *Bal Populaire* to the Casino: Class and Leisure in French Films of the 1930s", *Nottingham French Studies* vol. 31 no. 2 (Autumn 1992), 52-69.

Vincendeau, Ginette (1992b) "Noir is also a French Word: The French Antecedents of Film Noir" in Cameron (1992), 49-58.

Vincendeau, Ginette (1993) "Anatomy of a Myth: Jean Gabin", *Nottingham French Studies* vol. 32 no. 1 (Spring 1993), 19-29.

Vincendeau, Ginette (1995) (ed.) *The Encyclopedia of European Cinema*, London: B.F.I. / Cassell.

Vincendeau, Ginette (1996) " 'Avez-vous lu Freud?': Maurice Chevalier dans *Pièges* de Robert Siodmak" *Iris* no. 21 (Spring 1996), 89-98.

Vincendeau, Ginette (1998) *Pépé le moko*, London: British Film Institute.

Virilio, Paul (1987) "Lumières de la ville" in Boulegne (1987), 155-159.

Wakhevitch, Georges (1977) *L'Envers des décors*, Paris: Robert Laffont.

Waldman, Harry (1998) *Paramount In Paris*, Lanham: Scarecrow Press.

Walker, David H. "Cultivating the *Faits Divers*: *Détective*" *Nottingham French Studies* vol. 32 no. 1 (Spring 1993), 71-83.

Walsh, Michael (1996) "National Cinema, National Imaginary", *Film History* vol. 8 (1996), 5-17.

Warehime, Marja (1996) *Brassaï-Images of Culture and the Surrealist Observer*, Baton Rouge: Louisiana State University Press.

Warner, Marina (1993) *L'Atalante*, London: British Film Institute.

Weber, Eugen (1995) *The Hollow Years: France in the 1930s*, London: Sinclair Stevenson.

Weinburg, David (1977) *A Community on Trial: the Jews of Paris in the 1930s*, Chicago: Chicago University Press.

Westwood, Sallie and Williams, John (eds.) (1996) *Imagining Cities*, London: Routledge.

Willet, John (1978) *The New Sobriety: Art and Politics in the Weimar Period.*

Willet, John (1984) *The Weimar Years: A Culture Cut Short*, London: Thames and Hudson.

Williams, Alan (1992) *Republic of Images: A History of French Filmmaking*, Cambridge, Mass.: Harvard University Press.

Williams, Raymond (1975) *The Country and the City*, New York: Oxford University Press.

Wilson, Elizabeth *The Sphinx in the City: Urban Life and the Control and Disorder of Women*, London: Virago.

Wilson, Elizabeth (1992) "The Invisible Flaneur", *New Left Review* no. 191 (January/February 1992), 90-110.

Wilson, Elizabeth (1995) "The Rhetoric of Urban Space", *New Left Review* no. 209 (January/February 1995), 146-160.

Wilson, Elizabeth (1997) "Nostalgia and the City" in Westwood and Williams (1997), 127-139.

Winspur, Steven (1991) "On City Streets and Narrative Logic" in Caws (1991), 60-69.

Witta-Montrobert, Jeanne (1980) *La Lanterne magique. Mémoires d'une script*, Paris: Calmann-Lévy.

Wollen, Peter (1991) "Cinema/Americanism/the Robot" in Naremore and Brantlinger (1991), 42-69.

Woolf, Janet (1990) *Feminine Sentences. Essays on Women and Culture*, Oxford and Cambridge: Polity/Blackwell.

Zeldin, Theodore (1993) *A History of French Passions vol. II*, Oxford: Oxford University Press.

Zola, Émile (1996) (date of original publication 1890) *La Bête humaine*, Oxford: Oxford University Press.

Zola, Émile (1992) (date of original publication 1880) *Nana*, Oxford: Oxford University Press.

Zolotow, Maurice (1977) *Billy Wilder in Hollywood*, London: W.H. Allen.

Index

Notes, Appendices and Filmography have not been indexed apart from the biographies in the notes and the titles of the appendices. Page numbers in italics refer to these biographies and titles.

Film Culture in Transition

General Editor: *Thomas Elsaesser*

Double Trouble: Chiem van Houweninge on Writing and Filming
Thomas Elsaesser, Robert Kievit and Jan Simons (eds.)

Writing for the Medium: Television in Transition
Thomas Elsaesser, Jan Simons and Lucette Bronk (eds.)

Between Stage and Screen: Ingmar Bergman Directs
Egil Törnqvist

The Film Spectator: From Sign to Mind
Warren Buckland (ed.)

Film and the First World War
Karel Dibbets and Bert Hogenkamp (eds.)

A Second Life: German Cinema's First Decades
Thomas Elsaesser (ed.)

Fassbinder's Germany: History Identity Subject
Thomas Elsaesser

Cinema Futures: Cain, Abel or Cable? The Screen Arts in the Digital Age
Thomas Elsaesser and Kay Hoffmann (eds.)

Audiovisions: Cinema and Television as Entr'Actes in History
Siegfried Zielinski

Joris Ivens and the Documentary Context
Kees Bakker (ed.)

Ibsen, Strindberg and the Intimate Theatre: Studies in TV Presentation
Egil Törnqvist

The Cinema Alone: Essays on the Work of Jean-Luc Godard 1985-2000
Michael Temple and James S. Williams (eds.)

Micropolitics of Media Culture: Reading the Rhizomes of Deleuze and Guattari
Patricia Pisters and Catherine M. Lord (eds.)

Malaysian Cinema, Asian Film: Border Crossings and National Cultures
William van der Heide

Film Front Weimar: Representations of the First World War in German Films of the Weimar Period (1919-1933)
Bernadette Kester

Camera Obscura, Camera Lucida: Essays in Honor of Annette Michelson
Richard Allen and Malcolm Turvey (eds.)

Jean Desmet and the Early Dutch Film Trade
Ivo Blom